Into the Land of Bones

The Joan Palevsky Imprint in Classical Literature

In honor of beloved Virgil—

"O degli altri poeti onore e lume . . ."

Into the Land of Bones

Alexander the Great in Afghanistan

Frank L. Holt

UNIVERSITY OF CALIFORNIA PRESS

Berkeley   Los Angeles   London

*The publisher gratefully acknowledges the
generous contribution to this book provided by
the Classical Literature Endowment Fund of the
University of California Press Associates, which
is supported by a major gift from Joan Palevsky.*

University of California Press
Berkeley and Los Angeles, California

University of California Press, Ltd.
London, England

First paperback printing 2006
© 2005 by The Regents of the University of California

Library of Congress Cataloging-in-Publication Data
Holt, Frank Lee.
    Into the land of bones : Alexander the Great in Afghanistan /
Frank L. Holt.
        p.   cm.—(Hellenistic culture and society ; 47)
    Includes bibliographical references and index.
    ISBN-13: 978-0-520-24993-6 (pbk. : alk. paper)
    1. Alexander, the Great, 356–323 B.C.   2. Afghanistan—
History, Military.   I. Title.   II. Series.
DF234.57.H65 2005
939'.6—dc22   2004024131

Manufactured in Canada

14 13 12 11 10 09
10 9 8 7 6 5 4

For James Lafayette and Catherine Roberts Drinkard,
Loving in-laws who gave me the gift of a lifetime

CONTENTS

ILLUSTRATIONS

MAPS

PREFACE

This book grew out of a public lecture delivered soon after the terrorist attacks of September 11, 2001, just as American and Coalition forces were beginning to move against Afghanistan. My efforts to describe the kinds of military and political problems likely to be encountered there sobered an audience eager for optimism. After all, the greatest general of all time took a beating when he invaded Bactria (modern Afghanistan) to punish its warlords back in the fourth century B.C.E. The experiences of Alexander the Great, though long ago, still resonate, and they suggest that America's resolve will be sorely tested in that truculent land. Even now, three years later, the war is not over. The Taliban have not been eliminated as a threat to security in the region. Al-Qaeda remains as ruthless and resourceful as ever, which our leaders freely admit with their anxious and ubiquitous terrorism alerts. Where, we wonder, is all this heading? The invasion/evasion strategies of both sides in this conflict have long and tortured histories. Those odds, unfortunately, favor our enemies as much now as when the invaders were Macedonian, British, or Soviet soldiers. This does not mean that Coalition troops lack skill, dedication, honor, or heroism. They simply do not have history on their side. To change *that* will take a little luck, a lot of blood, and much more time.

I thank those who encouraged me to write this book. It is sometimes a risky proposition to draw parallels between past and present, for history never repeats itself as plainly as some fairy tale beginning "Twice upon a time . . ." Events are unique; yet, meaningful patterns do exist and ought to be examined for the insights they can offer. Otherwise, historians are but entertainers rather than educators. I have tried, not always successfully, I am sure, to monitor my use of perhaps ephemeral terminologies, such as "evildoers" and "Coalition partners," when describing ancient circumstances. This effort was made all the more difficult by my having read a great deal about current policies and events, which tends to influence a writer's thinking and vocabulary. The result may lead to charges of "presentism" in my work, but a lively dialogue between ancient and modern can scarcely avoid it. As usual, I have written with two groups in mind, both of them dear to me as a scholar and scribbler: my fellow professional historians and the general public. I hope that the one group will indulge my efforts to find an engaging prose style, and that the other will appreciate the need to document everything as completely as possible.

I have enjoyed, most of all, the encouragement and assistance of my family. Linda has again been my best critic and closest collaborator. I could not function without her skills as a passionate reader and professional typist. Laura has once more contributed her insights and enthusiasm. On a number of occasions, Patrick

McDaniel has patiently rescued me from computer crises. I thank the wonderful editors with whom I have worked at the University of California Press, especially Kate Toll and Laura Cerruti. I appreciate the comments of the press' outside readers, which helped me to reshape the book. My university and department have provided a stimulating intellectual environment in which to work; I am especially grateful to Professor Joe Pratt for his continuing interest in my research. Beyond my university family, I owe debts to two scholars who inspire me daily: the indefatigable Professors Stanley Burstein and Peter Green.

Finally, this book provides a welcome opportunity to thank two remarkable persons. James and Catherine Drinkard have been an important part of my life ever since I showed up at their door to date their daughter thirty-four years ago. For all that they have done for me, I dedicate this book to them.

Houston, Texas
August 2004

CHAPTER ONE

Introduction

I've only to pick up a newspaper and I seem to see ghosts
gliding between the lines.
Henrik Ibsen

THE CROSSHAIRS OF HISTORY

Afghanistan, the world's inexhaustible wellspring of warlords
and terrorists, cannot escape the crosshairs of history. In each of
the last three centuries, superpowers have trained their sights on
this tragic land, determined to impose upon it a new world order
successively British, Soviet, and American.[1] Such endeavors usually begin with confidence and end with catastrophe. First, with
exuberant expectations, the British Empire gathered in 1838 a
grand army to quell the unruly Afghans.[2] The goal was simply
to replace one ruler (Dost Muhammed) with another (the exiled
Shah Shuja) more amenable to British interests. "There have
been few military campaigns in British history," writes Major
General James Lunt, "which were more ineptly planned and

more incompetently executed than the first Afghan War; and that is saying a good deal."³ These 15,200 soldiers took with them 38,000 servants, together with brass bands, bagpipes, polo ponies, packs of foxhounds, and thirty thousand camels burdened with supplies. The officers of one regiment required two camels just to carry their cigars, and a single brigadier needed sixty beasts to haul his personal belongings. Even so, the expeditionary force soon ran short of provisions and had to pay premium prices for a flock of ten thousand sheep. The army ate everything, including the sheepskins fried in blood. The camels proved less helpful. They died in such numbers that one general pronounced them useless except for burial practice, an ominous remark indeed.⁴

Under General Sir John Keane, the British celebrated some early successes at Kandahar and Ghazni, then reached Kabul in August 1839 (see Map 1). There they placed Shah Shuja on the throne. This foreign intervention, however, stirred growing resentment among the native peoples even as most of the British troops swaggered back to India. Tribal opposition mounted across Afghanistan, erupting disastrously when terrorists butchered a prominent British official named Alexander "Bukhara" Burnes. In January 1842, the empire's remaining 4,500 soldiers and their 12,000 camp followers retreated from Kabul in a long wintry death-march that only one European survived.⁵ Shah Shuja fell to assassins on April 5, and the country disintegrated into feuding bands led by tribal warlords. Dost Muhammed reclaimed his throne, for what it was worth, and Afghanistan reverted to its original status. But for the making of 15,000 ghosts, nothing at all had changed.

Later in the same century, the British took another turn at taming Afghanistan. Never successful at unifying his nation,

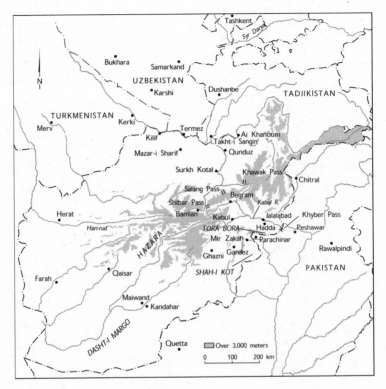

1. Modern Afghanistan

Dost Muhammed died in 1863.[6] He had outlived his three favorite sons, so the two dozen remaining settled into a spirited civil war that alarmed both the neighboring British in India and the Russians in central Asia. These anxieties fueled the infamous Great Game, in which both parties competed for influence over Afghanistan using all manner of spies and covert operations. When it appeared to the British that their own position was weakening among the tribal factions in Afghanistan, military intervention again seemed necessary. The Second Afghan War (1878–1880) commenced with a swift invasion by 33,500 troops on three fronts that promised complete success.[7] Revenge sweetened the air, but the atmosphere soon changed. Cholera swept through the ranks as daytime temperatures soared above one hundred degrees in the shade. Commanders were warned not to visit troop hospitals because they might not be able to bear the shock of what they would see. Fortunately, the war soon ended—or so everyone thought—in 1879. The British government, conducting two wars at once, was glad to declare its victory in Afghanistan. The cause had been just, the casualties from combat relatively low, and the naysayers happily hushed. But then, as in the previous war, a high British official was butchered in Kabul. Reprisals came swiftly as the angry occupiers rounded up rebels and hung them ten at a time.

The war caught fire again and burned brightly. At the battle of Maiwand (July 27, 1880), a British force of 2,500 men suffered a devastating defeat near Kandahar. Reinforcements under Lieutenant General Sir Frederick Roberts soon arrived, including a mobile city of 10,000 soldiers, over 7,000 camp followers, more than 4,700 horses and ponies, nearly 6,000 mules and donkeys, and over 13,000 other transport animals. The march of this army from Kabul and its triumph at Kandahar made Roberts ("flawless in faith and fame") a rare hero in the course of this raw and unromantic war; however, in the end, the general warned the West that Afghanistan should be left alone.[8] He added prophetically: "It may not be very flattering to our *amour propre,* but I feel sure I am right when I say that the less the Afghans see of us the less they will dislike us. Should Russia in future years attempt to conquer Afghanistan, or invade India through it, we should have a better chance of attaching the Afghans to our interests if we avoid all interference with them in the meantime."[9]

A century later, the Russians did indeed dispatch over 100,000 troops to install a puppet government in Afghanistan (1979–1989).[10] The twentieth century naturally brought new weapons to bear on the tribal warlords, who still controlled the countryside. Land mines killed and crippled Afghan civilians in unbelievable numbers (and still do); Soviet jets, helicopters, and tanks pounded guerilla forces armed and led much as they had been against the British. As before, the invaders seemed certain at first of an easy victory: "It'll be over in three or four weeks," Leonid Brezhnev promised Anatoly Dobrynin.[11] For years the Soviets had prepared for such an invasion, building useful roads and runways allegedly to help the Afghans, while the West pulled back and put its money into Pakistan.[12] Taking up the cause once espoused by Lord Roberts, the United States finally seized upon this Soviet intervention as a winning endgame in the long cold war. Détente crumbled with President Jimmy Carter's recall of his ambassador to Russia, a boycott of the 1980 Olympic Games hosted by Moscow, a grain embargo, and a mounting U.S. military budget. On the day of the Soviet invasion, Carter's national security advisor, Zbigniew Brzezinski, advised the president, "We now have the opportunity of giving the USSR its Vietnam War."[13] Under President Ronald Reagan, the CIA's operations in the region became its largest in the world as thousands of Soviets and millions of Afghans fell or fled. American money and munitions kept the mujahideen (jihadist) warlords trained and equipped for their bloody crusade.[14]

In 1986, Mikhail Gorbachev delivered his famous speech

likening Afghanistan to "a bleeding wound"; this pronouncement signaled Russia's weakening resolve to dominate
Afghanistan. To hasten the outcome, the United States decided
later in the same year to supply Stinger antiaircraft missiles to the
mujahideen via Pakistan.[15] Terrorists today still have access to
aging stockpiles of these dangerous weapons, but at the time the
gamble seemed worthwhile: Soviet air losses mounted rapidly to
118 jets and 333 helicopters.[16] The quagmire deepened. Finally,
on February 15, 1989, the last Russian soldier retreated across the
Amu Darya, leaving behind more than 13,800 Soviet dead as another superpower abandoned its hopes to subdue Afghanistan.[17]

For the next twelve years, victorious Afghan rebels struggled
for control of the ravaged country. One warlord masquerading
as prime minister callously bombarded the capital city on a daily
basis, killing some 25,000 of his own people.[18] Nations that had
armed and trained these warlords to defeat the Soviets showed
little interest in this dismal civil war. Chaos, crime, and corrup-
tion took hold and inflamed new resentments against the West.
Helpless and hopeless, many Afghans welcomed a stern "law
and order" movement touted by a militia of black-turbaned religious students called the Taliban (Seekers).[19] Led by Mullah
Muhammad Omar and financed in part by the billionaire Osama
bin Laden, who had once assisted the CIA in its transfer of
weapons to the mujahideen, the Taliban captured Kabul in September 1996.[20] The fighting continued as thirteen other factions,
including the Northern Alliance, stubbornly resisted the Taliban; but most of Afghanistan eventually fell under the authori-
tarian rule of these fundamentalists. Defying the outside world,
these extremists blew up the gigantic Buddhas carved in the cliffs
of Bamian, beat women senseless who failed to wear their

burqas, and abetted the insidious growth of the al-Qaeda terrorist organization. Then dawned a deceptively fine day in September 2001 that defined a new era among nations. Out of crystalline autumn skies screamed four jetliners on paths of unspeakable destruction. Suddenly the sights of another superpower swung around to Afghanistan.

Intervention came quickly and with new weaponry. Within a month, a thick alphanumeric soup of sophisticated aircraft boiled above Afghanistan. Crews aboard B-1 and B-52 bombers spewed tons of munitions into the mountain hideouts of the Taliban and al-Qaeda. Joining the fray were EA-6 Prowlers, F-14 Tomcats, F-15 Eagles, F-16 Falcons, F-18 Hornets, A-10 Thunderbolts, MC-130 Talons, KC-135 Stratotankers, UH-60 Black Hawks, HH-53 Jolly Green Giants, AC-130 Spectre gunships, and even RQ-1 A/B Predator drones flown by absentee pilots seated at computer screens in Riyadh.[21] Stirring the pot were but a handful of Special Forces on the ground. Unlike the 100,000 Soviet invaders airlifted in the twentieth century, or the immense traveling cities dispatched by the British in the nineteenth, America and its coalition partners relied upon space-age technology to fight an asymmetrical war in and above Afghanistan.[22] Rather than pack their cigars on camels, U.S. pilots could reach the battlefield at Mach 1 and return that same day for a smoke at their bases a thousand miles from central Asia. Even so, a few American personnel found themselves on Afghan ponies, fighting low and slow as if back in the regiments of Lord Roberts. Secretary of Defense Donald Rumsfeld proudly proclaimed the horseborne assault on Mazar-i-Sharif "the first U.S. cavalry attack of the twenty-first century."[23] In the opinion of General Tommy Franks, the image of those horsemen seemed as iconic as the

Marines raising Old Glory on Iwo Jima: "It was as if warriors from the future had been transported to an earlier century."[24] The tactic worked, and brought the latest superpower its first victory in the war. The Taliban fled, al-Qaeda soon abandoned its main terrorist training camps, and foreign invaders sanctioned—once again—the regime of a friendly ruler in a rebellious land.

The complete history of this latest invasion has not, of course, been written.[25] So far, one senior U.S. intelligence official (notably anonymous in his critique) claims that "the conduct of the Afghan war approaches perfection—in the sense of perfectly inept."[26] For his part, the general in command of the war declared even its worst engagement (Operation Anaconda) to be "an unqualified and absolute success."[27] Fresh battle lines are already being entrenched in books even as the real combat continues. What happens next none can say, although the past warns us that early triumphs in Afghanistan might yet end tragically. The fighting and humanitarian crises continue; many of the enemy's leaders and warlords remain at large or lurk in the shadows as momentary allies.[28] Assassinations still occur with unsettling frequency in Kabul and other cities. Anarchy torments the countryside while NATO boasts but three working helicopters to perform its mission.[29] Calls for more troops go unanswered. As early as the summer of 2003, Americans began openly to question whether U.S. forces were spread too thin, giving al-Qaeda and the Taliban too much hope that yet again the West might fail in the long run to make any lasting difference in Afghanistan.[30] Nearly every day, the news from central Asia stirs up painful reminders. The hoofbeats of our anachronistic cavalry have awakened the spirits of another time and kicked the dust from their tombs. Here and there, at Kandahar and Kabul, Herat and Begram, the desolate posts of the British and Soviet dead have become datelines again in tragic stories of war and occupation.

Few people today realize just how long this has been going on. The invasions led by Britain, the Soviet Union, and the United States stretch across centuries and carry us from an age of mules and muskets to one of helicopters and cruise missiles. Yet these modern struggles in Afghanistan are merely the latest phase of something far more ancient, a calamity thicker in ghosts than almost any other in history. Genghis Khan, "the atom bomb of his day," devastated the region when his Mongol hordes rode through in the thirteenth century c.e.[31] Tamerlane followed in the fourteenth century, and Babur (founder of the Moghul dynasty) in the sixteenth. In what has been called "the great hiving-ground of world-disturbers," these medieval wars presaged the modern misfortunes of Afghanistan.[32] One recent study, however, traces the problem back even further, to the fifth century c.e.: "The breakdown of law and order following the invasion of the White Huns perhaps initiated that self-reliant parochialism which is at the root of the fierce tribal and microgeographical independence and mutual hostility which characterizes the structure of Afghan society in recent centuries. Even the unifying influence of Islam [since the seventh century] has been unable to break down this attitude."[33] This broad frame of reference across fifteen centuries says a lot about the continuity of certain conditions in Afghanistan, but it still falls short of the truth by at least eight hundred years. The long rhythms of Afghan history do show some periods of relative calm during which cities grew, trade routes pulsed, irrigated agriculture expanded, and the arts flourished, but between each renaissance we find an era of ruin brought on or exacerbated by the parochialism, tribalism, fierce independence, and mutual hostility mentioned above. These social conditions, not to mention the physical challenges of a harsh terrain and environment, stretch back as far as our earliest written sources will carry us. In these respects, the twenty-first century C.E. differs very little from the fifteenth or fifth C.E. or even the fourth B.C.E.

A DEEPER PERSPECTIVE

What George W. Bush has called "the first war of the twenty-first century" actually began on a different autumn day more than twenty-three hundred years ago, when Alexander the Great launched the initial invasion by a Western superpower to subdue Afghanistan and its warlords.[34] Accounts of that campaign read eerily like news from our own day. Alexander, too, acted in the context of a larger Middle East crisis inherited from his father. King Philip II of Macedonia (reigned 359–336 B.C.E.) left his son an unresolved conflict against a major powerhouse based in what is now Iraq.[35] For many years, the Greeks had felt threatened by a regime whose palaces, power, and propaganda seemed to embody everything that divided the peoples of Europe from Asia. Philip's nemesis was the Persian Empire of the Achaemenid kings. Often despised and demonized by the Greeks, Persia had gobbled up the great powers of the past (the Egyptians, Lydians, Chaldaeans) as well as many lesser principalities (those of the Hebrews, Arabs, Phoenicians). The rulers of Persia took the title "King of Kings" to announce their authority over a wide range of local princes, chiefs, and potentates. Back in the fifth century

B.C.E., 120 years before the reign of Philip, Persian forces had even invaded Greece by marching through the domain of Macedonia to attack Athens and other city-states. Celebrated battles punctuated that epic struggle at Marathon, Thermopylae, Salamis, and Plataea. Herodotus became the Father of History by recounting this epic showdown.[36]

Macedonia and its related Greek neighbors often did not get along, but the specter of the Persian Empire overshadowed their differences and, in the fourth century, drove them together in a makeshift alliance led first by Alexander's father. Philip was a seasoned war veteran who took equal pride in his diplomatic expertise. He surrounded himself with an aggressive staff of generals and advisors who shared his vision of the world. Together they mapped out a bold plan to invade Persia using Macedonian troops backed by a coalition of Greek states (the so-called League of Corinth).[37] In 336 B.C.E., Philip sent an expeditionary army into the western fringes of the Persian Empire; he intended to follow at the head of a much larger force. The objective seems to have been relatively straightforward: push back the frontiers of the Achaemenid Empire and cripple the Persian king's military power without necessarily crushing him.

Philip's son took a much harder line and put no limits whatever on his own mission in the Middle East. When Philip fell to an assassin's dagger in 336 B.C.E., before reaching Persia himself, Alexander held the Persians partly to blame. Rightly or wrongly, he later accused the Achaemenid king of sponsoring turmoil in Greece and of financing the plot against his father's life.[38] Young Alexander therefore made it clear that regime change was to be the new goal of his war against Persia. Before that could transpire, however, Alexander needed to rally his nation and rebuild his father's old alliance through incentives and intimidation (on the ancient sources, see the appendix).

Philip's assassination had pitched the world onto a wobbly new axis, but Alexander somehow kept it spinning. He began his reign under a vexing cloud as some opponents openly questioned his right to take office. It was a dangerous time for a disputed succession. Alexander naturally relied upon many of the senior advisors and officers of his father's administration to help him through this crisis. Barely twenty years old, Alexander had next to restore allegiance to the Panhellenic (all-Greek) league, because a few wavering states publicly doubted the untested new king's experience and abilities. Between 336 and 334 B.C.E., reluctant allies were chastised and, when necessary, punished.[39] The war against Persia, Alexander announced, would be renewed. In fact, an aggressive preemptive policy would be put into play throughout the Middle East. Alexander made it clear that Persia's King Darius III must disarm and surrender or risk a fight to the finish. Under no circumstances could the alleged tyrant keep his throne.

True to the demands of his time, Alexander personally led his troops through the harrowing battles and sieges that toppled the regime of Darius. Macedonian kings led by example at the forefront of their armies, enduring all the risks of every ill-advised assault while earning all the renown for every brilliant success. More than any other battlefield commander in history, Alexander stayed ahead in this unforgiving ledger of leadership. At the Battle of the Granicus River in 334 B.C.E., he survived a brisk bout of hand-to-hand combat that smashed his helmet and killed his horse (see Map 2). His followers surged into the enemy ranks and

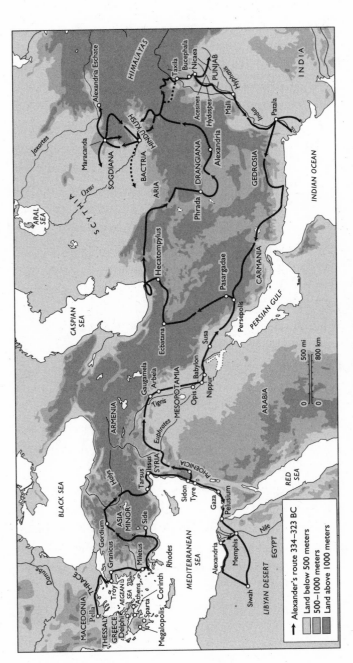

2. The world of Alexander.

routed the Persian forces. A year later at the Battle of Issus, Alexander suffered a thigh wound while leading the victorious charge that broke the ranks of Darius's huge army and forced the enemy to flee. During the capture of Gaza in 332 B.C.E., a catapult missile hit Alexander in the shoulder.[40]

Through all such duress, Alexander fought the Persians at close range in a conspicuous display of Homeric-style machismo. Darius, too, fought boldly at the head of an army that vastly outnumbered the Macedonians and Greeks, but Alexander proved the better tactician on every occasion.[41] This was never truer than at Gaugamela (near modern Irbil in Iraq) in 331 B.C.E., where Alexander routed his royal opponent for the final time. Darius fled into hiding, but his palaces fell one by one to the Greek and Macedonian invaders, who marveled at their opulence. How, they wondered, could a leader so wealthy and pompous command a military that proved so much less dangerous than expected? Even so, the victors remained uneasy about Darius's escape, and there were still remnants of the Persian grand army that had to be rounded up and disarmed. These matters preoccupied Alexander and his allies even as another crisis matured farther to the east. The Greeks and Macedonians were slow to appreciate the threat posed in what we now call Afghanistan, and reluctant to make this problem their top priority.

Known in antiquity as Bactria, Afghanistan emerged as a danger zone in direct response to Alexander's mounting power throughout the Middle East. From the perspective of the native peoples, Alexander and his followers represented an intrusive, alien culture offensive to local traditions.[42] Alexander was later decried as an "unbeliever" who brought evil to the East and drenched the land with blood.[43] Many Persians rejected

Alexander's claims of legitimacy as a liberator; they questioned the sincerity of his efforts to respect Persian religion and to promote a true partnership with local princes.[44] So, as the invaders battled deep into what is modern-day Iraq, and their forces occupied the entire region, Bactria became the refuge of what Alexander called, in turn, a rogue regime that harbored warlords and terrorists. Using rhetoric that still resonates today, Alexander denounced these men as lawless savages, the enemies of civilization. In what he called a new and dangerous world, Alexander warned his followers that these resourceful criminals would continue to exploit differences of religion, language, and culture to rouse attacks against innocent victims. They must be confronted with overwhelming military force, and stopped; their leaders must answer—dead or alive—for their crimes.[45] Not to act was to jeopardize the safety of Greece itself. "This is a noble cause," proclaimed Alexander to his armed forces, "and you will always be honored for seeing it through to the end."[46] Then, backed by unbridled support, the most powerful leader of the time led the most sophisticated army of its day against the warlords of Afghanistan. Ask those ancient Greek and Macedonian ghosts to reflect upon our situation today, and they might feel strangely at home. The old dictum "Plus ça change, plus c'est la même chose" (The more things change, the more they remain the same) ought to be the official motto of Afghanistan.

When in turn the British, Russians, and Americans each seized Kandahar in southern Afghanistan, they occupied a city founded by Alexander himself and still bearing the Arabic version of his name. When U.S. troops charged on horseback against the Taliban strongholds of Mazar-i-Sharif, they rode past the crumbling walls of Alexander's main camp, and the capital of the Greek kingdom that endured there for centuries. When American newspapers printed datelines from Ai Khanoum accompanied by photographs of a Northern Alliance gun emplacement on the heights of this remote village, practiced eyes could see the ruins there of an ancient city where Greek settlers once wrestled in the gymnasium, watched tragedies in the theater, worshiped the gods of their ancestral pantheon, and warred for control of Bactria for nearly nine long generations.[47] This book moves back and forth between modern Afghanistan and ancient Bactria to tell the story of an extraordinary place and the people who have struggled there. Its purpose is to place our present ordeal into a broader perspective, to provide a useful historical and cultural background for those who ask: Into what long history have we suddenly thrust ourselves and our armed forces? On what sort of ground—savage, sacred, or civilized— have we pitched our tents and taken our stand against terrorism?

We cannot answer such questions without facing up to a few challenges. First, it does no good to whitewash the present or the past. War is an ugly business, one of the most repugnant actions to which we humans regularly resort en masse. This is why every group convinced of its necessity works so hard to justify it to others. We rally to the conviction that a given alternative would be even uglier: terrorism, tyranny, starvation, or whatever else the abstracted enemy might be. When war looks like the lesser evil, we can embrace it warmly as though it at least has a good heart beneath its horrid exterior. To that end, we historically have found our greatest heroes in war, giving courage and sacrifice their most recognizable milieu in matters military rather than artistic, political, or philanthropic. Whatever else war might achieve for good or ill, whether in victory or in defeat, its extreme nature produces heroes whose glory helps us to ennoble the conflict. We need to believe that brave soldiers do not die for nothing, a sentiment that lies behind some of the grandest and most moving speeches ever made, such as Lincoln's remarks at Gettysburg and Pericles's oration at Athens. If lost lives were worth something, then the struggle that claimed them must be worthier still.

The emotional process is understandable, but wars and warriors thereby become difficult to judge dispassionately, much less to criticize. We meet that crisis head-on when we try to understand objectively the war in Afghanistan waged by Alexander, one of history's most heroized leaders. Alexander deserves our admiration for many of his personal qualities, such as his bravery, tactical genius, and tenacity. But to glorify the king and his conquests beyond their due cannot help us today: that path only blinds us to harsh realities that are easier to forget than to face again. If, for example, we indulge in the kind of ersatz history popular just a generation or so ago, we would see Alexander's invasion through the wistful eyes of men like Sir William Woodthorpe Tarn (1869–1957).[48] This gentleman-scholar argued tirelessly that Alexander was a high-minded prince of peace who was the first human to believe in the unity and brotherhood of all mankind. The wars conducted by Alexander had no base purposes such as egomania or greed, but rather the heartfelt desire to bring love and the benefits of a superior civilization to the wretched natives of ancient Iraq, Iran, and Afghanistan. Military conquest never had a kinder, gentler, or nobler objective than the one attributed by Tarn to Alexander: "Alexander's aim was to substitute peace for war, and reconcile the enmities of mankind by bringing them all—all that is whom his arm could reach, the people of his empire—to be of one mind together: as men were one in blood, so they should become one in heart and spirit."[49] Furthermore, Tarn insisted that in one place, and one place only, his hero's dream of peace and world brotherhood eventually came true: that place was allegedly Afghanistan!

The charming past recreated by Tarn answered all his wishes for the kind of world he could not himself enjoy in the first half of the violent twentieth century.[50] Tarn's worshipful vision of Alexander's world remains popular today in some circles, but it ill serves those who want an honest appraisal of the past as a signpost for the future.[51] Tarn's sanitized and sanctified account of Alexander's campaigns in and around Afghanistan must give way to the uglier version presented in these pages. Beneath the whitewash, bloodstains run deep.

Second, we must acknowledge that the wars waged in Afghanistan by Alexander, Britain, the Soviet Union, and now the United States share some salient features that may not bode well for our future. For example, all these invasions of Afghanistan went well at first, but so far no superpower has found a workable alternative to what might be called the recipe for ruin in Afghanistan:

1. Estimate the time and resources necessary to conquer and control the region.
2. Double all estimates.
3. Repeat as needed.

Afghanistan cannot be subdued by half measures. Invaders must consider the deadly demands of winter warfare, since all gains from seasonal campaigns are erased at every lull. Invaders must resolve to hunt down every warlord, for the one exception will surely rot the fruits of all other victories. Invaders cannot succeed by avoiding cross-border fighting, since the mobile insurgents can otherwise hide and reinforce with impunity. Invaders must calculate where to draw the decisive line between killing and conciliation, for too much of either means interminable conflict. Finally, all invaders so far have had to face one more difficult choice: once mired in a winless situation, they have tried to cut their losses through one of two exit strategies:

1. Retreat, as did the British and Soviets, with staggering losses.
2. Leave a large army of occupation permanently settled in the area, as Alexander did.

Neither option seems acceptable to the United States, which must therefore learn from its predecessors' mistakes and seek another path.

That process must take into account the same problems encountered throughout Afghan history, beginning in antiquity. As one scholar has adroitly observed in a study of Alexander's cities, "the requirements of imperial rule in Central Asia are laid down by nature, and were as valid in the time of Alexander (and earlier) as in that of Queen Victoria."[52] Alexander therefore drew a timeless map of the region, both politically and militantly, which still can be recognized spread across planning tables in modern military headquarters. But that is only the beginning. Alexander's reputation as a military genius, though richly deserved, cannot mask some of the miscalculations he pioneered in Bactria. He led his men into a war whose mission necessarily evolved. This often confused his troops and contributed to great disappointments. Morale suffered as men realized that they had been given false expectations about the nature of the resistance and the timetable for their return home to their families. In Bactria, allies and enemies were often indistinguishable until it was too late. Alexander's soldiers had been trained to wage and win major battles, but the king now shifted them into new and uncomfortable roles: they juggled awkwardly the jobs of conqueror, peacekeeper, builder, and settler. One minute they were asked to kill with ruthless and indiscriminate intensity, the next they were expected to show deference to the survivors. Enemies might suddenly become allies and exercise authority over Macedonians and Greeks. Some of Darius's generals and satraps (governors) regained power as Alexander's appointees. Alexander was the first ruler to underestimate the deleterious effect of such a conflict on his armed forces.

Third, let us not forget that Afghanistan has always been an inherently unstable territory. Even now, it barely qualifies to be called a nation in any conventional sense. Sure, it has (at times) a figurehead leader, flag, currency, and provisional constitution, but its traditions of local independence overwhelm all grander political notions. After all, Afghanistan is a collection of peoples who speak three times more languages (over thirty) than there are paved airfields (ten) in an area the size of England and France. It is an impoverished land with little to lose by resisting foreign intruders. Only 12 percent of the land is arable, and even then its main crop, opium, is illegal. Most of the population lacks access to safe water and sufficient food. Malnutrition has been a constant. About a quarter of the population has malaria, and perhaps half suffer from tuberculosis. The life expectancy for Afghans remains less than forty-five years. Poor but proud and defiant, the people there are not intimidated easily. The vaunted power of the West has little leverage beyond the immediate range of its weapons.[53]

In Afghanistan, a little rebellion always goes a long way. A force composed of a mere 10 percent of the population can use the rugged terrain and hostile climate very effectively against larger, better-armed forces. And that insurgent 10 percent, forever present, can swell in an instant to 90 percent or more. Nor can the populace be cowed by capturing its heartland. Afghanistan has no center to speak of, and no clear edges. Afghanistan's few large cities all perch on its periphery: Mazar-i-Sharif in the north, Herat in the west, Kandahar in the south, and Kabul in the east. They all lie nearer to other nations than to each other. Indeed, many segments of the population feel a closer kinship to ethnic groups outside Afghanistan than to compatriots within. The borders are nominal, not natural. They are porous to such a degree that rebels can easily drift across and regroup among friendly brethren. Under these conditions, whether cities fall or not, an invader can never really know who is winning the war.

That explains why we stand today (albeit for different reasons) where the Soviets did in 1980, the British in 1879 and 1839, and even the Greeks and Macedonians in 329 B.C.E. To see our way forward, we must first take a long look back. For recent history, that task is relatively simple. Accounts of the British and Soviet experience in Afghanistan are numerous, and some analysts have made good use of them. Unheroized historical studies of

Alexander's invasion are considerably rarer, though no less vital. The events of 9–11 and their aftermath have given new urgency to that research, and this book is one result. The following pages provide a fresh look into Alexander's invasion; this book is written for those who seek a millennial perspective on one of the defining conflicts of our time.

CHAPTER TWO

Hunting the Enemy

CITY OF BONES

In the spring of 329 B.C.E., at the age of twenty-six, Alexander set up camp in a city rumored to be the oldest in the world. Zariaspa lay beside the Bactrus River and served as the administrative capital of Bactria, an old province of the Persian Empire; for these reasons, the city itself was generally referred to simply as Bactra (without an *i*). Today the site, called Balkh, is a sprawling ruin in northern Afghanistan with miles of crumbling walls enclosing a small village in a dusty tract.[1] In Islamic tradition, old Noah himself founded this city after floating through the Great Flood. Thousands of years later, Balkh was still "a splendid city of great size" (though already declining) when Marco Polo passed by in the thirteenth century C.E.[2] Gradually, its population shifted fourteen miles eastward to Mazar-i-Sharif, particularly after the establishment there of the popular shrine of Hazrat 'Ali, son-in-law of Muhammad, in 1481.[3] It was at Mazar-i-Sharif that the

United States and its allies won their first victory in Afghanistan (with the cavalry charge mentioned in chapter 1), and at the tomb of 'Ali that large crowds celebrated the event.[4] Ironically, many Muslims revere an alternate burial place for this same 'Ali, a rival shrine located at Najaf in Iraq—the scene of so much strife in an even more recent war.[5]

Neither Najaf nor Mazar-i-Sharif existed as cities in the fourth century B.C.E. When Alexander rode by on his way from Babylon to Bactra, Islam had not yet redrawn the maps of ancient empires. Zoroastrianism prevailed in much of the Persian realm conquered by Alexander, and Bactra was the holy city of its prophet.[6] A famous golden shrine of Anahita, worshiped by Zoroastrians as a goddess of fertility and purifying waters, still stood astride the Bactrus River when the Greeks and Macedonians arrived.[7] In later legends, Anahita would become the wife of Alexander and use her powers to help her husband win his wars.[8] In reality, the only thing her cult could do for the king was to preside over the nourishing waters that refreshed his troops in this arid land. The Bactrus River, and the dozens of irrigation canals drawing from its stream, gave life to a land otherwise parched by encroaching sand dunes, dust storms, and daytime temperatures simmering above 110°F.

Inside the city, the sparkling oasis turned ugly. Decaying bodies and bleached human bones lay scattered in the streets. One of Alexander's men reported seeing packs of dogs gnawing at the dead, while a few stalked and snapped at fresher meals still alive but helpless against the hounds.[9] The outraged Greeks shuddered as they witnessed this alien spectacle. It was not, of course, the ordinary sight or smell of death that unsettled these veterans of Alexander's wars. They had made careers of wading through

blood pooled deep in captured cities and bodies piled high on bat-
tlefields. They had massacred entire populations when so ordered, or when the rush of victory carried them too far to stop.
They had certainly witnessed on many occasions the glut of dogs
and carrion birds on the dead and dying of war.

Bactra was different. Alexander's army had not stormed its
gates or scaled its walls. The dogs inside were not growling over
the bones of battle casualties. The thing that so shocked the
Greeks and Macedonians was that they had entered, unopposed,
a city quite alive with normal trade and human traffic, its people
going about their daily affairs with a wary eye on the newcomers but not the slightest regard for the carnage around them. As
part of their religion, the Bactrians literally tossed their dead to
the dogs and even hastened the process by letting these hounds
execute their old, sick, and invalid citizens. No one intervened.
In fact, the dogs were kept for just this purpose. In their own language, the locals called their hounds something like Devourers
or Undertakers and let them do a dirty but sacred job that in
Greece would be the work of a tomb or funeral pyre. Alexander
and his troops denounced the use of Devourer dogs as a barbaric
custom, whereas the Bactrians in turn could not believe that anyone would be so depraved as to set a dead person afire. Alexander had cremated his father back in Macedonia; no one in Bactria could imagine such a sacrilege. What were the two cultures
to do, now that fate had thrown them together? How should the
living henceforth treat their dead, now that one of the world's
youngest conquerors had arrived in one of the world's oldest
cities?

To Alexander's credit, his policy was generally to respect local
customs and religions. This had been true in Egypt, where the

king paid homage to the bewildering beliefs of that exotic civilization. Indeed, Alexander would in time be mummified and buried there.[10] When the Indian sage Calanus fell ill in Alexander's camp, the king allowed—even assisted—the preparation of an elaborate funeral ritual culminating in the man's astonishing self-immolation on a blazing pyre.[11] At Pasargadae in Persia, Alexander took special care to restore the aged tomb of Cyrus, and he later punished those who defiled that hallowed ground.[12] Alexander accommodated all sorts of local traditions on his long march from Greece to India, but at Bactra he bristled and would not budge: the Devourer dogs had to go. This decision gave the first hint of an epic struggle that would become as political and religious as it was military. Bactria would be treated unlike any other part of Alexander's immense empire. The Greeks and Macedonians saw it as particularly alien and developed a singular distaste for its population. In the eyes of Alexander's troops, nowhere needed civilizing more than this bleak landscape where warlords hid in the hills and a cruel religion brutalized the streets.

Of course, the tired and ill-tempered invaders were not entirely fair. As one Greek author complained when he later read of the Devourer dogs, Alexander's compatriots "tell us nothing but the worst" about the native peoples they met in central Asia.[13] Their biased accounts left out the extraordinary local achievements revealed to us today through the great efforts of archaeologists. The region was certainly urbanized, wealthy, and well irrigated. We must therefore be wary of the ancient propaganda that the conquering Greeks first brought civilization, high art, and economic prosperity to the backward Bactrians. In fact, the land was enjoying one of its periodic golden ages. Thus, Alexander's army did not find the region in quite the ruined condition that exists today, although the invaders soon did their part to level its towns and cities, burn its croplands, and scatter its population. For a time, the Greeks and Macedonians themselves turned Bactria into a tempestuous wasteland that had to be rebuilt in order to regain something of its former (unacknowledged) glory. That cycle would continue down through the ages, with repeated invasions and periods of rehabilitation, as noted in chapter 1. Some of these eras were worse than others (the Umayyads and Mongols stand out for the long-term effect of their incursions), but it began with Alexander: the extent to which he actually brought high civilization to Afghanistan is the extent to which he destroyed what had been there since the Bronze Age.

Just a few weeks before Alexander arrived in Bactra, a warlord named Bessus held a raucous war council in the city. If we can trust a deserter's account of that meeting, passed down through the centuries, this Bessus put on quite a show.[14] Amid great feasting and drinking, Bessus tried to rally the martial spirit of his assembled friends and followers. He boasted of their power and belittled that of the invaders. He invoked the gods of the land to aid his cause and reminded his listeners of his own personal stake in their war against the Greeks.

Two years earlier, Bessus had fought against Alexander in the Battle of Gaugamela (October 1, 331 B.C.E.) near modern-day Irbil in Iraq.[15] At that time, Bessus was the satrap of Bactria under Darius III, the "King of Kings" who ruled the Persian Empire. The Persian king and his satrap were kinsmen, and Darius desperately needed Bessus and the renowned cavalry from Bactria to help stop the relentless progress of the Greeks and Macedonians.[16] Alexander's troops had already captured the western third of the empire, and at Gaugamela the fate of everything else would be decided in a few desperate hours of dusty fighting. Darius's plan, captured after the battle, clearly assigned Bessus and the Bactrian contingent the main task of meeting— and destroying—Alexander's personal assault against the Persian left wing.[17] During the battle, Bessus and his soldiers fought well, but found themselves pinned down while Alexander charged through a gap in the line and chased Darius from the field. With his own cavalry still intact, Bessus disengaged. According to one modern analysis of Bessus's conduct that day, "no commander could be blamed for ordering a withdrawal in such circumstances. Later he [Bessus] could reasonably claim that others had let him down, that it would have been suicidal to remain where he was, and that he had not been defeated."[18]

When Darius and Bessus met again, what remained of the Persian army and its officers must surely have struggled to explain how they had lost to an invading force five times smaller than their own. Whose cowardice had caused such a debacle? No doubt Bessus was still defending his actions when, at Bactra in 329 B.C.E., he argued along the lines quoted above and blamed everything on Darius: It was Darius's incompetence, not his own poor judgment or Alexander's generalship, that had gotten everyone in this mess.[19] That is why Bessus had arranged the assassination of Darius in 330 B.C.E. The Persian King of Kings had first been deceived, arrested, and shackled and then shut into a locked wagon to be hauled along like a doomed animal.[20] The Bactrian cavalry saluted Bessus as Darius's royal successor, calling him Artaxerxes V. In time, as Alexander drew near, the conspirators stabbed Darius and left him for dead. They hastened to the safety of Bactria's hills, as warlords are still wont to do.

Alexander had not taken this news well. He had beaten Darius, torched the largest palace at Persepolis to settle old scores, and begun to see himself as the rightful new King of Kings in conquered Persia. The brutal murder of Darius deprived Alexander of his coup de grâce and destabilized the newly won empire. The war should have been over, but instead this criminal Bessus claimed Darius's throne—*Alexander's* throne—and defied the superpower to stop him. Alexander would have to invade Bactria to bring this madman to justice. To prepare the way, the king made a speech at Hecatompylus (cited in chapter 1), in which he denounced Bessus and his cabal as a threat to the civilized world. This operation would carry the leader of the Greek and Macedonian world well beyond the original mandate of the League of Corinth. Technically, the alliance had finished its job with the fall of Persia. If necessary, however, Alexander was prepared to go it alone against Bessus. He allowed the unwilling to turn back homeward and paid the rest handsomely to sign on as volunteers with his Macedonians. That is why Alexander needed to frame an essentially personal war in terms of a new, grander, more abstract cause. This was no longer to be a war of conquest and Hellenic retribution against a rival state, but rather an unavoidable struggle to keep the peace and protect all nations of law from organized criminals. Alexander meant to hunt down the outlaw Bessus and all who harbored him, not conduct a conventional war against a foe deserving the title of King Artaxerxes V.[21]

Alexander had to take some diplomatic gambles in order to strengthen his case against Bessus and his followers. In a precarious balancing act, he simultaneously acted the part of Macedonian king, leader (hegemon) of the Greeks, and ruler of all Persian territories. Rather than sweep away every vestige of Darius's old regime, Alexander adopted some elements of Persian royal dress and protocol. He also chose a few Persians to hold high office. This put a less imperious face on the occupation of Persia and provided some leverage against the rhetoric of Bessus, but it angered many of the Greeks and Macedonians. Alexander nevertheless rushed into a policy of reconciliation toward men of dubious reliability. Even some of Darius's murderers were pardoned and put into positions of authority, an expedience that Alexander very soon regretted.[22]

Bessus, of course, was the key exception: he would have to pay an extraordinarily painful and public price for his royal pretensions. Rather than barge straight into Bactria, Alexander circled his prey. He fought a campaign in the area of modern Herat in western Afghanistan because the native governor there, named Satibarzanes, had, after surrendering, suddenly renounced his allegiance to Alexander and massacred the foreigners stationed in his province. Alexander's policies were already backfiring. This man was clearly acting in conjunction with Bessus, so Alexander moved quickly to isolate the danger. The insurgents were soundly defeated, although Satibarzanes escaped.[23] Alexander's generals would deal with him later. Meanwhile, Alexander appointed another Persian as governor. The army then swept south into the district of Drangiana. At Phrada (modern Farah), the recent attempts by Alexander to legitimize his power in Persia exposed a serious rift in his entourage. Traditionalist Macedonians resented some of Alexander's new policies, such as his appointment of former enemies to prestigious posts and his wearing of Persian regalia. An assassination plot formed in response to the king's apparent betrayal of his own people. The conspiracy failed and the traitors were executed. The most prominent victims were the great Macedonian generals Philotas and his father, Parmenio, who, in spite of their apparent innocence, were purged nonetheless in order to clear the king's court of naysayers. A fresh coterie of loyalists closed ranks around Alexander; the Afghan wars would swiftly advance the careers of men like Craterus, Hephaestion, Coenus, Perdiccas, and Ptolemy.[24]

After escaping this danger, Alexander renamed the place Prophthasia (Anticipation) to commemorate the failure of the plot. His march resumed south and then eastward along the high-duned fringe of the Dasht-i Margo (the Desert of Death). He had hoped to run down Barsaentes, another of Darius's killers who had abused his pardon and sided with Bessus. The Persian, however, had too great a lead and vanished (like many of the Taliban) into what is now Pakistan.[25] The Greek and Macedonian army passed by Kandahar, a site built up by Alexander and still bearing his name (derived from Iskandariya, *Alexandria* in Arabic).[26] The center of so much strife during the invasions by Britain, the USSR, and now the United States, old Kandahar guarded strategic routes leading southeast to the Indus Valley, and northeast to the region of Kabul. Alexander took the same road later traveled by Lord Roberts in 1880; the Greeks and Macedonians thereby arrived at winter quarters in the vicinity of modern Begram, where the king fortified the camp as yet another Alexandria.[27]

Since declaring his intention to punish the outlaw regime of Bessus, Alexander had marched fifteen hundred miles over eight months in a wide arc through what is now the southern half of

Afghanistan. Parts of the journey had penetrated a miserable purgatory with "plagues of midges, mosquitoes, houseflies, and poisonous snakes and hurricane-force winds."[28] Worse was soon to come in a region habitually short of food. No matter what the climate or circumstances might be, Alexander had to procure every day the equivalent of 255 tons of food and forage, plus 160,000 gallons of water, just to keep his army alive and moving forward.[29] On the other (northern) side of the Hindu Kush Mountains, Bessus and his followers were destroying everything that might feed the invaders. The rebels knew that the Greeks and Macedonians would consume all their provisions as they struggled over the high passes of the mountains, arriving in Bactria's heartland exhausted and hungry. The scorched-earth plan, a good one under the circumstances, recognized that warfare in central Asia depends upon logistics, and that attrition can deal the hardest blows of all.[30]

The fabled Hindu Kush Mountains, mistakenly called the Caucasus by Alexander's men, soar as high as seventeen thousand feet (see Map 3). The lower slopes sustain modest vegetation, mostly scrub and grasses, but barren rock prevails above fourteen thousand feet. In winter, the snow line descends to six thousand feet and blocks the passes; blizzards are common, and snow falls even during summer at the higher elevations. The spring melt usually commences in March or April, gradually freeing the passes and sending torrents of icy water and boulders tumbling down every streambed. As early as possible—too early, in fact—Alexander threaded his army through these mountains. He had three possible routes: the western, through Bamian and the Shibar Pass; the central, via the Salang Pass; and the eastern, by way of the Panshir Valley and the Khawak Pass. The path

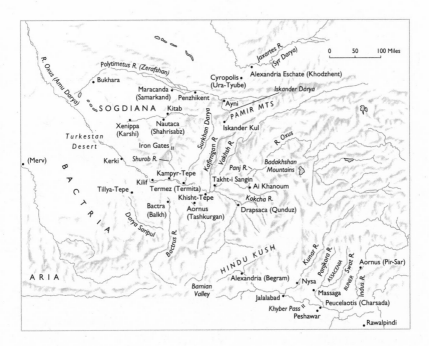

3. Ancient Bactria

through Bamian, where the giant Buddhas later towered near a pilgrim's trail, until blown up by the Taliban, offered the easiest and most obvious choice, so Alexander probably refused it to surprise Bessus. The central course was shortest but by far the steepest, and it was never practical until the 1.6 mile Salang Tunnel, the highest in the world, was cut by the Soviets.[31] The longer route over the Khawak Pass seems to have suited Alexander's purpose in the spring of 329 B.C.E.[32]

The Greeks and Macedonians struggled for two weeks through deep snow before the passes fully cleared. The food ran out, and starving men naturally resorted to every extreme: they caught and ate raw fish, chewed on local plants, and finally ate their own baggage animals to survive. Like the British in the First Afghan War who ate sheepskins fried in blood, the invaders persevered. Because firewood could not be gathered, they devoured the carcasses uncooked and stumbled on toward Bactra. Either their king had miscalculated his army's needs, or he had moved of necessity and entered the mountains while the weather was still dangerous.[33] Perhaps complicating Alexander's operations was an extraordinary anomaly in the climate. Recent analyses of Fennoscandinavian tree-ring data demonstrate that some of the coolest summers of the past seventy-four hundred years (5407 B.C.E.–1997 C.E.) occurred in precisely the years 330–321 B.C.E.[34] What so dramatically cooled the north at this time is not certain, but the effects may have contributed to Alexander's trouble by producing unexpectedly early and longer winters, with heavier snowfalls, in 329–327, as well as a contemporary famine in Greece caused by widespread grain shortages.[35] This data need not mean that the central Asian summers were comfortably cool, only that they may have been shorter and somewhat less horrendous while winters were correspondingly more severe.

Though in much distress, the Macedonian and Greek invaders made it across the mountains and found comfort in the Bactrian towns of Drapsaca (modern Qunduz?) and Aornus (modern Tashkurgan?).[36] Bessus and the Bactrian cavalry were nowhere to be seen when Alexander's troops emerged tired and famished from the icy clutches of the Hindu Kush Mountains. Had the rebels used the guerilla tactics for which the Afghan warlords are now famous, the Greeks and Macedonians might have suffered a major setback. But Bessus employed only half a winning strategy: he cut off Alexander's supplies, but also should have attacked at opportune moments. As it turned out, Bessus was not in position to strike the invading army; he seems to have denuded the likeliest invasion route while ignoring the others. Alexander's risky move paid off. He and his troops refreshed themselves and regrouped while Bessus, a few miles west at Bactra, held his hasty council of war.

Whatever Bessus's exact words in his arrogant speech to his warrior band, he and the Bactrians were extremely worried.[37] Blame Darius all he might for Gaugamela, brag of his own prospects as King Artaxerxes V, scoff at Alexander's rashness, but as many as a hundred thousand foreigners had gotten into Bactria and were fast approaching, unopposed.[38] When Bessus laid out the next stage of his strategy, enough wine had been drunk to make it sound quite sensible: They would retreat north through the desert, cross the Oxus River, and make their stand in the region of Sogdiana. The Oxus (modern Amu Darya) would hold back the Greeks and Macedonians while Bessus recruited allies from the nomadic peoples of the vast northern steppes.

To this plan, one banqueter, named Gobares, dared object. In a speech probably embellished in the retelling over the ages, Gobares sprinkled his appeal with local proverbs still popular today, such as "still waters run deep" and "his bark is worse than his bite."[39] This eloquence was meant to convince Bessus to give up and take his chances with Alexander, who could at times be incredibly merciful. Gobares questioned the legitimacy of Bessus's authority, an indication that Alexander was already winning among some Persians the political battle for Darius's throne. Bessus, of course, would abide none of this talk; when he drew his sword in anger, Gobares fled Bactra and reported the whole affair to Alexander. The Macedonian king hastened to the capital city, that bizarre oasis of Anahita littered with human bones, only to find Bessus already gone.

VICTORIES

At Bactra, the Greeks and Macedonians nonetheless got some very good news.[40] The generals who had remained behind near Herat to capture or kill Bessus's ally Satibarzanes now rejoined the army and reported what had happened. There had been a significant battle during which Satibarzanes had paused, taken off his helmet, and challenged any opponent brave enough to fight him in single combat. Old white-haired Erigyius, who shared the Macedonian command with three others (including a Persian, Artabazus), stepped forward and accepted the offer. During the fight, Satibarzanes missed with his spear and Erigyius charged, driving his lance into the enemy's throat and out the back of his neck. Thrown from his horse, Satibarzanes continued to fight though still impaled. Erigyius grabbed the lance and pulled it free, then thrust it forcefully into Satibarzanes's face. The latter could do nothing but help drive it deeper to hurry his death and end his own suffering.

At Bactra, Alexander and his soldiers marveled at the mangled head of Satibarzanes, which Erigyius carried around as a trophy of war.[41] The deed had won the battle and ended the insurrection around Herat, preventing those rebels from reinforcing Bessus as the warlord had planned. The same dramatic news may have been what compelled Bessus to withdraw into Sogdiana in search of other allies, and no doubt it demoralized the Bactrian cavalry, which had counted on Satibarzanes's support.

When the Bactrians learned that Alexander had crossed the Hindu Kush, that Satibarzanes was dead, and that Bessus planned to retreat north across the Oxus and abandon Bactria to the invaders, most of the native horsemen simply slipped away to their homes.[42] It could not have been a substantial band that followed Bessus to Sogdiana. At Bactra, Alexander considered these facts and decided to forge ahead as quickly as possible to finish Bessus before the assassin could redress his losses. Acting, of course, as the rightful King of Kings, Alexander appointed Artabazus—the Persian just back from the victory against Satibarzanes—to be the satrap of Bactria.[43] The message was clear: join Alexander's cause, like Artabazus, and receive all the perquisites of the old Persian Empire; or live as outlaws, like Satibarzanes and Bessus, and endure the righteous punishments of the civilized world. No one could be neutral.

The march from Bactra to the Oxus River crossed a harsh stretch of desert that would again test the resilience of the Greek and Macedonian army.[44] The invaders had nearly frozen and starved just a few weeks earlier in the mountains, and now during high summer they had to hike through nearly fifty miles of searing wastes where Anahita's water could not sustain them. Local informants advised Alexander to travel only at night, both to escape the worst temperatures and to navigate the desert by the stars. To keep the journey down to two nights, the king lightened the army's load by leaving its baggage at Bactra in the care of Artabazus. Still, it was a disaster. The sand glowed with heat, mirages danced, and the dry air sucked every drop of moisture from the mouths of the suffering men. Water bags emptied too soon, and discipline failed. Soldiers gorged themselves on stores of oil and wine, only to vomit away what they had foolishly drunk. With growing numbers of men dehydrated or already dead, Alexander pressed forward to the Oxus River and lit signal fires to guide and encourage the troops. Relays of water bearers went back into the desert to assist the weakest stragglers. Unfortunately, many drank so excessively that they had "choking fits" and died. Alexander reportedly waited by the trail, without refreshing himself, to welcome each survivor as he staggered into camp. The political battle to win over the Bactrian people was going well, but the land itself was literally killing the Greeks and Macedonians.

The next obstacle was the Oxus River, the longest and largest in central Asia. As today it defines much of the northern border of Afghanistan, in antiquity it separated Bactria proper from Sogdiana. The region of Sogdiana stretched north to the Jaxartes River (modern Syr Darya); it was attached administratively to Bactria as an extension of the province (satrapy). At his crossing point, Alexander measured the river's width at about three-quarters of a mile. Scholars have long disputed the exact location. In antiquity, the key crossings were located at Kerki, Kilif, Kampyr-Tepe, and Termez. Kerki was probably too far west for Alexander's purposes. Of the remaining possibilities, the importance of Termez in later history (it became a key Islamic trading center) has swayed many to settle upon it. Legends do link Alexander to the founding of Termez, but such associations carry no decisive weight in that part of the world. Termez is certainly a reasonable guess, now with its Friendship Bridge (at times an Orwellian misnomer), but Kampyr-Tepe and Kilif cannot be ruled out as the spot where Alexander first encountered and crossed the Oxus. In fact, Kampyr-Tepe is the only crossing site where pottery has been found that is contemporary with Alexander's reign. The challenge would have been the same at any locale.[45] Bessus had burned all the boats, and the powerful current made it impossible to set pilings in the deep riverbed. In any case, no wood could be found with which to construct a makeshift bridge. The only solution was the age-old practice of fashioning flotation devices by stuffing straw into leather tent covers and water skins. By stitching them tightly, these maintained enough buoyancy to float swimmers lying upon them across the river. The whole operation took five or six days.[46]

During this time, Alexander received fresh intelligence about Bessus's situation. The warlord had not fulfilled his promise to oppose the invaders at the "wall of the Oxus." In fact, with each leg of Alexander's relentless pursuit, Bessus found himself more alone. The man claiming to be Artaxerxes V experienced (ironically and perhaps justly) the same plight as Darius after Gaugamela: he fled, unable to mount a fight, and lost the last of his fretful lieutenants. Word of Alexander's kindness to Gobares, the man who had defected after opposing Bessus's speech at Bactra, encouraged other rebels to slip away to the oncoming army. It was easy, under the circumstances, to favor for the moment Alexander's claim to the Persian realm over that of the retreating Bessus. Warlords tend to pledge allegiance as the occasion warrants, whatever the alleged religious and political crimes of the enemy. This remains Lesson One today: "There are no immutable loyalties or alliances in Afghanistan, whatever ethnic or religious umbrella they may be formed under and however fervent the oaths that seal them."[47] Bessus betrayed Darius, and others revealed themselves willing to betray Bessus in turn.

Alexander could afford, therefore, to send part of his army back home. Some old and unfit Macedonians received their formal discharges on the banks of the Oxus. They would not have been dragged across the desert from Bactra if Alexander had not believed they might be needed to fight Bessus; clearly, the military situation had changed and the king could be charitable. An additional contingent of Greek mercenaries from Thessaly also went home, but they were apparently fired. They may have been held responsible for breaking discipline during the recent desert march and for grumbling about the hardships. Anticipating an arrest instead of a battle, Alexander resumed his march into Sogdiana with almost a thousand fewer men.[48]

Then something strange occurred—if we may believe some of the ancient sources.[49] As the invading Greeks and Macedonians approached a town, its inhabitants surrendered in great celebration. They spoke a degenerated form of Greek and claimed to be the descendants of the Branchidae, a Greek clan that had been deported from Miletus (in western Asia Minor) by the Persian king Xerxes in 479 B.C.E. They happily welcomed Alexander within the walls of their town, expecting nothing like the so-called liberation they were about to receive. On this sesquicentennial of their exile, the Branchidae learned just how long their fellow Greeks could hold a grudge. Alexander's army decided that the Branchidae were traitors living under the protective custody of the Persians, to whom they had once betrayed a famous temple in Miletus. The Branchidae remained, therefore, enemies rather than friends, criminals rather than compatriots. Alexander and his soldiers plundered the town and butchered every single person. No mercy was shown to the defenseless citizens, not even those begging as suppliants. The massacre was complete. Next, in a spasm of rage reminiscent of the Romans at Carthage, the invaders destroyed every vestige of the town and even leveled the surrounding woods and sacred groves. The stumps themselves were pulled up and their broken roots burned out of the ground. What roused such passions we cannot know. Perhaps Alexander's army needed a bloody catharsis after its recent travails; perhaps the men were spoiling for a fight against anyone in their path; perhaps the king wished to play to the home crowd in Greece after acting so much lately as a legitimate king of Persia. Whatever the reason or reasons, the first atrocity had occurred in a campaign that would soon become a breeding ground for senseless brutality.

Having executed these traitors to the Greek cause, Alexander's attention turned back to the treason of Bessus. A message arrived that three prominent rebels (Spitamenes, Dataphernes, and Catanes) had locked Bessus in chains somewhere in the neighborhood of modern Kitab in Uzbekistan. Having stripped their former leader of all his regalia, the warlords wished to surrender the captive to King Alexander for punishment. Two versions exist of the transfer to Alexander's custody. In one, Spitamenes personally delivered the prisoner bound and naked, led around by a collar and chain. Spitamenes made a little speech on the occasion, professing his loyalty to the memory of Darius, for which Alexander praised him.[50] In the other version, the hero is Ptolemy. This account certainly derives from Ptolemy's own memoirs, written when he became the king of Egypt at the outset of the Hellenistic age.[51] Ptolemy could not resist the opportunity to elaborate at great length—indeed, exaggerate—his role in bringing Bessus to justice. When Alexander learned of Bessus's arrest, the king assigned Ptolemy the mission of riding ahead with a picked force of five thousand men to secure the prisoner. This was Ptolemy's first high-profile command, and he wished to make the most of it. Better to describe himself as the key figure, rather than give that honor to Spitamenes, whose daughter later married the general Seleucus, a political rival of Ptolemy.

Fearing the capricious nature of the so-called barbarians, Ptolemy dashed to the rendezvous lest Spitamenes and the others should change their minds and release their captive. Ptolemy's troops covered the ten-day journey in only four. Sure enough, claimed Ptolemy, the conspirators were having second thoughts. As the invaders approached, Spitamenes and his followers allegedly rode off, leaving Bessus behind in a small village. Ptolemy surrounded the place and ordered its inhabitants to surrender Bessus, which the frightened villagers naturally did, after what had happened to the Branchidae. Informed of Ptolemy's success, Alexander sent instructions on the treatment of the prisoner. Bessus was to be stood bound and naked by the right side of the road on which Alexander would pass. The captive should be wearing a wooden collar as a symbol of his disgrace.[52] A few days later, the king stopped beside the would-be usurper and demanded an explanation of his crimes. All accounts agree that Bessus offered a lame defense: he had taken the title "King of Kings" intending only to pass it, in turn, to Alexander.[53] His long flight belied the excuse, and the penalty would be horrific. First, he was tortured while a herald announced his various evil deeds. Then he was placed in the custody of Darius's brother, Oxathres, and sent to prison in Bactra. There in the coming winter, Bessus would be dragged before a sort of Loya Jirga and literally defaced.[54]

According to Persian custom, the rightful King of Kings should be a handsome man; Darius, for example, had been "the best-looking and tallest of all men."[55] Usurpers, therefore, were brutally disfigured before they were killed, in order to render them thoroughly unfit for the throne they had coveted. Later in Bactra, where Bessus had so recently held his war council under the name Artaxerxes V, the captive's ears and nose were cut from his face. There could be no doubt then which man was king. Alexander appeared before the crowd young and ruggedly handsome. He was clean shaven, short, and muscular, with his head habitually cocked to the left. His hair and complexion were fair; his voice deep and harsh; his eyes clear and tending toward blue.[56] After the death of Darius, Alexander had begun to wear some of the regalia of the Persian kings, notably the diadem, striped robe, and belt.[57] Surely with startling effect, beside him stood Bessus chained and bleeding, a broken man. Lord Byron might have been looking at Bessus stripped of his royal robes and name (rather than thinking of Napoleon) when he penned these lines:

> 'Tis done—but yesterday a King!
> And arm'd with Kings to strive—
> And now thou art a nameless thing:
> So abject—yet alive![58]

But not for long. In one account, Oxathres presided over the crucifixion of Bessus and the desecration of his corpse. In another, Bessus was strapped between two bent trees and ripped to pieces when the saplings sprang upright.[59] Even the greatest admirers of Alexander felt shock at this savagery.[60] One is reminded of the haunting photograph showing the Afghan president Muhammad Najibullah hung from a traffic kiosk in Kabul after the Taliban captured, castrated, and then killed him in 1996.[61] Victory is the proud parent of vengeance in the wars of Afghanistan.

CHAPTER THREE

A Desperate Struggle

EXPLOSION

In the summer of 329 B.C.E., a strange calm settled over Bactria and Sogdiana. The threat of war had passed. A compliant Persian held the post of Bactrian satrap; the dangerous Bactrian cavalry had demobilized; farmers and herdsmen had returned to their ancient tasks. The last of the warlords had backed down and betrayed their leader. As a result, no rival contested Alexander's right to rule the empire of Darius III. This first invasion of Bactria-Afghanistan by a punitive superpower could hardly have seemed easier.[1] Except for the horrid weather and challenging terrain, the operation involved fewer risks, surely, than anyone had predicted. Satibarzanes had put up a fight, but not Bessus. No Bactrian city, not even Bactra, had closed its gates and forced a siege. On the other side, the only destruction of croplands resulted from Bessus's orders, not Alexander's. The only locals killed by the Greeks were the descendants of other Greeks. No

Bactrian except Bessus was tried and condemned to death. There seemed for just a moment an exquisite chance that the intervention might actually end well. The United States senses that possibility now, as once did the Soviets; the British felt it twice. It is, historically, a dangerous feeling.

Since the political contest between Alexander and Bessus involved a throne in far-off Mesopotamia, it probably mattered little to the Bactrians which man eventually sat upon it, so long as nothing much changed in their own homeland. They wanted most to be left alone, returning to local matters of family, faith, farms, and flocks and petty feuds about them. Alexander, however, was not quite ready to leave them to their work. This adventurous king never missed a chance to examine another frontier. He liked to offer sacrifices at the extremities of his empire, especially along major rivers.[2] Just ahead of the army, the Jaxartes (modern Syr Darya) flowed along the border of the Sogdian extension of Bactria, thus defining the northeast frontier of the old Persian Empire. The king wanted to add his personal monuments to those of his predecessors and, at the same time, to reconnoiter a critical expanse. Preemptive measures seemed in order.

Beyond the Jaxartes stretched the open steppes of central Asia, where various independent Scythian tribes lived out a nomadic existence.[3] These hardy peoples, renowned for their fighting spirit and horsemanship, sometimes joined forces with their sedentary neighbors to the south. Bessus had staked his last hopes on such an alliance, and that gave Alexander very good reason to bar the door. Like the present borderlands nominally separating Afghanistan from Pakistan, Uzbekistan, Tadjikistan, and other nations, the Jaxartes frontier offered rebels a place to hide, smuggle, and recruit. Alexander intended to fortify this frontier and prevent any such collusion in the future by setting up a permanent military barrier between Sogdiana and the Scythians. The king had done this sort of thing before; in fact, he began his reign in 336 B.C.E. with a Balkan campaign north to the Danube River, where he bullied some Scythian tribes that threatened interference in his realm.[4] It had worked wonders back home, but he was not in the Balkans any more.

At his leisure, Alexander moved his army northward through Sogdiana. He may have been following the old caravan route that threaded the Iron Gates and emerged in the territory of Nautaca south of Maracanda (modern Samarkand). The long pursuit of Bessus, though anticlimactic, had taken its toll on the cavalry horses. Therefore, in the fine horse-rearing country around Karshi (site of a critical air base used by the Soviets and, later, by U.S. Task Force Dagger), Alexander requisitioned fresh mounts for his men.[5] This may, in retrospect, have touched a nerve among a local population always sensitive to any loss of livestock. More unwelcome intrusions soon followed.

Alexander's army paused briefly in Maracanda, the largest city in Sogdiana. Inside its impressive circuit of walls and strong citadel, the king left a thousand men as a garrison.[6] About 180 miles farther to the northeast lay the Jaxartes frontier. Alexander's plans for this area were no doubt already taking shape, and the king's preparations could not have been overlooked by the indigenous population. Near the river there existed only one substantial city, an old Persian foundation named Cyropolis (perhaps modern Ura-Tyube), plus six walled towns. Though impressive, Cyropolis stood twenty-five miles south of the crucial river, too far to effect the kind of control that the king now en-

visaged. Given the surplus population available from these settlements, Alexander decided to construct a new, powerful military post right on the Jaxartes (probably at modern Khodzhent).
Surrounded by almost seven miles of defensive walls and named
Alexandria Eschate ("the farthermost Alexandria"), it would
henceforth guard the edge of his empire.[7]

This was apparently more meddling than the locals were
willing to bear. Plans for the new city signaled a permanent
Greek presence on the Sogdian-Scythian border. This would diminish the commercial and administrative standing of Cyropolis and probably meant that area croplands and pasturage would
be attached to Alexandria Eschate as dependencies. In other
ways, militarily closing the frontier would disrupt traditional
patterns of life in an environment where rivers naturally at-
tracted disparate peoples together rather than divided them.
Scythians and Sogdians-Bactrians enjoyed a symbiotic relationship, especially through economic interactions and occasional
military alliances. The Persian Empire had accepted this fluid
state, but Alexander would not.[8] He intended to isolate the region from its neighbors. It was becoming obvious that the new
ruler of Persia had his own ideas about the governance of Bactria.
Wary warlords like Spitamenes began to wonder about their
trade of Bessus for Alexander. Their formal summons to attend
the Afghan council at Bactra to witness the punishment of Bessus
emphasized the inauguration of a new regime and put the Bactrians ill at ease about their uncertain futures.[9]

Without warning, the entire region exploded into armed resistance. An unsuspecting party of Greek soldiers out collecting
supplies was suddenly attacked. Those not slain were taken prisoner into the nearby mountains. Stunned and then furious,

Alexander led a retaliatory strike against the insurgents, whose numbers quickly swelled to twenty thousand.[10] In the forefront of the fighting, the king took an arrow through his leg that splintered the bone. He had not suffered an injury since leaving the Mediterranean coast, and his men reacted bitterly to the sight. They stormed the enemy stronghold, killing most of the defenders.[11]

The uprising spread rapidly to Cyropolis and the neighboring towns, whose inhabitants murdered Alexander's garrisons and closed the towns' gates. Alexander dispatched one of his best generals, Craterus, to put Cyropolis under siege. Meanwhile, though wounded, the king began a systematic attack against each of the six outlying towns. As they fell one by one, huge fires and plumes of smoke announced to the next in line that Alexander was coming. Without mercy, the angry Greeks and Macedonians slaughtered the males and reduced the women to slavery. Hardly innocent, the Sogdians also proved treacherous, reneging on pledges and luring the invaders into an ambush under a flag of truce. Returning to Cyropolis, Alexander pressed the siege begun by Craterus. The king noticed that a streambed ran under its walls, carrying water inside through several channels. With a small commando force, Alexander personally slipped through the conduits and entered the city. He and his men broke open a gate and admitted their comrades. Many of Cyropolis's fifteen thousand defenders were killed.[12]

Across the land, tens of thousands lay dead and countless others were wounded or captured. The ferocious, close-order fighting spared no one; even Alexander suffered another serious injury. The king fell unconscious when struck in the head and neck by a large stone. For many days, his vision blurred and he could barely speak. The scab on his wound kept opening, prolonging his painful recovery. This wound, perhaps the first reported case of transient cortical blindness, combined with the leg injury to make it impossible for Alexander to walk, ride a horse, see clearly, or speak audibly.[13] He was in bad shape at a terrible moment, for the news became grimmer by the hour.

A similar thing later happened in 1879 when Lord Roberts sent out foragers from Kabul to bring in supplies for the winter. Local villagers refused to give up willingly what they needed themselves, so Roberts tried next to seize some local chieftains in order to force their cooperation. The British came under immediate attack, compelling Roberts to storm the nearest villages, burn down the houses, and plunder the grain and livestock. Town by town, the insurrection spread. Roberts split his forces and attacked the villages in a bloody cycle of retribution. Officers wondered aloud what had gone wrong: "A change has indeed come over the vision of our dream—last night we were all cock-a-hoop, thinking ourselves fine fellows, and that all we now had to do was to walk around and burn some villages; and within twenty-four hours we are locked up, closely besieged, after a jolly good licking and all communications with the outer world cut off."[14] Alexander's troops could have expressed the same shock as they counted up their losses. Almost overnight, what seemed a successful invasion had turned into a debacle. The Greeks and Macedonians were unprepared for the consequences of Alexander's actions, and they realized too late that the fighting extended all the way back along their lines of communication to Bactria. The cakewalk had become a death march.

Alexander must have felt himself trapped and cut off from the outside world when, beleaguered at the Jaxartes, he learned that his huge garrison at Maracanda was also under serious attack. Adding insult to Alexander's injuries, Spitamenes and his associates—the captors of Bessus—had taken up arms and brought the Bactrian cavalry back into the war.[15] None of these insurgent warlords, called *hyparchs* (commanders) by the Greeks, claimed to be a king. They ruled, in a rough sense, no more than isolated locales. Some controlled a valley, others a mountain fortress or string of villages. When not in revolt, they normally served as local princes or chiefs, levying fighting men and taxes for the Bactrian satrap who, in turn, answered to the King of Kings. They commanded their own contingents in war. This loose arrangement gave each hyparch a great deal of autonomy and preserved the powerful sense of localism so natural in places like Afghanistan. An easygoing loyalty to the state and its representatives could vanish in a flash once parochial interests seemed threatened. When such "commanders" (a title still popular among Afghan warlords) repudiated their oaths to a king or state, they might at times band together against a common foe or break off and fight alone at the head of their own followers and kinsmen.[16] From Alexander's day, we know a few of the strongest by name: Ariamazes, Austanes, Orsodates, Catanes, Dataphernes, Itanes, Oxyartes, Sisimithres, and Spitamenes.

These men are precisely reminiscent of the clan warlords common to modern Afghan history. *Terrorists* might seem too strong a term for them, but the word does apply in many ways. They singly and collectively acted as expatriate agents intent upon undermining an established government through violence and intimidation, often aimed indiscriminately at civilians as well as soldiers and officials. As modern commentators point out, all sorts of groups might fall into this category, some of them vilified and others openly admired: al-Qaeda, the Kenyan Mau Mau, the French Resistance, Irish nationalists, and so on.[17] To Alexander's army, the Bactrian and Sogdian hyparchs became true terrorists, and Spitamenes the worst among them; but to the native peoples, Alexander and his generals fully deserved the title.[18] There were no discussions of anything like Geneva Conventions, no apologies for the abuse of prisoners, no public oversight of military actions or expenditures. On all sides, atrocity answered atrocity in the brutal arithmetic of war and retribution.

Wars in the fourth century B.C.E. concentrated their horrors into a narrow space of slashing blades, piercing shafts, and massive blunt-force traumas. Scarcely anyone could kill an enemy without staring him in the eye; everything became personal and desperate within the shower of a victim's blood and the sound of his gasping breath. If most soldiers truly fear the bayonet more than the bullet, then ancient warfare stands out for its frenzied close-range slaughter with primitive weaponry. The Bactrians and their Scythian allies wielded stones, bows, battleaxes, spears, and swords. Some of the bows were powerful compound types; the arrows usually were tipped with bronze, three-edged points. Scythian riders developed a handy carrying device called a gorytus that combined a bow case and a quiver. They also experimented with armored cavalry of a kind later made famous in the Middle Ages.[19] Spears of varying lengths were employed either as thrusting weapons or as javelins; the latter were fitted with leather throwing-thongs to increase range and accuracy. Bactrians carried a short sword hung from the right hip and laced to the leg. They wore a waist-length corselet made of thick leather reinforced with metal. A skirt of leather strips protected the groin and thighs. Some Bactrian fighters donned helmets, while others preferred a lighter, hooded headgear.[20] All in all, the Bactrians and Scythians looked so frightening with their wild, unkempt hair and great shaggy beards that one Macedonian general suggested fighting them only in the dark of night.[21]

For their part, Alexander's armed forces encompassed a wider array of tactical units operating under a sophisticated command structure, the most advanced in that era, thanks largely to innovations begun by Philip II.[22] The Macedonian cavalry and infantry derived from territorial levies. Originally, the cavalry formed the elite arm, particularly the mounted Companions (Hetairoi) of the king. The term *Companion* highlighted a close association with the king endowing status and privilege. To avoid slighting the infantry, the Macedonians wisely extended the title to a special brigade called the Foot Companions (Pezhetairoi); when that name was later granted to the Macedonian infantry as a whole, the former Foot Companions claimed the designation Shield Bearers (Hypaspists) and later Silver Shields (Argyraspids). These carefully recruited and trained Shield Bearers were more mobile and versatile in battle than the king's six (later seven) brigades of Foot Companions, so they performed the crucial task of linking together the fastest (Companion Cavalry) and slowest (Foot Companions) elements of the Macedonian army. They acted, too, as commandos in special situations, such as the arduous mountain campaigns in Afghanistan. Most Macedonian infantrymen wore armor, including helmets and cuirasses. Their national weapon was the sarissa, a long spear reaching eighteen feet and weighing about fourteen pounds. Its menacing blade was balanced by a useful butt spike, which could itself be swung around and wielded if the sarissa's shaft were broken. Massed in precise formations, men carrying these sarissas cut deep into the ranks of the enemy.[23]

Alexander's cavalry fought using swords and sarissas. Because the stirrup was unknown at the time, cavalrymen had to take care not to be unseated while charging, slashing, or thrusting. The king's mounted forces underwent a transformation in response to the Bactrian campaign. The old squads (ilae) of two hundred riders were organized into larger battalions (hipparchies) of two or more ilae. These units better served the powerful detachments sent out by the king to hunt down the insurgents, and they stood a better chance against attacks by the first-rate horsemen of Bactria and Scythia. Overall command of the cavalry, once vested in a single Companion, had to be divided for security reasons after the execution of Philotas.[24]

Alexander also deployed a great number of allied and mercenary troops. Lacking Macedonian reinforcements, the king grew increasingly dependent on the use of Greek mercenaries while in Bactria. Furthermore, to preserve his dwindling Macedonian manpower, Alexander singled out these mercenaries to be left behind as garrison forces and colonists. This caused resentment among the Greeks forced to remain in Bactria and led to some dissension in the ranks. Another source of friction would be the king's decision before leaving Bactria to supplement his armed forces with additional native recruits.[25] His army thenceforth mixed three volatile elements, but the extreme demands of the Bactrian war left Alexander no choice. He had to assume the risks or retreat from the region.

SHOCK WAVES

To meet the crisis erupting behind him, Alexander sent a large detachment of infantry and cavalry to save Maracanda from Spitamenes. That the king placed an interpreter rather than a general in overall charge of this mission shows a tragic miscalculation: he believed that the Bactrian rebels could be talked into laying down their weapons. Meanwhile, Alexander himself attended to the more serious matter, or so it seemed, of building Alexandria Eschate and beating off the hostile Scythians threatening his men from the opposite bank of the Jaxartes. These nomads saw the new fortress as a foot upon their necks, and they joined with the Bactrians and Sogdians who had risen up against it.[26] While the Greeks put up walls as fast as they could, the Scythians fired arrows in their direction and taunted Alexander to come after them. The king, of course, was trying to hold his temper long enough to heal properly and fortify the city. After a few weeks, he still had trouble convincing his closest friends that he was healthy enough to fight. The religious omens for battle were also unfavorable. The king, however, could not be dissuaded.

To cross the Jaxartes River under enemy fire, Alexander could not rely solely upon the method he had used at the Oxus. He did not have five days to transport his army on individual floats; besides, such an operation would expose his swimmers to devastating volleys of Scythian arrows, literally like sitting ducks. The king needed a more complex system that protected the personal floats with a flotilla of large rafts. Both devices were made from stuffed leather hides (tent covers and water skins), but the rafts incorporated a number of rigged-together floats on which a sturdy deck could be constructed. The rafts required a crew to handle them, but they were capable also of carrying strong contingents of troops and even some of the horses.[27]

His enemies were spoiling for a fight, and Alexander obliged them. He used long-range catapults to drive back the Scythians and clear a landing. The startled nomads watched in horror as one volley tore completely through a comrade and all his armor. Aboard the rafts, contingents of archers, slingers, and more catapults kept up a steady barrage as groups of infantry and cavalry paddled across. General J. F. C. Fuller describes Alexander's deployment as being "like a line of amphibian tanks followed by unarmoured landing craft."[28] The current was surprisingly swift and played havoc with the flotilla, but once the operation had begun there was no turning back. The Scythians gave ground as Alexander established a strong perimeter around his landing zone. Recovering, the nomads next tried their classic maneuver of attacking in a circular motion. Archers on horseback wheeled around the flank of the Greeks and Macedonians, firing and then retreating out of range. Alexander solved the problem with a clever maneuver of his own, throwing into the enemy's path a mixed force of cavalry and light infantry. This broke the Scythian attack and befuddled their leaders, who retreated in frustration. The invaders pursued them for miles into the desert before halting to slake their thirst from brackish springs. Triumphant, they returned to Alexandria Eschate. Many fell ill with dysentery, however, since the water they had drunk was foul. Their ill-starred king lay wretched among them.[29]

Recovering yet again, Alexander faced one of the greatest shocks of his life. The 2,360 soldiers he had sent to Maracanda had blundered into a withering ambush, and of their number many had not survived.[30] Their story, which the troubled king tried to keep from the rest of his army, reveals how drastically unprepared the Greeks and Macedonians were for this kind of war. The commanders of the expeditionary force, none of whom returned, included the Persian interpreter Pharnuches and three Macedonian generals: Andromachus, Menedemus, and Caranus. They reached Maracanda, expecting Pharnuches to negotiate with Spitamenes, but the Bactrian warlord had already retreated west along the Polytimetus (modern Zerafshan) River. Too clever to be pinned down, Spitamenes proved himself a master of guerilla warfare. He managed to join forces with six hundred Scythian cavalrymen in just the sort of alliance Alexander had meant to forestall. These reinforcements inspired Spitamenes to set a trap for the Greeks and Macedonians hot on his heels. He lured them out toward the desert and then used his superior cavalry repeatedly to strike the enemy and retreat out of range, just as the Scythians had done against Alexander at the Jaxartes. Unfortunately, the king was not present to counter the maneuver. His generals were stymied.

This cat-and-mouse game went on until the invaders, cut to pieces, tried to withdraw to the protection of some woods near the Polytimetus. Adding to the panic, dissension arose among the commanders. Pharnuches technically may have been in charge under the original orders of Alexander, when the mission seemed focused upon negotiations, but the situation had radically changed. It had become a wholly military problem, and a desperate one at that. The experienced Macedonian generals, however, were reluctant at this point to take responsibility; leadership collapsed, leaving each man scrambling for his life.[31] Some troops swam desperately to a small island in the river only to be surrounded and shot down. Spitamenes executed all the captives. The Greeks and Macedonians who managed to escape in other directions carried with them the news of the defeat, the worst in Alexander's reign. Every officer had perished, and naturally the rank and file gave confused and contradictory accounts to their astonished king.[32]

Alexander reacted with the fastest march of his life, covering the 180 miles to Maracanda in just over three days.[33] Craterus followed with the slower units. Spitamenes meanwhile had attacked Maracanda again, but he quickly withdrew at Alexander's approach. The king's pursuit took his army past the ghoulish battlefield and out to the edge of the desert. Spitamenes had too great a lead, however, so Alexander let him go. Turning back, the king buried his dead comrades under a huge mound and gave a sinister order: sweep through the valley of the Polytimetus, seize every fort and village, systematically demolish them, burn all the crops, and kill anyone who might sympathize with Spitamenes.[34] These repressive measures only fueled greater resentment, confirming for the Bactrians and Sogdians that indeed they had been right to resist the meddlesome invaders in the first place. Much of Sogdiana lay in ruin, whole towns and villages had been wiped out, the death toll spiraled upward, and the refugee crisis must have been enormous. Some scholars estimate that 120,000 Bactrians were killed.[35]

In the so-called fog of war, Alexander's men jabbed, sliced, torched, and bombarded in a frenzied swath. Innocents no doubt perished in the heavy use of firepower, just as American warplanes have accidentally bombed Afghan allies, coalition partners, and even several wedding parties. Twice in one week (in

December 2003), U.S. forces killed groups of Afghan children while trying unsuccessfully to target individual warlords. Such events take a heavy toll not only on indigenous peoples but also on the luckless soldiers whose orders place them in these winless circumstances. Trying to curb the power of the warlords and prevent their alliances with the Scythians, Alexander had inadvertently intensified (at a dear price) the very calamity he had meant to avoid. The outcome was an escalating cycle and scale of violence. This happened, too, in the nineteenth century, when a British major-general butchered every man, woman, and child in the village of Killah-Chuk to avenge a detachment of his army.[36] Throughout the 1980s, Soviet military doctrine sanctioned devastating attacks against the rural populations of Afghanistan that also are reminiscent of Alexander's actions. For example, whenever the mujahideen ambushed a convoy, Soviet forces immediately bombed all surrounding villages as retribution. They destroyed harvests and felled trees. Ground assaults on settlements near suspected rebel hideouts were often designed to leave no survivors; sometimes soldiers operated under orders to slaughter even the cattle, horses, dogs, and cats.[37]

Earlier in the twentieth century, intrusive Russian settlements in central Asia sparked a Muslim uprising associated with the so-called *basmachi*. These peasants and their local leaders massacred the Russians and mounted a long, vicious campaign against further colonization. They used mobile cavalry forces that hit hard and then vanished; insurgents easily blended into the village populations that supported their cause. The Russians responded with equal brutality, destroying towns and looting farms. The Soviet press labeled the *basmachi* as bandits, just as the Greeks did the Bactrians.[38] The parallels run deeper: "The principal weakness of the *basmachi* movement was its lack of unity. The various detachments operated independently of each other under the leadership of ambitious and jealous chieftains."[39] These same problems soon hampered Spitamenes.

With winter fast approaching, the king left three thousand infantry on guard in Sogdiana while he trudged the bulk of his army back to Bactra. Provisions had been stockpiled there, and Alexander had arranged to receive embassies and reinforcements during the idle weeks. Alexander also convened the general assembly that witnessed the mutilation of Bessus.[40] The king must have felt some satisfaction in these proceedings, however grotesque, but he knew that a far more dangerous enemy had suddenly materialized. Spitamenes proved to be a most cunning and charismatic leader. Unlike Bessus, he combined a strategy of attrition with well-timed guerilla attacks. Spitamenes did not hesitate to take the offensive, as at Maracanda, where his threat to Alexander's critical supply line showed keen intelligence.[41] Alexander's directive to scorch the Polytimetus Valley on the eve of winter may have been logistical payback. From that point on, both men went at each other's throats by aiming lower, at the stomach.

After the bitter setbacks in Sogdiana, the arrival of twenty-two thousand fresh Greek soldiers (the equivalent of two divisions) provided a welcome boost to manpower in the region. No doubt Alexander had originally summoned these men, all Greek mercenaries, to reinforce his planned invasion of India; unpredictably, the immediate crisis in Bactria pressed these forces into a different role, for which they cannot have been prepared. As they mingled with the king's veterans in Bactria, the exchange of news linked one edge of Alexander's empire to the other. From the Greek homeland, these mercenaries brought word of a grave situation. Rallying around Sparta, an anti-Macedonian movement had attempted to free the city-states from the domineering hegemony exercised by Alexander and Antipater, his regent in northern Greece. Emotions had run high from the beginning, when the Macedonians had first bullied their so-called partners into a full, if reluctant, cooperation in the overthrow of Darius. In Athens, for example, fiery orators attacked each other either for kowtowing to Alexander's policies or, conversely, for endangering the city's welfare by antagonizing the powerful king. As Alexander marched ever farther from Greece, it was Antipater's job to keep this dissension under control while safeguarding Macedonia's grip on the Balkans. To that end, he raised an army of forty thousand troops and drove south. Near Megalopolis, Antipater soundly defeated the Greek uprising. Hostages were seized and sent east to face Alexander's judgment. The anti-Macedonian rebels, for the moment, had failed.[42]

The hostages arrived at Bactra along with the twenty-two thousand Greek mercenaries. This large company therefore knew firsthand about the troubles in Greece, and surely men from both sides of that conflict were numbered among the soldiers. In fact, the eight thousand Greeks sent by Antipater himself may have been mercenaries from the losing side who were too dangerous to leave unemployed in the homeland. The king could no doubt put them to some use conquering India. As it turned out, Alexander now had just the assignment for potential troublemakers—they would help conquer, and then garrison, the wilds of Bactria and Sogdiana.

Perhaps predisposed to resent Alexander's administration, many of the new mercenaries were surely unhappy campers in central Asia. Having told their stories of affairs back in Greece, they listened in turn to the shocking accounts from survivors of the Sogdian insurrection. They learned that the very city in which they were bivouacked had only recently been purged of something called Devourer dogs. They certainly shuddered at the news of the Branchidae massacre. Many could have witnessed the public butchering of Bessus, only to wonder what Spitamenes must be like. They would know soon enough. It was their turn to tackle the insurgents of Afghanistan, and they no doubt hoped to fare better than the men who had died by the thousands just a few weeks earlier.

Today we find ourselves in a position to appreciate just how desperate was the struggle in ancient Bactria. For his part, Alexander felt absolutely committed to the daunting task of suppressing the warlords of the region. His miscalculations at the outset of the mission could not deter him in his duty, as he saw it, to safeguard the civilized world. He did not hesitate to bring the full arsenal at his disposal to smash any who opposed him. He recognized no one's neutrality. In his zeal, of course, he sometimes made matters worse both on the front lines and on the home front. It was no easy task to hold together an alliance that lacked a unified vision of what the world should be like after the fall of Persia. The League of Corinth clearly had no stake in the affairs of far-off Afghanistan, and many states worried that this war only made Alexander more arrogant and reckless, and that he lacked even the slightest regard for the league's waning influence.

For the soldiers serving in Alexander's national army, there was also a growing sense of desperation. The campaign had seemed to be over back in Iraq, and then again with the capture of Bessus. The fighting, however, kept flaring up—no longer in massive battles, but in ambushes and raids that took a steady toll exceeding even that of the all-out war against Darius. Far from home in a land that bewildered them, these troops faced a long, uncertain future quite different from the tour of duty they had anticipated. The veterans had not seen their families for years, and they were not particularly sympathetic to the new recruits, who had not helped in the war thus far but had remained back home and in some cases jeopardized everything with their anti-Macedonian uprising. The tension in the ranks of Alexander's army was building, soon to explode.

The indigenous peoples of Bactria, Sogdiana, and Scythia suffered horribly as well. Wars are more eagerly waged against enemies perceived as backward, brutish, and beyond salvation except by forced improvement or death. Unfortunately, the advice that Aristotle reportedly gave to Alexander before the war seemed to reflect the general thinking of the time: "Deal with the Greeks as their leader, and with the Barbarians as their master. Take care of the former as friends and kinsmen, while treating the latter as you would plants or animals."[43] The Greek moralist and biographer Plutarch later went so far as to claim, "Those vanquished by Alexander were happier than those not, for the latter had no one to end their miserable existence, whereas Alexander compelled the losers to live happily."[44] As so many other imperialist states have done through the millennia, the Greeks dehumanized the victims of their aggressions: the natives *needed* conquering because they were by nature inferior. One modern historian echoed this ancient pronouncement when he wrote that the defeated peoples of the Persian Empire, "whatever their latent capabilities, often had not at the time the intellectual, political, or social energy of the Greek."[45] A sniff of this haughty attitude comes across today in the boast by some pundits that the United States would bomb Afghanistan forward, not back, into the Stone Age.[46]

Those being invaded, of course, would probably take a different position on this matter. In fact, archaeological explorations have now dispelled many of the misleading comments made about the Bactrians by ancient Greek writers. We see evidence of complex cities supported by sophisticated irrigation systems, the latter wholly ignored in classical sources.[47] We find high art and extensive trade networks. Indeed, Bactria had been a center of civilization long before the rise of the Greek cities, in spite of the barbarian image painted by hostile invaders. We must remember that our literary sources provide an incomplete picture of a region under attack.

The very notion that a generous band of Greeks and Macedonians had achieved something noble by crushing Persia would seem ludicrous to Alexander's enemies in Bactria. The defense of their families and possessions called for many desperate sacrifices, even in the face of overwhelming military force. Whole settlements simply refused to allow foreigners to interfere in their local affairs. The warlords themselves, like the Greeks and Macedonians, took great pride in their martial skills, sense of honor, and fierce independence. They fought back using the age-old guerilla tactics of the region, sometimes alone and sometimes in makeshift alliances. Naturally, the insurgents considered their cause to be just and often found help among the quiescent general population caught up in the struggle. Many rural communities immediately assumed the worst whenever the invaders came their way, so men, women, and children would flee to remote mountain hideouts to wait out the danger. Families and clans huddled like hunted animals in caves or forests, which only convinced the foreigners that indeed the natives were by nature wild, crude, uncivilized people who subsisted as savage bandits.[48] Even their strange religion put off the invaders. Alexander's army feared what it could not understand, and it was the implacable foe of everything it feared.

CHAPTER FOUR

The Hydra Heads of Bactria

A PROPHECY

In the early spring of 328 B.C.E., Alexander's veteran army and its twenty-two thousand Greek reinforcements embarked on another attempt to subjugate Bactria. Given the widespread danger, the king could not hope for much success using conventional strategies. To march his huge army from place to place, as he had done to overthrow Persia, would be an aimless exercise in central Asia. There were no enemy palaces to storm and pillage, no great concentrations of hostile troops to engage, and no single head of state to capture or kill. The opposition moved and melted all around the invaders, testing Alexander's resolve while taking measured risks. This posed a novel challenge for a military superpower better suited to win big battles along a linear path of world conquest. The so-called hammer-and-anvil tactics made famous by the Macedonians could not be relied upon here, for the enemy could not be pinned against the anvil long enough for the hammer to strike.[1]

Alexander faced the same dilemma as modern tacticians whose high-tech hammers have so often pummeled fruitlessly, as was the case throughout the Soviet invasion, where "fighting Afghans was like nailing jelly to a wall; in the end there was just a wall full of bent nails."[2] In December 2001, General Tommy Franks believed that al-Qaeda's soldiers were trapped between "a hammer and an anvil" at Tora Bora in eastern Afghanistan.[3] In spite of a massive U.S. bombing campaign, bin Laden and most of his fighters slipped away. Millions of dollars worth of laser-guided hammers crushed mountains but not the mortal enemy. Later in the Shah-i Kot Valley (Operation Anaconda), a bold hammer-and-anvil battle plan fell apart when U.S. air-power accidentally strafed the allied hammer. The Afghan warlord Zia Lodin therefore pulled his men out of the fray, leaving the forces of the U.S. anvil exposed to heavy fire from al-Qaeda. Losses were high, and another hard lesson was learned about joint operations with local leaders.[4]

Alexander's genius and adaptability led him to try a more diffuse, mobile response to the insurgency. This strategy imposed greater responsibility on the king's officer corps and pushed his troops to endure prolonged danger and privation.[5] The experience changed history but also the men who made it. This new phase of the operation began when Alexander divided his forces in a bold effort to smother the rebellion.[6] To patrol Bactria south of the Oxus River, the king ordered four brigade commanders (Polyperchon, Attalus, Gorgias, and Meleager) to comb the countryside and keep the peace. These four may have operated under the supervision of Craterus, a senior marshal whose activities west of Bactra in this period are attested.[7] Alexander himself led the rest of the army back into Sogdiana. Finally getting ahead of the learning curve, the king this time crossed the desert without incident and, to avoid a problem experienced earlier, ordered his men to dig wells near the Oxus River to find clean water. The river here was notoriously burdened with silt, and the wary invaders could not be certain that hostile natives and their herds had not poisoned or polluted it. Freshly sunk wells offered Alexander and his forces the only sure means of finding safe water to drink. Out of one shaft flowed a fatty substance so strange that the Macedonian general Ptolemy summoned his king and the royal soothsayers. Anxious for a good omen, Alexander was advised that the effusion was indeed a gift from heaven, but that it portended troubled times. For once, we may today agree with an ancient prophecy: the substance was petroleum.[8] Alexander's men had inadvertently discovered one of the prime moving forces of modern history; ironically, the glum prophecy about it is the very first reference to oil in Western literature.[9]

After crossing the Oxus, the king divided the troops with him into five columns, one for each of the main valleys stretching north from the Oxus between the outstretched fingers of the Pamir Mountains. The natives had abandoned their towns and villages down in the valleys in order to seek refuge in the surrounding mountains. To hit them hard and fast, a coordinated assault spread outward. The king's close friend Hephaestion led a sweep up the valley of the Panj River; Ptolemy cleared the Vakhsh, Perdiccas the Kafirngan, and Coenus the Surkhan-Darya. Artabazus, the satrap of Bactria, was sent along to assist Coenus. Alexander took the fifth column around the west flank toward Maracanda.[10] Near the site of the Branchidae massacre a year earlier, the king discovered a mountain stronghold commanded by Ariamazes.[11] This warlord had allegedly collected thirty thousand people and ample supplies into caverns high on a precipitous rock. Alexander first sent Cophes, a son of Artabazus the satrap, to talk the rebels down from their lair. This failed. Ariamazes scoffed at the idea of surrender, daring the Greeks and Macedonians to come after him "if they could fly." Always sensitive to taunts, Alexander canvassed his army for mountain climbers and bribed the best of them to risk the ascent. He promised that the first soldier to reach the snowy summit would be paid a princely bounty of twelve talents (about 680 pounds of good silver), and that those following would be paid on a descending scale of rewards. The climbers who survived would earn their money.[12]

Weighted down with weapons and food, the volunteers used ropes and iron spikes to scale the back of the sheer mountain out of sight of the defenders. The perilous climb took at least twenty-four grueling hours. More than one in ten fell to his death, but the others got above the caverns and signaled their anxious king far below. Alexander then taunted Ariamazes in turn, telling him to look upward and see that, indeed, the invaders could fly. The rattled hyparch lost his nerve and surrendered the fortress, putting himself, his family, and all his followers into Alexander's hands. The king coolly singled out the most prominent persons, including Ariamazes, to be scourged and crucified at the base of the mountain. The rest became slaves.[13] To forestall the emergence of another warlord there, Alexander placed the captured stronghold under the direct control of Artabazus, his regional satrap.[14]

Each of the five columns completed its mission and, during the summer months, made its way to the rendezvous at Maracanda. The generals reported on their operations, but our sources provide none of the details. As usual, we learn only of the king's exploits, not those of his subordinates. Surely other insurgent warlords suffered fates similar to Ariamazes's. Alexander next sent the detachment under Coenus and Artabazus to hunt down Spitamenes, who was reported to be among the Scythians. Hephaestion and his troops drew the task of resettling the ravaged territories. Meantime, the king and his other officers scoured the more remote districts of Sogdiana in search of any remaining pockets of resistance.[15] This operation may have entailed a strong sweep up the Polytimetus (modern Zerafshan) River, with units branching out through the steep valleys of its tributaries. Alexander meant for the entire population to witness the power and range of his army. Curiously, Alexander legends still flourish up in those remote valleys where the king left his mark. There is an Iskander Darya (Alexander River) that flows out of Iskander Kul (Lake Alexander). Locals believe that Alexander built a golden dam to form the lake, and that flecks from the dam can still be panned downstream at Ayni and Penzhikent. They further report that, with every full moon, Alexander's trusty steed Bucephalus rises from the lake and traverses the night sky.[16]

In the resettlement mission carried out by Hephaestion, the refugee populations routed out of the hills were herded back to their villages and put to work. Garrisons were established at critical points. Apportioned among these military colonies were Greek mercenaries plus numerous rebel slaves such as the followers of Ariamazes. One of the settlements arising from Hephaestion's commission may have been the strategic post at Ai Khanoum, the Northern Alliance stronghold mentioned in chapter 1. An earlier community existed there, but perhaps in this period the place was strongly fortified by the Greeks with walls and a defensive ditch. From the acropolis, sentries could watch far to the south, as well as safeguard to the north and west the confluence of the Oxus and Kokcha Rivers. Its new citizenry of Greek soldiers enjoyed all the amenities of the town, while a huge workforce of natives tilled the soil and tended to the mundane tasks. In a few generations, Ai Khanoum would become a thriving, cultured Greek city, but its humble origins were strictly military.[17] Alexander had not backed away from the policies associated with the earlier foundation of Alexandria Eschate.

With four hefty Greek and Macedonian detachments patrolling Bactria, several others probing deep into Sogdiana with Alexander, Hephaestion overseeing the resettlement plan, and the force under Coenus and Artabazus hunting Spitamenes in Scythian territory, the entire region echoed with military activity. It might have seemed that the worst had passed, with just a few weeks of mop-up before retiring to winter quarters. In the spring, the army might finally quit Bactria and push on to other tasks or return home. But the resourceful Spitamenes would not relent. He crafted a bold plan to deny the Greeks and Macedonians their winter provisions. Somehow slipping past everyone, the unpredictable warlord struck directly at the most unlikely place: Bactra, serving simultaneously as Alexander's main headquarters, the provincial capital, and the army's winter camp. This attack was no mere stunt, but rather an effort to disrupt the pivotal node of the king's complex logistics.[18]

First, Spitamenes's Bactrian followers and their Scythian allies surprised and destroyed a Greek garrison guarding the western approaches to Bactra. The insurgents killed all the defenders but took the hapless commandant as their prisoner. The raiders then plundered the villages around Bactra, specifically driving off the cattle that had been gathered near the city to feed Alexander's troops during the winter.[19] Spitamenes naturally did not besiege the capital, and never intended to do so. Bactra had legendary defensive walls, and insurgent warlords rarely succeed in such intensive, long-term operations.[20] His plan was simpler. As the crucial herds were being rustled by Spitamenes, a group of soldiers inside Bactra decided to intervene. In one account, Alexander's regional general, Attinas, led three hundred cavalry in pursuit but fell into an ambush just as the Greeks and Macedonians had done the year before near Maracanda. There were allegedly no survivors.[21] The other version indicates that Peithon led the mission to recover the cattle.[22] This man was in charge of making arrangements for the care and feeding of the king and his court. This shows that, indeed, preparations were under way for winter quarters, and that Peithon bore some responsibility for the cattle and other supplies being taken by Spitamenes.

Joining Peithon were a group of sick and wounded soldiers from the base hospital, some of the royal pages who attended the king, and about eighty Greek mercenaries on garrison duty. Also present and willing to fight was Aristonicus, the most famous musician of that era.[23] He played a harplike instrument, the kithara, and habitually sang for the entertainment of Alexander and his companions. For at least twenty-two years, Aristonicus had been internationally famous, so he could not have still been young. Yet he put aside his kithara and rode off with the others to clash with Spitamenes. Whether these volunteers accompanied the general Attinas, or followed separately, historians do not know. They allegedly succeeded at first in retrieving the plundered supplies and killing many of the insurgents, but they too were ambushed while returning. No one would assume command amid all the confusion, and the losses were again heavy. Peithon suffered an injury and fell captive, the mercenaries lost three-quarters of their number, and brave Aristonicus died "more like a soldier than a singer." Alexander honored him with a statue at the shrine of Delphi in Greece.[24] Although these losses cannot compare numerically with the disaster in 329 B.C.E., the effect proved substantial nonetheless. Alexander's careful plans unraveled, and the stigma of this reverse soon ignited pent-up resentments among his own generals. One of them would die by the king's own hand within a matter of weeks.

Spitamenes had pulled off a stunning incursion; but burdened with cattle, he could not evade all the dispersed elements of the king's grand army. Craterus intercepted the rear echelon of the rebels near the desert, apparently west of Bactra, and defeated the Scythian allies. The charmed Spitamenes escaped, however. Alexander now faced the disappointing prospect of fighting another year in Bactria, the most recalcitrant corner of his vast empire. He was learning a hard lesson about the elusiveness of victory in Afghanistan.

For a second time in 328 B.C.E., Alexander reunited the Sogdian wing of his army at Maracanda. He met with emissaries from some of the more distant Scythian tribes, politely rejecting their suggestion of a marriage alliance.[25] At age twenty-eight, the king was still a bachelor, an anomaly for polygamous Macedonian royals, although he was soon to find his first bride. At the moment, however, his mind was on logistics. Spitamenes's raid on Bactra convinced Alexander to revise his arrangements for the winter months. First, the king and his army descended upon a protected game park in Bazaira. The Persians called such an enclosed preserve a *paradeisos* (paradise), a place where royalty could hunt from stands and blinds in a beautiful setting of forests, springs, and pastures. This one had been kept undisturbed for four generations. Unlike the small, recreational hunts Alexander loved so well, this hunt saw thousands of hungry Greek and Macedonian soldiers quickly bag and butcher about four thousand beasts; the army banqueted on the spoils and returned to Maracanda.[26]

Second, Alexander replaced Artabazus as the satrap of Bactria, allegedly at the latter's own request because of old age.[27] While one ancient source claims that Artabazus was nearly one hundred years old, other evidence indicates that he was at least thirty years younger.[28] Even at sixty or seventy, Artabazus remained within the age range of active officers serving in Alexander's armed forces.[29] It seems, therefore, that Artabazus's age was greatly inflated in order to justify his retirement. If the decision was truly his own, this may suggest that Artabazus had worn himself out during the grueling campaigns of 329–328 B.C.E. and could think of no better excuse. Leading a contingent of Bactrian and Sogdian soldiers, he had been serving mainly as a liaison officer attached to Coenus's command. Even if the king should allow Artabazus to rest, as it were, behind a desk at Bactra, it was now apparent that vigorous leadership might be needed there in light of Spitamenes's recent attack. Artabazus may have had enough campaigning and begged off as best he could by exaggerating his extreme old age. Yet, it is difficult to imagine that Alexander did not know Artabazus intimately, since the king had taken the man's daughter as a concubine. It is interesting, too, that Alexander decided henceforth to assign Macedonians to the position of Bactrian satrap. This raises the real possibility that

Alexander himself initiated the Persian's retirement. Perhaps the king had already anticipated leaving behind a huge army of peacekeepers in Bactria, a force that would have to be commanded by a Macedonian. To replace Artabazus, the king appointed a senior officer named Cleitus, a Companion of proven abilities who would never actually serve; he had only days to live before his king would kill him. That crisis would force Alexander to choose yet another Macedonian satrap, named Amyntas, to govern what one source called "the most powerful part of the king's empire."[30]

Third, faced with unexpected supply problems following Spitamenes's raid, the king abandoned the thought of wintering again at Bactra. He dispatched Hephaestion south to restore order in and around the old city of bones.[31] Under the circumstances, the rest of the army would remain dispersed in Sogdiana. The men would live off the land in mobile groups that had the added advantage of denying Spitamenes access to any available supplies there during the winter. Logistics were to play a large role in determining the winner of this interminable war.

A DEATH

The death of Cleitus stands out as one of the great tragedies in Alexander's reign. Kings do not often kill their close friends in a fit of rage, and even W. W. Tarn could not easily excuse the deed. The best he managed was to acknowledge "the wild beast" in Alexander and to praise in a backhanded way "the power of will that could usually keep such a beast chained."[32] Not murdering more often became one of Alexander's virtues. Perhaps Tarn was thinking subconsciously of Cleitus's last words to Alexander, which included the lament: "I am thrown to wild beasts!"[33] The doomed man did not mean the king, of course, but rather the impossibly stubborn and warlike Bactrians over whom he was supposed, somehow, to rule as governor.

Praising Alexander, Plutarch insisted that none of the king's contemporaries was up to the challenge of winning this tiresome war: "Who but Alexander would not have wearied and given up marshaling and arming his troops, besieging cities, chasing down peoples in numerous revolts, desertions, and riots; pursuing faithless leaders to Bactra, Maracanda, and Sogdiana as if cutting off the heads of the Hydra, which always grow back twice as thick."[34] The mythical Hydra provides a defining image of Afghan warfare through the years. The ability of the foe to regenerate itself demoralizes even the most self-assured invaders. This kind of hydralike warfare exacts a heavy toll on everyone, and its effects are psychological as well as physical. The smashing victories of Alexander's troops against the armies of Darius had occurred years earlier, closer to home. The battles of the Granicus River (334 B.C.E.), Issus (333), and Gaugamela (331) each had that quick, dramatic, conclusive quality that the Greeks so relished.[35] Even the long coastal sieges at Halicarnassus (334 B.C.E.), Tyre (332), and Gaza (332) had at least ended decisively. In those campaigns, the veterans with Alexander had grown accustomed to a comforting expectation: when they fought someone, they absolutely prevailed; and the defeated enemy *always stayed defeated.* This arrogance of power, as so often since, lost its punch in Afghanistan. The place and its people took no heed of recent history, ignored the strength and sophisticated modernity of the invaders, and cared little for the time-honored conventions of treaties and truces. They fled like bandits if confronted with overwhelming force, then attacked whenever the odds were better. You could never tell if you were winning the war or not. Meanwhile, the casualties mounted and it became more and more obvious that even with a so-called victory, a substantial number of Greeks and a few Macedonians would have to stay behind in Bactria as a peacekeeping force. Cleitus hated the thought of presiding over them. He may also have strongly resented that his new post placed Artabazus's native forces under his command.

At a court banquet in Maracanda, Cleitus freely expressed his displeasure.[36] The guests, as was customary, had drunk too much wine and were letting off steam in a boisterous atmosphere. Gritty warriors boasted of their prowess in Homeric fashion, each one competitive and unduly sensitive to any perceived slight from his peers. Entertainers and sycophants catered to the vanities of their favorites, especially the king, who was known to lavish gifts on his flatterers.[37] Alexander once gave a fawning actor ten talents (569 pounds of silver), and a doting poet received ten thousand gold coins.[38] The stimulus of alcohol, ego, and instant reward clouded everyone's good judgment and sometimes pushed Alexander's guests over the edge. On this occasion, the king indulged his growing pretensions of divinity and denigrated, by comparison, the achievements of his father Philip II; he also allowed a poet to compose a song ridiculing the recent defeat of his generals by Spitamenes.[39] For the older men of Philip's generation, these insults cut deep. Cleitus stepped forward and dared to praise not only Philip but also himself—reminding everyone present that he had saved Alexander's life six years earlier when a Persian was about to smash the king's head in battle. Against the braggadocio of the great captain, Cleitus champi-

oned the team. Every soldier had done his part. Why should
Alexander steal all the glory, and why should some noncombat-
ant be allowed to belittle the fighting men?

It does appear strange that the king would encourage such a
tactless display, especially the entertainer's performance mocking
dead comrades. Imagine in 1842 a British burlesque of the tragic
retreat from Kabul, or in 1880 a spoof of the battle at Maiwand.
Consider the firestorm following the impromptu remarks made
about President Bush by Natalie Maines of the Dixie Chicks, and
the effect had the trio actually sung derisively of American soldiers dying in combat.[40] To explain Alexander's conduct, some
historians have suggested that the defeat being lampooned was
the Polytimetus disaster: by allowing the ridicule of incompetent
generals, the king himself escaped blame for what went wrong
and appeared grander by comparison.[41] The same could also be
said of Spitamenes's more recent attack on Bactra. Furthermore,
the conspicuous bravery there of the musician Aristonicus made
a tempting theme for the performer called upon to sing at Maracanda. An entertainer had upstaged the career officers in that
battle, a fact that Alexander commemorated in another artistic
medium. No doubt this irked many drunken veterans who faced
death every day. On their behalf, Cleitus spoke passionately.

Tempers flared. Insults flew, and then objects from the table.
Alexander grabbed for a weapon to silence Cleitus while calmer
men tried to intervene. The king cried out for help, thinking that
the fate of Darius had now befallen him. Alexander's marshals
did not know how to restrain their agitated king without indeed
seeming to disarm and arrest him. Philotas and Parmenio had
been executed for doing considerably less. In a regrettable frenzy,
Alexander snatched a bodyguard's spear and ran Cleitus through

on the spot.[42] The king's remorse became legendary, but he lost more than his temper that night. Henceforth, wary Companions guarded their tongues and advised their leader less frankly. Alexander grieved in seclusion for three days without taking food or water.[43] When he emerged, everyone naturally absolved him of blame. The philosopher Anaxarchus solemnly proclaimed that anything done by Alexander was de facto above reproach; the king officially could do no wrong. People therefore blamed the whole incident on Cleitus and got back to the business of fighting.

Amyntas took over the position of satrap, inheriting the troops once under Artabazus's command (including native recruits).[44] Alexander left Coenus and Amyntas to winter in Maracanda with a large contingent of cavalry, two Macedonian brigades, and other units. They were to keep a watchful eye on northern Sogdiana. The king himself led part of the army to a fertile region called Xenippa (perhaps near the area of modern Karshi).[45] Once he had dispersed the soldiers, foraging became more effective, although the hardships on the natives must have been immense. In addition, quartering soldiers among the general population prevented Spitamenes from resupplying in friendly districts. Should he try, the warlord and his forces could be detected as though they had tapped the web of a waiting spider. The idea was to trap such rebels or drive them into the clutches of one of the concentrations of Greek and Macedonian troops stationed near Maracanda.

At Xenippa, about twenty-five hundred Bactrian insurgents did attempt to melt into the local population for the duration of the winter. Alexander's approach, however, convinced the native villages to expel their rebel guests. Flushed from cover, the guerillas fled north, straight into the arms of Amyntas. In a fierce engagement, both sides suffered heavy casualties before the Bactrians scattered again. As they fled south, the trap closed tight and they surrendered to Alexander. The king next moved to Nautaca (around modern Shahrisabz) to wait out the worst of winter.[46]

Meanwhile, Spitamenes himself took the field when he realized that Alexander's army intended to occupy all of Bactria and Sogdiana, leaving Spitamenes's kinsmen and allies no safe haven for the winter. Alexander's strategy had turned the tables. Spitamenes's logistical crisis drove him to attack a frontier garrison, whose alarm quickly brought Coenus to the scene. Spitamenes and his Bactrian followers, plus reinforcements of about three thousand Scythian cavalry, fought Coenus in a major battle near a place called Gabae. The Greeks reported, rather fantastically, only thirty-seven casualties on their side compared to over eight hundred enemy dead. A number of the Bactrians surrendered to Coenus, but Spitamenes escaped once more. The unexpected turn of events incensed the Scythians, who naturally plundered the possessions of their former allies and reconsidered their affiliation with Spitamenes. As Alexander reinforced his web, a growing sense of despair repaid Spitamenes in kind: as he once had betrayed Bessus, so his associates now betrayed him. The Scythians beheaded Spitamenes, sending the gory trophy to rest beside that of Satibarzanes in Alexander's camp.[47]

Another ancient account insists that the Bactrian warlord's wife actually delivered the head to Alexander. Spitamenes loved her dearly, the story goes, and kept her at his side throughout the strenuous war with Alexander. She finally wearied of the toil and danger. Begging her husband, for her sake and that of their three

children, to make peace with the invaders, she aroused Spitamenes's suspicions. He threatened her life, but her brothers in-
terceded. After a brief estrangement, she returned to his camp.
One night he came to bed drunk. She seized the moment, hacked
off his head, and carried the grotesque thing to Alexander. The
king allegedly was delighted at this turn of fortune but immediately sent the bloodstained murderess away "lest she set a bad example for his mild-mannered soldiers."[48] Let us assume, in light
of so many atrocities, that Alexander meant his comment to be
sarcastic. Spitamenes's daughter Apama apparently did not of-
fend: she later married the Macedonian general Seleucus, became the only successful queen among the host of captured Persian women, gave birth to a great Macedonian monarch, and
received honors from many Greeks in spite of her father's triumphs and her mother's treachery.[49]

The betrayal of Spitamenes certainly eased the burdens
weighing on Alexander. The Bactrian warlord had made life
miserable for the invading Greeks and Macedonians by leading
one part of a scattered movement that reminds us of the modern
mujahideen. The radical religious fundamentalism may be missing, for it is hard to tell about the ancients, but all the rest is there:
charismatic leadership, fierce local loyalties, shifting alliances,
guerilla tactics, gritty endurance, and inborn xenophobia.[50] Spitamenes did not, as some historians carelessly say, spearhead a na-
tionalistic uprising. His aims had nothing to do with nationalism,
any more than did those of the mujahideen who fought the Soviets and then each other. Spitamenes disliked the disruptive interference of the Mediterranean invaders and tried to force them
out. His associations with most of the other rebels were loose and
opportunistic, not centralized; he took no title that would suggest

nationalist aspirations of any kind. While he was not a king like Darius, or even an aspiring head of state like Bessus, scholars nevertheless consider Spitamenes "the most formidable opponent who ever faced Alexander."[51] His strategy and tactics anticipated those that have distinguished the campaigns of modern Afghan militants: the element of surprise, the avoidance of warfare waged from a fixed position, the use of terror, the exploitation of weather and terrain, the application of primitive technologies to achieve unexpected results. His successes compelled Alexander to try tactics that are today still used by some modern invaders, such as the Soviet counterinsurgency measure of destroying food, agriculture, and pastoralism.[52] Spitamenes was foremost among all the Hydra heads that menaced the invading Greeks and Macedonians. Others naturally rose up in his place, but they lacked his genius for mobile guerilla warfare. They had sharp teeth but poorer vision and shorter necks.

At some point in late autumn or early winter, Alexander attacked one or two of them in their caves and fortresses. The ancient sources for these operations jumble the names and facts together, but it seems likely that the king undertook some daunting attacks high in the mountains.[53] Like the citadel of Ariamazes, captured in early spring, these strongholds took advantage of the steep terrain. One hyparch, named Sisimithres (who may also have been called Chorienes), rallied his armed followers and entrenched them beyond a cramped, fortified pass at the Iron Gates. This site was apparently reinforced by a wall like the one built later, still visible today. As a further refuge, the natives sheltered in a rocky fortress protected by a narrow defile and a raging river. Supplies had been hoarded there, and the families of various other warlords joined Sisimithres in what seemed an impregnable hideout. Among these refugees was another unusual Bactrian woman who intrigued the Greeks: the mother of Sisimithres, who was also the wife of Sisimithres and mother of his two sons.[54]

In freezing cold and deep snow, Alexander's troops first assaulted the fortified pass. The position was heavily defended, but the king brought up battering rams. These impressive machines operated under the protection of long-range fire from Greek archers and slingers.[55] Once the invaders broke through, they labored to bridge the ravine and waterfall protecting the fort. During the day, the king oversaw the siege operation; at night, the work progressed under the supervision of three Macedonian generals: Ptolemy, Perdiccas, and Leonnatus. This methodical, round-the-clock enterprise both alarmed and fascinated the rebels. A framework of piles and wickerwork supported a rising fill of earth, inexorably bringing Alexander's artillery within range of the fortress. The king used torsion catapults to pummel the horrified Bactrians. Some extraordinary evidence of this military operation may have been found recently. Archaeologists in September 2002 discovered at the Iron Gates on the Shurob River a stone catapult ball. This artifact has been described as perhaps "the only weapon from Alexander's army ever recovered."[56]

Sisimithres realized that he could not defend his fortress against the advanced technology of the invaders: Alexander's engineering and firepower were too much. Sisimithres received emissaries from Alexander who advised him to surrender, hinting that the king was anxious to quit the region and advance east to India. Sisimithres, like so many other warlords, wanted nothing more than the withdrawal of the Macedonian's army, but his obstinate mother-wife convinced him to hold out longer. As the enemy's catapults and battering rams came closer, his nerve failed. Exasperated, he finally surrendered his citadel, its inhabitants, and their massive winter stockpile of food.

This time, unlike earlier in the year, there were no crucifixions or enslavements. The days of torture, mutilations, trophy heads, and terrorism against civilians came to a temporary end.[57] Instead, Alexander embarked on a new policy that paid rich dividends. He showed mercy to Sisimithres and soon restored him to power. Perhaps the king felt it necessary to gamble again on winning the loyalty of these warlords. Surely the betrayal of Spitamenes made this prospect easier, signaling as it did the warweariness of most Bactrians and Scythians. Even so, Alexander had to avoid being lulled into danger, as he had been following the arrest of Bessus. Bactrian hyparchs had a history of doubledealing. To be safe, Alexander enlisted two of Sisimithres's sons into his army, where they could serve as hostages. What probably swayed Alexander more than anything else were signs that the population at large had had enough. The villagers of Xenippa communicated this change of heart when they refused to shelter the Bactrian rebels. The lesson is timeless, even for the modern Afghan mujahideen: "When the local populace has to bear the reprisals with no apparent end in sight[,] . . . the local populace that remains often just wants to be left alone by all sides. The Mujahideen in this area lost a great deal of local support and, consequently, intelligence information and early warning."[58] Without such support, the warlords of Bactria lost something that Alexander eagerly gathered in inverse measure—hope.

CHAPTER FIVE

Love and War

LITTLE STAR OF HOPE

As the twenty-eight-year-old king rested his army at Nautaca, in
the vicinity of modern Karshi, his troops shivered, famished and
fatigued after another brutal year of fighting. For some, this was
their seventh winter away from the beaches of Greece, their third
since invading Afghanistan. Icy Nautaca made even Bactra seem
inviting, but Alexander's troops would have preferred the at-
tractions of earlier winter quarters in posh places such as Egypt
and Persepolis. There were no fine palaces here to promote long
evenings of rest and relaxation. Cold nights seemed haunted by
fresh memories of disaster: the failures of leadership against Spitamenes at the Polytimetus River and at Bactra had cost the lives
of thousands; the drunken quarrels among their generals had escalated into the king's murder of Cleitus. Alexander appeared as
courageous and charismatic as ever when he endured all the
hardships of mountain warfare alongside his men, but talk of his

divinity and the way he conciliated the Persians put some distance between the king and his veterans. There was already much to grumble about, and more just weeks away.

Still, the torrent of bad news could now be tempered by an occasional turn of good fortune. Alexander knew how relieved his soldiers were to receive the severed head of Spitamenes and the surrender of Ariamazes and Sisimithres. Word spread quickly when the Scythians also turned in the warlord Dataphernes, bound in chains just as he had bound Bessus. At some point in the war, Alexander personally slew the rebel Orsodates with a well-aimed bowshot.[1] Generals responsible for restoring order in neighboring provinces arrived at Nautaca with timely news of their success.[2] Once more, Alexander and his troops could sense an opportunity to end this Bactrian invasion on favorable terms. That chance had vanished before, but it could not be allowed to elude them again. Alexander considered his options and seized the moment with single-minded determination. Not everyone would approve his decision, but they would applaud its consequences.

Whether inspired by the recent offer of a Scythian bride or stunned by the beauty of a young Bactrian captive, Alexander resolved to marry a local woman from a prominent warlord's clan. He chose a daughter of Oxyartes named Rauxnaka, meaning "Little Star" in Persian and pronounced *Roxane* by the Greeks.[3] Oxyartes (his name reflects ancestral ties to the nearby Oxus River) was one of the Bactrians who betrayed Darius and threw his support behind Bessus. He remained with Bessus until the latter's arrest, then presumably joined the insurgency against Alexander. We cannot be sure whether he rode with Spitamenes or operated independently, but soon after Spitamenes's death he surrendered and became useful to Alexander as a negotiator. His family took refuge with Sisimithres, whose capitulation Oxyartes may have arranged.[4] Among those who surrendered with Sisimithres were Oxyartes's children, including the famously alluring Roxane. She caught the king's eye and became the subject of idealized fantasies as far-fetched and sentimental as anything on the romance market today. Her marriage to Alexander quickly inspired a celebrated painting by Aetion, a contemporary of the young couple who exhibited the work to admiring crowds at the Olympic Games in far-off Greece. Centuries later, the Roman writer Lucian saw the painting in Italy. His description of Aetion's sentimental masterpiece would later give rise to copies by Botticelli and Sodoma: "The scene is a very lovely chamber, and in it there is a bridal couch with Roxane, a most beautiful maiden, lounging upon it. Her eyes look down modestly as Alexander approaches. There are smiling Erotes [cupids]: one of them is standing behind Roxane, removing the veil and displaying the bride to her groom; another, like a good servant preparing her for bed, is taking the sandal from her foot; a third holds Alexander's cloak and strenuously draws him toward Roxane as the king offers her a crown."[5] Lucian adds that some of the cherubic cupids are shown sporting with Alexander's armor to emphasize the king's other great love—war.

The image of the demure Roxane intruding sweetly and irresistibly into Alexander's life of conquest makes good melodrama and pleasing art, but we must be very careful not to gloss over the hard realities of her plight. Part of the heroization of war is the marginalization of women so that the suffering of noncombatants can be systematically neglected. Interesting examples can be found not only in the ancient effort to treat Roxane's predicament as a diversionary love story but also in modern portrayals of women in Alexander's wars. Take, for instance, a splashy movie poster advertising the 1955 Robert Rossen film *Alexander the Great.*[6] The lavish illustration shows massive armies in battle and cities burning. Hundreds of men animate the busy scene, along with precisely four women. The female figures, scarcely clothed, are being abducted as the prizes of battle. Three are being carried off, slung over a warrior's shoulder or hoisted around the waist. Fair enough—but all three of these captives appear absolutely delighted by the event, their faces brightened by the rapture. The fourth woman does not smile, but rather lies on the ground, gazing upward at Alexander, completely starstruck and pining for her hero. Billing the film as "THE MOST COLOSSAL MOTION PICTURE OF ALL TIME!" the advertisers give the horrors of war and pillage the ridiculous semblance of spring break among the wild and willing.

A better model for the real Roxane might be the second-most famous of all Afghan women. Nearly everyone knows the photograph of the Afghan girl with the haunting green eyes. She first appeared on the cover of the June 1985 issue of *National Geographic,* staring out of the most famous image in the magazine's long and storied history.[7] The world so empathized with that face that the editors resolved, after seventeen years of inquiries, to find her again. No one knew her name. She had disappeared back into the bedlam of the modern Afghan wars, an anonymous needle in a haystack of 3.5 million refugees and 1.5 million dead. Persistent searchers finally located her, reportedly living in a village near the camps made notorious by the al-Qaeda terrorists.[8] She came forward reluctantly, unaware of her fame and uncomfortable with the attentions of Westerners. Devout and defiant, she told her story without smiling and then turned away the publicity so craved by her contemporaries elsewhere in the world. Her name, as it turns out, is Sharbat Gula. As well as anyone can remember, she was born in about 1973 to a Pushtun family that included three sisters and a brother. Soviet warplanes killed her parents, and at the age of about six, she became a refugee in Pakistan. It was there in 1984 that the photographer snapped her picture, a presumptive intrusion that angered her. Now married and a mother, she clings to her simple life with typical reticence. She embraces Islam and the burqa. She even has a good word to say about the Taliban. Her saga lends a famous face long without a name to ancient Roxane, a famous name long without a face.

Like Sharbat Gula, Roxane knew firsthand the ravages of war. Scholars estimate that she was born in about 340 B.C.E., making her sixteen years younger than young Alexander.[9] Her world seemed always unstable in spite of her father's place among local tribal leaders. Before Roxane was five, two of her Persian kings had already been killed.[10] By the time she was seven, the next monarch was fighting for his life against her future husband. At about ten, she learned that her father had joined in the murder of Darius and, with Bessus, was falling back to defend their Bactrian homeland. Roxane probably had no idea that she and her family were considered part of a terrorist threat.

She hid from the invaders like countless others, high up in the mountains. When eventually she fell into enemy hands, Roxane was called upon to perform a native dance for the conquerors. From among the troupe, Alexander singled her out; by sharing a loaf of bread cut by his sword, they formally married.[11] Many of the guests wondered: Why her? Why here? What the Macedonians knew of Bactrian wives dispelled many of these women's charms; the infamous consorts of Spitamenes and Sisimithres had discomfited the foreigners. Were there no Greek or Macedonian women worthy of their king, whose father, Philip, had married seven times? In fact, before departing Macedonia, young Alexander had been begged to take a bride and produce an heir.[12] The life of a Macedonian king could never be assured given the risks he must take, and the realm's security depended on a successor. Alexander, however, had refused this advice. Across thousands of miles of hazardous marches and military action, the bachelor king had never relented. Then suddenly in the wilds of central Asia, he wed a warlord's daughter. Was this passion or politics? With Alexander, nothing is ever certain. He treated the women of Darius's family chivalrously, but married none until much later. He politely declined the proffered daughter of a Scythian king. He probably had a mistress named Barsine, the daughter of Artabazus, who had recently retired as Bactria's satrap. To keep up royal appearances, he allegedly maintained a Persian harem equal in number to the nights of the year. Still, rumors circulated that he really preferred men or felt no sexual urges at all.[13] Always an enigma, the king's personal life confounds us. Perhaps he did feel some love or lust for Roxane, but no doubt she also served his need for a symbolic reconciliation with the Bactrians. As much a bribe as a bride, Roxane brought the warring factions together.

Unlike the legend coupling the king and the goddess Anahita, this historic union linked Alexander to the flesh and blood of Bactria. The impromptu marriage brought the king into one of the prominent clans of the region, where he could build a personal network of new loyalties. Just as he had played the part of a Persian king to undercut the power of Bessus, now he took on

the role of a Bactrian kinsman to undermine the rebels still opposing him.[14] It was a bold gesture, but one that would not be
agreeable to most modern heads of state. British monarchs, Russian premiers, and American presidents simply do not wed the
children of worrisome Afghan warlords. Nor did Alexander's
policies sit well with his soldiers. To make matters worse, the
king also promoted a son of Oxyartes to a high post and vigor-
ously recruited Bactrians into his own army. This siphoned away
soldiers from the resistance but naturally alarmed many Greek
and Macedonian veterans.[15]

Through all this, Roxane suffered. She was uprooted from her
native land to lead a life allegedly of luxury, love, and adventure.
But hers was a match made in haste, not heaven. No one asked
her blessing. Far from being a fairy princess, the luckiest of little
Afghan girls, she was destined to be Alexander's widow far
longer than she was Alexander's wife, and finally to be murdered
for being the mother of Alexander's heir. She died without ever
being accepted into her husband's world. For years, the couple
could not even carry on a conversation without the aid of inter-
preters.[16] If given the choice, she might actually have refused the
crown offered to her in Aetion's romanticized painting. Like
Sharbat Gula, Roxane may have wished to remain anonymous,
married quietly to a local villager rather than to a conqueror
from an alien and hostile culture.

After two months in winter camp, the restless king hurried
back into action before the arrival of spring in 327 B.C.E. Two
long years earlier, the Greeks and Macedonians had crossed the
Hindu Kush while winter still gripped these mountains, and
they had suffered greatly for it. This time in Sogdiana, the army
blundered straight into a horrifying tempest with far worse con-

sequences.[17] The first day of the march gave no forebodings of disaster. On the second day, the skies turned dark and threatening. On the third, lightning flashed everywhere and created a surreal, frightening aura. Thunder deafened the startled troops. Suddenly, rain and hailstones pummeled the soldiers, who crouched for shelter beneath their shields. As ice accumulated on the shields, they became too heavy and slippery to hold. The men grew tired and drenched. As they broke ranks and sought shelter in the woods, everything quickly turned to solid ice. Light failed and panicking men got lost. More than two thousand allegedly perished in a macabre scene, with bodies locked in ice as if the dead were still chatting and chattering together to keep away the chill.[18] As he had done during the logistical nightmare at the Oxus in 329 B.C.E., Alexander rallied the stunned survivors and promised relief. The former rebel Sisimithres rushed supplies and flocks to feed the cheerless Macedonian army, the first material payoff from Alexander's milder policies. The king later answered this kindness by raiding Scythian territory and driving off thirty thousand cattle as a recompense for Sisimithres.[19]

The first Bactrian warlords, men like Oxyartes and Sisimithres, had now joined Alexander's forces and proven their loyalty. A few remained on the loose, Catanes and Austanes chief among them. Alexander ordered a trusted Companion to hunt them down. Commanding a large force of three infantry brigades plus cavalry, Craterus took on the main body of rebels while a lieutenant (Polyperchon) cleared the region called Bubacene somewhere near the modern Surkhan-Darya Valley. Craterus killed 1,620 of the enemy, including the warlord Catanes (notoriously the best of the Bactrian archers); Austanes was captured and delivered to Alexander.[20] The situation finally resembled again the first march into the heartland of Bactria, with the native population at least pretending to accept Alexander's sovereignty. Meanwhile, the king had returned to Bactra, eager to organize the next phase of his campaigns. Plans for an invasion of India, long deferred, absorbed the general staff. Before Alexander left, however, two more crises arose. Like the murder of Cleitus, these problems revealed how powerful were the volcanic forces building within the king's inner circle. Naturally, they erupted in Bactria.

MORE OPPOSITION

In the spring of 327 B.C.E., Alexander's attempt to reconcile the factions surrounding him touched another nerve. Since Bessus's first challenge, Alexander had added to his traditional Greek and Macedonian responsibilities the various roles of Persia's rightful king. This entailed the appointment of some Persians to satrapal offices, the adoption of some aspects of Persian court protocol, and the wearing of some Persian regalia. Alexander could scarcely have governed otherwise, although these concessions galled his jealous countrymen. Many openly resented his marriage to Roxane and the honor this bestowed on the warlord Oxyartes.[21] As more and more such foreigners joined Alexander's entourage, a court in which even Greeks and Macedonians often could not get along became an ethnic and cultural riot. Persians, for example, always performed *proskynesis* before their kings.[22] This act of deference required a form of bowing down while blowing a ceremonial kiss. To a Persian subject, this homage signified the superior social rank of the king, not his divinity. The Persian King of Kings was never worshiped as a god (except, of course, in his role as pharaoh among the Egyptians). In the Greek world, however, this same act expressed adoration of a deity. Unless Alexander was indeed a living god, this servile debasement appeared inappropriate to all traditionalists in his retinue. Thus, to practice *proskynesis* before Alexander seemed as unthinkable to one group as not doing so was to another.

At Bactra, Alexander decided to confront this issue once and for all. The marriage to Roxane may have highlighted the problem, since Alexander was henceforth drawn more directly into the social nexus of the native peoples. In this new situation, he could have abolished *proskynesis* and tried to explain why to his Persian courtiers and kinsmen, or he might simply have accepted (as he did in the end) that some persons would perform it and others not. The first option would surely diminish his local stature, and the second had already caused embarrassment when some Macedonians ridiculed the Persians for displaying such servility. Unable to segregate his court and unwilling to lose status before the Persians, Alexander attempted a third course—to have everyone, including the die-hard conservatives, adopt *proskynesis* more or less voluntarily. We cannot know whether the inscrutable king acted purely out of practical concerns, or whether there was also a touch of megalomania in his choice. Certainly, he underestimated the hostile reaction.

By prearrangement at a banquet, some of the king's Greek and Macedonian Companions drank a toast to his health and then performed *proskynesis*.[23] The expectation was that everyone else would casually follow suit. One person refused to participate, however, and his abstention was immediately brought to the king's attention. The lone holdout was Callisthenes of Olynthus, who served as the court historian (some would say propaganda minister) of Alexander's reign. He was the nephew of Aristotle, Alexander's tutor, and he enjoyed a small intellectual following of his own. Like many scholars, Callisthenes could at times be arrogant and obstinate; some said he lacked common sense.[24] His objections to performing *proskynesis* are not entirely clear. In his unfinished history, he openly embraced the idea that Alexander was the son of Zeus. He may have drawn the line, however, at appearing to worship the king, or he may have simply disliked the proliferation of Persian rituals at Alexander's court. Whatever his reasons, his public opposition annoyed the king and aborted the experiment of a unified court ritual.[25]

Alexander's pique at Callisthenes may have played some part in the next crisis. At Bactra, some of the royal pages plotted to kill Alexander.[26] These teenagers formed an elite corps of noble attendants drawn from the leading families of Macedonia. By design, they developed an especially close relationship with the king, joining him in the hunt and guarding him as he slept. As part of their training, they fell under the tutelage of the scholarly Callisthenes, whom some of them ardently admired. One of these pages, named Hermolaus, had apparently breached royal etiquette during a hunt in Bactria by spearing the king's prey. Alexander bristled at the affront and ordered that Hermolaus be whipped in front of his peers. Naturally, the youth had already assimilated the heroic ethos that took deep umbrage at any public slight; the question is whether his tutor encouraged deadly retribution. Hermolaus may have had other grievances stemming from Alexander's growing orientalism. A personal grudge alone does not really explain how Hermolaus convinced his closest friends to organize so bold a conspiracy. The king's marriage to a Bactrian, his integration of so-called barbarians into the army, his Persian attire, his ridicule of fallen generals, and his fondness for *proskynesis* all broke faith with the Macedonian birthright of these ambitious boys. They may have shared the conservative point of view of their mentor Callisthenes but also may have been more impulsive. Covertly, they each contrived to draw guard duty on the same night in order to assassinate Alexander as he slept. The king, however, drank till dawn and never went to bed.

The next day, the story leaked. Years earlier, during the first stage of the invasion into Afghanistan, one of Alexander's top generals (Philotas) had been executed—not because he had plotted against the king, but because he had not taken a rumored plot seriously.[27] No one was going to make that mistake again. Zealous loyalists interrogated, tortured, and executed Hermolaus and the other young suspects. No evidence linked Callisthenes directly to the conspiracy, but Alexander arrested him nonetheless. The man had come to symbolize opposition to the king's evolving powers and policies, as ill-starred Cleitus once had done. Again, the court blamed the whole mess on the arrogance and stubbornness of the victim; no one took the tutor's side as he slowly died in prison.[28] Samuel Johnson's lines on human vanity would make a suitable epitaph for poor Callisthenes:

> Deign on the passing world to turn thine eyes,
> And pause awhile from letters to be wise;
> There mark what ills the scholar's life assail,
> Toil, envy, want, the patron, and the jail.[29]

When the tumultuous spring had passed, the king ordered ten thousand infantry and thirty-five hundred cavalry to garrison Bactria while the rest of the army marched away with him to

India.[30] These numbers are staggering and belie any suggestion that the region had been fully pacified. Such an enormous army of occupation had no equivalent in any other province of Alexander's empire. In fact, over 43 percent of all infantry and over 95 percent of all cavalry posted to foreign garrisons were stationed in what is now Afghanistan, even though the king's realm at that moment stretched across more than nine other modern nations, including Egypt, Turkey, Syria, Iraq, and Iran.[31] Without question, the hot spot of Alexander's world was Bactria.

Even this substantial military presence does not tell the whole story, since as many as ten thousand additional Greeks and Macedonians resided as permanent settlers among the Bactrians and their neighbors.[32] These old and disabled veterans dwelt in cities and colonies scattered throughout the area, left back to live out their days among the populations they had fought, in places that they loathed. It must have been a dreary prospect, judging by the desperation of these men to escape whenever the opportunity arose. It was natural, of course, for the army to slough off men no longer able to fight. However, such veterans may have felt like the worn-out Bactrians tossed aside to the Devourer dogs, whose bones they had once seen littering Bactria's largest city. When one of the Macedonians, a Companion named Menander, refused to stay at the garrison of which he had been placed in charge, Alexander executed the man to set an example for the others.[33]

Yet, for all its difficulties, this policy of massive settlement in Bactria distinguishes Alexander's invasion from those of the modern British, Soviets, and Americans. It gave his other policies a stern measure of durability, but at a huge cost and risk no modern state could bear. Essentially, Alexander practiced a form of population displacement. He drained off many of the young Bactrians of fighting age, both as conscripts to replenish his army and as hostages to guarantee the good behavior of their surviving families. He replaced these locals with a sizable number of Greek and Macedonian colonists, many of whom were no longer useful to him because of age, injuries, or dubious loyalty. Probably the king thought of this solution only after he had sent home the old veterans from the Oxus in 329 B.C.E., else he might have used them as well. His ideas were forged in the fires of the long Bactrian resistance. This shuffle of populations, not to mention the exhaustive war itself, choked out the native rebellion. It did not, however, please Alexander's settlers or bring about a brotherhood of mankind.

When Alexander finally marched back across the Hindu Kush Mountains in the direction of India, it was not the close of one chapter in his career and the beginning of another. He had spent more of his life—and lost more of his men—fighting in Bactria and Sogdiana than in any other part of the Persian world. And he was not yet finished. Alexander had known for years that he must invade the remote borderlands east of modern Kabul in order to finish the Bactrian war. At least one of Bessus's partners in crime, Barsaentes, had fled in that direction and remained at large among dangerous allies; another of Bessus's henchmen, Sisicottus, had originated in that region, where, no doubt, other rebels bided their time.[34] If his enemies could find powerful allies in Scythia, they could do likewise in India. The pending campaign in eastern Afghanistan must therefore be considered an extension of the war in northern Afghanistan. Strategic aims, as he saw them, guided the king's sweep toward the Indus River in a move that closely resembles the struggle in Bactria and Sogdiana precisely because it was part of that campaign. The chance to probe the boundaries of the exotic East was, for Alexander at least, a bonus; not many of his followers shared the king's enthusiasm for the unknown.

The trek back over the Hindu Kush went smoothly this time.[35] Alexander chose the easiest route over the Shibar Pass, which posed no great logistical problems. The winter snows had cleared, and one of his Alexandrias, founded near Begram in early 329 B.C.E., awaited the army on the other side of the mountains. While in this Alexandria, the king replaced the city's original commandant with someone more reliable, a Companion named Nicanor, and assigned Tyriespis the office of regional satrap.[36] He rounded up more locals to live in the city and left additional soldiers as colonists. Then his army swept through the valley of the Kabul River, which would also serve as the bloody trail of the British retreat in 1842.

Alexander split his forces to cover more ground, as he had learned to do a year earlier in Sogdiana.[37] Hephaestion and Perdiccas took half the Macedonians and all the Greek mercenaries as they led two columns along the main route past today's Kabul and Jalalabad. They had orders to suppress any resistance along the way and to establish garrisons. In 1878, during the same time of year, British forces undertook a similar mission. Their plan was to conduct any necessary punitive raids, fortify garrisons, and secure the main lines of communication between Kabul and Peshawar. At Jalalabad, for instance, British soldiers set up camp and, sensing no local opposition, began to improve the area by repairing roads and drainage. One cavalry unit, the Tenth Hussars, nonchalantly sent back for its band and tennis balls. They found themselves engaged in serious fighting all too soon.[38] Hephaestion and Perdiccas faced similar circumstances. They encountered little resistance and eventually threaded the famous Khyber Pass; together they reached the Indus early in December. As they set about assembling a pontoon bridge, a revolt erupted behind them. Like Satibarzanes and Spitamenes, a man named Astis, who had allegedly made his peace with the Macedonians, suddenly changed his mind. So, just when matters seemed under control, Hephaestion had to go back with a picked force to deal with this insurgent leader whose uprising cut across the invaders' lines of communication. After a thirty-day siege, Hephaestion captured the rebel stronghold at Peucelaotis (modern Charsada) and put Astis to death.[39]

Meanwhile to the north, Alexander's detachment endured a challenging march through cold, rugged terrain. Knowing that here, as in Sogdiana, many local hyparchs and their followers would simply flee deep into the remoter upland valleys to stay clear of the main army marching with Hephaestion and Perdiccas, Alexander led a rapid-strike force along a northern arc to intercept and engage them in their wintry fortresses.[40] The king augmented his cavalry with eight hundred mounted infantrymen to speed his assault and yet keep handy a heavily armored force for tough mountain and siege operations. The regular infantry followed as best it could under Craterus's command. The king attacked the first fortress into which the area's refugees had gathered, somewhere north of Jalalabad. The fighting resembled the situation earlier in Sogdiana. Alexander was wounded in the shoulder, though not seriously; some of his Companions (including Ptolemy and Leonnatus) suffered injuries as well. What followed was shameless butchery, part of a deliberate campaign of "sheer terror."[41] The Macedonians stormed the fort and took no prisoners; only those who fled immediately survived the whole-sale massacre ordered by Alexander. The king then razed the town to its very foundations. Craterus and the infantry destroyed all nearby settlements that hesitated to surrender.

Conspicuously, in light of the brutality otherwise associated with this whole operation, Alexander showered kindness on one community. At Nysa (just inside modern Afghanistan, northeast of Jalalabad), the king indulged his men's belief that they had found some kindred followers of the Greek god Dionysos. It had become exceedingly cold and the troops were worn out; the rank and file were grumbling again. So, when the natives of Nysa begged for terms, Alexander called off his attack and trimmed his demand for one hundred noble hostages. Entering the town, his homesick troops relaxed and enjoyed lavish entertainments that resembled a drunken Dionysiac revel. The feasting revived their spirits deep in the mountains in the dead of winter just as Sisimithres's feast had done for them the year before.[42] Their lives seemed as surreal as ever when they sobered and set out again.

Alexander's detachment next invaded the land of the Aspasians, whose terrified inhabitants burned their own homes and scattered into the mountains. The king ordered an indiscriminate slaughter of the slower folk. In the pursuit, Ptolemy managed to spear and despoil the local warlord. At the next town, too, the natives burned their belongings and fled; they had no idea that such desperate measures would not deter Alexander. The invaders were after the people, not their possessions. The king waited for Craterus to catch up, and ordered him to fortify the abandoned site to help militarize this frontier. As Craterus supervised the work, Alexander rounded up locals to populate the place along with settlers drawn from his unfit soldiers. While out foraging for supplies, Ptolemy discovered the main body of refugees and reported their incredible number to the king. Alexander sprang into action. He orchestrated a three-pronged attack that allegedly netted, after ferocious combat, some forty thousand prisoners and 230,000 of their oxen.[43] Though clearly an exaggeration by Ptolemy, these figures suggest that here (as on the Jaxartes frontier) Alexander's invasion deliberately affected every living thing in his army's path.

As Alexander crossed from valley to valley, he traversed the modern borders of Afghanistan and entered what is now known as the Federally Administered Tribal Areas and North-West Frontier Province of Pakistan. These remote areas have long been dotted with refugee camps of the type that once harbored Sharbat Gula. In his day, Alexander targeted the equivalents of such settlements as havens of warlords and seedbeds of resistance. His precise route has long been a subject of interest among explorers. The intrepid Sir Marc Aurel Stein (1862–1943) produced an engaging memoir of his personal quest, *On Alexander's Track to the Indus,* which is still widely read today.[44] Stein traced Alexander's path up the Kunar Valley, across to the Panjkora, and then down to Swat. Clambering over rocks and ruins, the Hungarian archaeologist identified as many of the battle sites as he could, based on ancient texts and modern terrain. His surmises are as good as any, and his gift for description brings to life the hardships endured by the ancient combatants.

In the Swat Valley, Alexander first besieged a place called Massaga, where he endured another injury.[45] The king's artillery and siege towers annihilated many of the defenders, including their commander. These machines must have been a wonder to see among the wild mountains of Swat. Measuring fifty by sixty feet at the base and rising to fifty feet, with assault bridges that lowered to unleash waves of archers and other troops, the Macedonians' wheeled towers were massive.[46] Stein marveled at how Alexander ever got them over the passes, but of course they were transported in pieces and modified on-site.[47] Still, the effort was immense and shows the foresight of the king.

The inhabitants of Massaga had hired seven thousand mercenaries from neighboring India; when the battle went badly, these pragmatic men accepted a truce and promised to serve in Alexander's army. The king, however, later changed his mind. In spite of the truce, he surrounded the mercenaries and executed them to the very last man.[48] This massacre was meant to terrify other towns into surrendering, but the natives despaired of fair treatment and took their chances fighting. One by one, their settlements fell, with great loss of life.

Even the mighty mountain fortress at Aornus (modern Pir-Sar?) could not hold out against the determined Macedonian invaders, who cherished the thought that Hercules himself had once failed to capture it.[49] Using the same methods that had succeeded in Sogdiana, Alexander's troops triumphed over man and nature. The king sent Ptolemy with a picked force to seize some heights after a difficult climb, reminiscent of the move against Ariamazes. Alexander began siege operations by constructing a raised earthwork like the one used against Sisimithres. The Macedonians thereby trumped Hercules by capturing the mountain. Many refugees died there either at the hands of Alexander's troops or by throwing themselves from the cliffs. The king celebrated his victory and soon afterward received the severed head of one last warlord, a rebellious leader in Buner whose weary followers killed him to stop the fighting.[50] The wintry campaign in eastern Afghanistan had thus played out as earlier in the north: the king met resistance with overwhelming force and ferocious retribution. He showed no mercy or conciliation until he had shed great quantities of blood. Once he had stormed all known fortresses and refuges, killed sufficient numbers of locals and their tribal leaders, and received the remaining rebels in parts or in chains, Alexander left behind heavy garrisons and got on his way. He rejoined Hephaestion and Perdiccas at the Indus bridge, confident in the situation behind them.[51] Within a year, however, the region flared up in renewed revolt—a poor omen for the future.

CHAPTER SIX

Dark Shadows

CHAOS

Alexander the Great never again set foot on the soil of Afghanistan. For the remainder of his short life, the king skirted the country in a destructive march down through Pakistan and back along the coast to Babylon in Iraq. Every miserable step of the way, the effects of the Bactrian war harassed Alexander and his exhausted army like one of the Devourer dogs. The troops grew tired and testy; they lost the will for further conquests. Men turned mutinous as the toil and bloodshed took their toll. They had been hating and hunting warlords for so long that systematic brutality became second nature. No one seemed the least bothered anymore by the massacre of civilians. Guerilla warfare and garrison duty seemed their new lot, a far cry from the heady days of heavy hauls from the plundered palaces of Persia. They looked around them and saw a very different army swollen with mercenaries and foreign conscripts. Many familiar faces were gone.

Disease had become more prevalent as they wandered farther and farther from the Mediterranean. They felt less confidence in their commanders, including even the king. He had changed like everyone else. His physical scars were accumulating at an astonishing rate, but his emotional and psychological damage seemed even greater. There were rumors that he drank himself unconscious for days at a time. He appeared moody, sometimes plunging into a vicious rage or sulking like a child. On other days, he loved his worst enemies. Posttraumatic stress syndrome made every survivor of the Bactrian campaigns an unpredictable victim.

Against the ugly reality of that experience stands the happy face of war painted on the shields of Alexander's army by many apologists. Who now believes Plutarch that the ancient peoples of Afghanistan considered themselves fortunate that Alexander found and conquered them, or that the king's only aim in slaughtering them was to end the enmities of humankind and substitute peace for war? To assert his authority and safeguard his empire from potential threats, Alexander acted unilaterally and accepted few restraints: the ends always justified the means. His stern actions anticipated those of modern invaders such as the Soviet armed forces, of whom it has been written:

> On the basis of accumulating experience over nearly three centuries, they have defined the preconditions for the successful occupation of Muslim territories and the suppression of local resistance as:
>
> 1. The effective isolation of the region.
> 2. The destruction of the local leadership, and especially its ability to achieve unity.
> 3. The erosion of popular support for any resistance through the destruction of the local social and economic infrastructure.[1]

Alexander worked down this same list beginning in 329 B.C.E., when he sought to isolate Bactria from its Scythian neighbors, to crush the insurgent Bactrian warlords, and to ravage the countryside as a means of breaking its support of the hyparchs. To his credit and shame, Alexander avoided half measures once he set his mind to the task. The king went far beyond the momentary capture of key cities, the coercion of a few tribal leaders, and the establishment of a foreign puppet leader. He scoured every dark corner of Afghanistan and its wildest borderlands. He tracked down every rebel. He established intrusive military foundations to seal off the frontiers. He raided and burned cities, villages, farms, forts, and even refugee camps. He punished civilians as if they were enemy soldiers. He invented total war and embraced it as the lesser evil.

Alexander's invasion of Bactria and its environs cost the lives of innumerable indigenous peoples. Estimates of men, women, and children killed begin at 120,000 and climb considerably higher. The king's known losses (up to 7,000 soldiers) seem small by comparison, but they represent a significant proportion of his available manpower. More important, the Greek and Macedonian casualties far exceeded anything endured in Alexander's campaigns up to that time. They demoralized the men beyond recompense. The losses against Spitamenes at the Polytimetus River were the worst for any military engagement in Alexander's reign; in fact, the king lost almost as many troops on that one day as in all the great battles and sieges that cumulatively overthrew Darius. Also noteworthy were the major losses due to the environment, which eclipsed those from battle. Such suffering had never afflicted the king's army as when it crossed the mountains and deserts of Afghanistan and blundered into the Sogdian blizzard. Yet, to explore the effect of this invasion of Afghanistan, we must go beyond the staggering body count and consider the fate of the survivors. What, for example, did the costly Bactrian campaigns really gain for the Greeks and Macedonians? Did they enjoy a peaceful old age in the homeland they had protected, or did war abroad become a way of life? Was the world a safer place for the conquered peoples? Did the threat posed by warlords and terrorism cease, or did the invaders and occupiers become terrorists themselves?

It is not easy to ascertain what transpired in ancient Afghanistan in the wake of Alexander's campaigns there. During his reign, anything that happened away from the king stood a poor chance of being recorded for posterity. After all, the main historians of the time were members of his entourage, who focused on their immediate surroundings and experiences. Their spotlight naturally followed the king and his court, leaving everything else in shadow. Thus, when Alexander marched away from places like Bactria, darkness swallowed the land, leaving us wondering about what later happened there. Some modern scholars assume only the best. For example, we often read that "settled conditions" in Bactria and Sogdiana brought about prosperity, peace, trade, and urbanization.[2] Others have argued more soberly that the situation Alexander left behind was unsteady and volatile. Hardly had the king gone away than messengers arrived in his camp to report renewed uprisings in places allegedly pacified. When such envoys drifted into the spotlight of Alexander's court, they brought hints of what was really happening elsewhere. On the basis of these clues, we can see that those left behind in Afghanistan remained in a state of war and turmoil, not peace and prosperity.

For example, in the summer of 326 B.C.E., a messenger arrived at Alexander's camp in the Punjab to announce that trouble had erupted along the borderlands of present-day Afghanistan and Pakistan. The king had departed that area only months earlier, but already the Assacenian tribesmen had murdered the hyparch assigned to them by Alexander. The king therefore ordered one of his Companions, Philip the son of Machatas, to assist Sisicottus (commandant of the Aornus garrison) in putting down the rebellion before it spread any farther. The extent of the problem is revealed by the fact that Tyriespis, the governor of the Kabul region, was also called upon to help stop the insurgency. Our sources make no mention of another regional governor, the Macedonian Nicanor, which suggests that he may have been killed early in the revolt.[3]

Meanwhile, Alexander's forces followed up a victory against the Indian rajah Porus by pushing east to the Hyphasis (modern Beas) River. There, the king's demoralized soldiers begged Alexander to take them back home. At this so-called Hyphasis Mutiny in the eastern Punjab, the army stubbornly balked for the first time in Alexander's life.[4] The king listened unhappily as Coenus, one of his key generals in the Bactrian war, dared to articulate the many grievances of the rank and file. The anxieties born of the Afghan campaigns predisposed the men to camp-side complaints, especially about the increasing likelihood that illness or injury meant permanent assignment to some wretched frontier garrison.[5] Matters were getting no better, and it gave no comfort that Alexander's special squad of surveyors (the Bematists) could tell them *exactly* how far they had marched from home. How much farther would they have to go to satisfy the king and keep Greece safe?

Alexander tried to cajole his men into crossing the Hyphasis River and marching deeper into South Asia. He delivered another of his rousing speeches, but the troops were no longer so easily convinced. The last time Alexander had promised them a closing campaign of only a few days had been at Hecatompylus four years earlier. They were to have quickly punished Bessus and been finished, yet here they were still fighting as fiercely as ever. Nothing would move the men to continue. Alexander therefore did the unthinkable: he stopped, bowing to the will of a force he could no longer control. The excited troops helped to set up altars like those at the Jaxartes frontier and then began the long march homeward. They had not gone far when Coenus died of disease. Suggestions that Alexander murdered him, as he had the outspoken Cleitus and Callisthenes, have no reliable foundation.[6] The general health of the army had deteriorated, and maladies of one sort or another carried off many victims.

Alexander took the long way back. Turning south through Pakistan, the king continued to maraud and massacre as he had done in Bactria. Philip the son of Machatas rejoined Alexander's main army and assisted in the campaign down the Indus Valley; his arrival back in our spotlight suggests that his mission against the Assacenians had been reported as successful.[7] That fuse had only been dampened, however, since the powder ignited again. We are not privy to the explosion, but not long afterward, the governor who had helped Philip against the rebellious Assacenians was summoned to Alexander's camp. Tyriespis faced vague charges of greed and arrogance during his governance of the region around Kabul. The frustrated king executed him. Whatever the exact nature of his crimes, they indicate a continuing crisis in eastern Afghanistan.

Alexander replaced Tyriespis with an unusual candidate. Because of some trouble in northern Afghanistan, Alexander had summoned his father-in-law, Oxyartes, to the same tribunal. It comes as no surprise that the king acquitted him. But, rather than send Oxyartes home, Alexander assigned him the vacated province of the dead Tyriespis.[8] This appointment exonerated the king's kinsman and, perhaps more important, removed him from whatever situation had aroused suspicions in his native territory. There were, indeed, extraordinary security concerns in that quarter, especially when an enormous rebellion broke out in Bactria at the erroneous news of Alexander's death in battle.

The new trouble started early in 325 B.C.E., when Alexander's troops showed no enthusiasm for yet another assault on a native town in Pakistan. The king therefore resorted to great risks in order to motivate them. Leading the attack, Alexander brashly mounted the battlements and leapt inside. He took on the Indian defenders almost single-handedly as his frantic soldiers rushed to save him. Before they could arrive, Alexander suffered a grievous wound in the chest that may have punctured his lung. Two Companions protected the fallen king while the rest of the army breached the walls and poured inside the town. The outraged Greeks and Macedonians slaughtered every soul living there.[9]

As Alexander slowly recovered from his injury, he received a disturbing report. The king had left a huge army of occupation behind in Bactria, but these twenty-three thousand Greek colonists did not willingly embrace their new military and political duties.[10] When rumors circulated that Alexander had died from his injuries, many of these soldiers in Bactria tried en masse to abandon their posts. About three thousand disgruntled veterans seized this moment to revolt because "they could no longer abide living there among the barbarians."[11] Amyntas the satrap (Cleitus's replacement) apparently lost control of the capital during an uprising led by a Greek named Athenodorus. To guide his followers out of Bactria, Athenodorus allegedly took the title of king (the unforgivable crime of Bessus) and urged the native Bactrians to support his cause. This bold uprising illuminates the continued volatility of Bactria.

These Greek rebels shifted loyalties without shame as though they had become warlords themselves. A Greek named Biton challenged Athenodorus's authority, luring the so-called king to a banquet. There a native Bactrian named Boxus joined the plot and assassinated Athenodorus. Historians have no idea who this Boxus might have been, other than a native opportunist not unlike some of the warlords in recent Afghan history. Around Jalalabad, for instance, several local leaders and their lieutenants vied in late 2001 for leverage and loot. They each allied with the United States against al-Qaeda, accepting American money and munitions to attack Tora Bora and, in the long run, to position themselves for postwar power. As it turned out, they seemed at the same time to be under strong obligation to Osama bin Laden, whom they allowed to escape before they attacked his hideouts.[12] Similarly, Boxus was apparently playing off the factions around him, hoping to profit when the occupiers pulled out of Bactria.

After the murder of Athenodorus, Biton convened an assembly at Bactra, as Bessus had once done and Alexander, too, in order to win over the troops. The crowd generally accepted Biton's assertion that Athenodorus had threatened him, but gradually suspicions arose about Biton's story. Many Greeks therefore armed themselves and planned to execute Biton, but another faction appeased them for the moment. This reprieve only spurred Biton to greater crimes; he plotted next against those who had saved him. Outraged, the Greeks seized both Biton and Boxus. The latter was summarily put to death; Biton received the same sentence, but was to be tortured first. During the torture, however, some of the Greeks "went crazy" and staged a riot. The prisoner Biton was released, naked and bleeding, a sight so pitiable that he was allowed to escape back to Greece.[13] Meanwhile, most of the other settlers stayed at their troubled posts, but only because they learned that Alexander had recovered from his injury. We are told that the Greeks in Bactria "longed for their Hellenic upbringing and way of life, abandoned as they were to the fringes of the empire, but they endured out of fear so long as Alexander was alive."[14]

Whether or not the melodrama surrounding Athenodorus, Biton, and Boxus has been hyped in the report given to Alexander, a very real tragedy lies behind it. We cannot doubt the disaffection of Alexander's settlers or the fact that Bactria remained a turbulent place where factionalism and warlordism thrived. The instability, however, now expressed itself through the actions of the newcomers as much as the natives. It may have been worse. We glimpse only the spectacle at Bactra without any evidence for the situation beyond the capital. Curiously missing in the entire story is Alexander's Macedonian satrap, Amyntas, whose disappearance seems ominous. Another governor, Philip, took office in Bactria. He, too, would soon vanish.[15] Similarly, a different Philip (the son of Machatas), who had put down the Assacenian revolt and been left to govern part of Pakistan, fell to assassins in 325 B.C.E. He was killed by the mercenaries stationed with him. The murderers were in turn executed by the dead man's Macedonian guards.[16] These events provide a grim, though incomplete, picture of how matters stood once Alexander's main army marched away.

CATASTROPHE

On the way back west through southern Pakistan and Iran, Alexander led a large portion of his army through the hellish wastes of the Gedrosian Desert. Their suffering and privation reached new extremes. Some experts argue that this ordeal had no real purpose beyond punishing the army for its weakness and insubordination in Afghanistan and Pakistan. A so-called reign of terror followed, during which Alexander purged his government of many deficient satraps and lesser officials.[17] Even the empire's minister of finance, a boyhood friend of Alexander named Harpalus, took fright and ran for his life—taking a mercenary army and part of the treasury with him.[18] The world around Alexander swirled with crises, and every solution raised new problems. The army soon erupted in protest when it appeared that Alexander had chosen to replace his weary Macedonian veterans with thousands of troops recruited from provinces such as Bactria.[19] One of Oxyartes's three sons, Itanes, served Alexander as a Companion in a special cavalry squadron. The commander of that elite unit was a Bactrian named Hystaspes. The success of such foreigners galled the Macedonians, who accused their king of "going barbarian" at the expense of his own proud heritage.[20] They had won the war but lost their king. Alexander executed the loudest complainers among his Macedonians and cowed the rest into momentary submission.

Dark shadows were gathering. In the autumn of 324 B.C.E., illness carried off the king's dearest friend, Hephaestion; the misfortune plunged Alexander into a deep depression that verged on mania. Wrestling with a world of problems, Alexander was running out of experienced, able-bodied compatriots to help him. The strain of his brutal wars and brittle peace finally overwhelmed the young king. In Babylon on June 10, 323 B.C.E., Alexander died at the age of thirty-two. Some persons naturally suspected foul play and poison, but most modern historians and medical experts point instead to malaria, pancreatitis, leukemia, porphyria, schistosomiasis, typhus, West Nile virus, or alcoholic hepatitis.[21] At the time, Alexander had not yet fulfilled his first obligation to his people; his Bactrian wife, Roxane, was pregnant, but no heir stood ready to take the place of Macedonia's king and Persia's conqueror. Roxane's life among the captives, queens, and concubines of Alexander's wars had its own tragic consequences. Somewhere in Pakistan, she had suffered a miscarriage. At Susa a few years later, still childless, she watched her husband marry Stateira, a royal daughter of Darius. Her situation became threatened, but like her father out in eastern Afghanistan, Roxane was a survivor.

Alexander's last official act was to entrust his royal signet ring to Perdiccas, one of his favorite generals. That seems innocent enough, but apparently Perdiccas and Roxane had already planned what to do in such an emergency. Before the news could spread of the king's demise, the pregnant Roxane lured Stateira (and her sister Drypetis, Hephaestion's widow) into a trap.[22] She did so with a forged letter bearing Alexander's royal seal, which only Perdiccas could have helped her do. Roxane murdered Stateira and Drypetis, Darius's daughters, and buried their bodies deep in a well. No chance remained that Stateira might also give birth to an heir or be used along with her royal sister to lay claim to Darius's empire. Perdiccas bet his future on Roxane and the possibility that a boy he could control would soon be born.

Around the corpse of Alexander, the dead king's paladins literally battled and bargained for power. Two camps fought respectively for the rights of Alexander's half-brother, Philip Arrhidaeus, or his unborn child, should it be a boy. The latter as king would be unable to govern on his own for many years, and the former had such infirmities that he, too, could rule only under someone's close supervision.[23] The opportunity to serve as puppet master for either (or both) of these royal candidates created a volatile competition. When Roxane bore a son, named Alexander IV, he and the invalid Philip Arrhidaeus were proclaimed joint kings under Perdiccas's supervision. The provinces of the empire were then distributed as inducements to the other leading generals.[24]

The succession crisis in Babylon meant opportunity once more in Bactria. Without hesitation, more than twenty-three thousand unhappy Greeks grabbed their gear and tried to go home. Alarmed at this news, the generals in Babylon agreed with Perdiccas that the settlers must not be allowed to abandon their Bactrian billets. Just as Alexander had once executed a man for refusing to stay in Bactria, Perdiccas declared himself willing to do the same even if it meant the extermination of all the homesick veterans. The determined settlers, "all of them experienced in war and noted for their courage," elected a Greek named Philon to lead their army of twenty thousand infantry and three thousand cavalry. Perdiccas ordered his ambitious subordinate Peithon to gather troops and crush these rebels.[25]

In December 323 B.C.E., Peithon marched east to Bactria.[26] In such a strange new world the Greeks and Macedonians now strove among themselves. A baby half Bactrian shared the throne of Macedonia, and in his name an army headed toward his mother's homeland with murderous intent to make the Balkan colonists stay there against their will. The child-king would never see Bactria; Macedonia would be his grave. His old and angry subjects in Bactria would never return to their Greek homes; their ghosts lie in Afghanistan still. The cosmos had turned upside down in the space of only a few years. In the process, the role of warlord in Afghanistan had shifted from native to Greek commanders.

Lipodorus, one of the rebel generals serving under Philon, played out the familiar type of the wavering subordinate in this second settlers' revolt. During the final battle between the armies of Peithon and Philon, this Lipodorus pulled his contingent of three thousand soldiers out of the fight and thereby gave the victory to Peithon. After the surrender of the long-suffering settlers, another massacre occurred. Peithon's troops broke their pledges, set upon the Greek prisoners, and slaughtered them in numbers hard to fathom. Our ancient source states that none of the captives survived, which would mean that at least twenty thousand perished (if we assume that at least the three thousand with Lipodorus were spared).[27] Even if exaggerated, such savagery recalls the war these very men had once survived, when they had slaughtered the Branchidae plus incredible numbers of Sogdians, Scythians, and Bactrians. Surely these veterans were not all annihilated, since it remained necessary for someone to garrison the region.[28] Even so, whatever the extent of the carnage, another blow had been struck against Alexander's original settlement policy in Bactria.

Back in 328 B.C.E., Alexander and four of his emerging generals had led those ill-starred soldiers across the Oxus River into Sogdiana. The oil they discovered on that occasion portended a troubled future, and their lives fulfilled the prophecy. Even the men who had marched away from Bactria seemed doomed. Three of the commanders had already died of disease (Coenus, Hephaestion, and Alexander) and the fourth (Perdiccas) was about to be killed by his own troops in a war against the fifth (Ptolemy). In the distribution of provinces agreed upon at Babylon, Ptolemy had eagerly taken Egypt because its wealth and geography guaranteed a measure of independence. He further expressed his ambitions by stealing the body of Alexander in order to bury it in Egypt. Perdiccas vowed to retrieve the mummified relic by military force. Ptolemy dug in his heels and awaited Perdiccas's invasion. Twice Perdiccas tried to force a passage of the Nile River near Pelusiun, but Ptolemy's soldiers repulsed each attempt. A third assault upriver near Memphis almost succeeded, but so many drowned that the demoralized survivors turned on Perdiccas. A stern delegation of lieutenants murdered Perdiccas in his tent.[29]

Perdiccas's assassination in 320 B.C.E. jeopardized the lives of Roxane and Alexander IV.[30] They were sent to Macedonia where Olympias, Alexander the Great's powerful old mother, took charge of raising the boy-king as a Macedonian. Many xenophobes distrusted the foreign Roxane and endeavored to efface the Bactrian heritage of her son. In 317 B.C.E., Olympias executed her stepson Philip Arrhidaeus, who was the royal colleague of her grandson, Alexander IV.[31] Two years later, Olympias suffered a similar fate at the hands of an ambitious general, Antipater's son Cassander. Because it now seemed possible that Alexander IV might reach the age of maturity and actually rule the empire, some of the generals and governors decided to intervene. In 311, they killed Roxane and her son.

The long, harrowing trail from Bactria to Babylon and then to a Balkan grave hardly seems to have rewarded Roxane for sharing a loaf of nuptial bread with Alexander the Great. Our knowledge of important persons such as Roxane suffers from a double deficiency: she was a woman in a patriarchal era, and she was a Bactrian, from the losing side of the war. Our histories ultimately depend upon Greek and Roman writers, and they certainly had a masculine prejudice driven by their emphasis on martial events. From their works, the names of nearly a thousand of Alexander's contemporaries are known.[32] Of these, only about fifty are women (roughly 5 percent).[33] And of these women, fewer than twenty represent the foreign cultures conquered by Alexander—and some of *them* are mythical, such as the queen of Meroe in Africa and queen of the Amazons in central Asia. We know too little about what happened to an entire generation of women whose lives would have been so different but for the wars of their fathers, husbands, brothers, and sons.

An epic cycle of civil wars and assassinations tore at Alexander's fragile world. The internecine bloodbath soon claimed every member of Alexander's family and extinguished the ancient ruling dynasty of Macedonia. Curiously, the blood of the beheaded rebel Spitamenes coursed through the veins of more than a dozen later kings, whereas Alexander's line ended with the murder of his only son by the jealous Macedonians. Subsequently, a few of Alexander's surviving generals felt free to proclaim themselves kings of various corners of the fragmented empire: Ptolemy in Egypt, Seleucus in Babylonia, Lysimachus in Thrace, Cassander in Macedonia, and so forth. During all this time, Alexander's legacy never led to peace. His treacherous generals and tired armed forces fought each other with the ferocity they had honed in Bactria. One indication of this sad state of affairs may be found in the history of the elite unit in Alexander's army called the Silver Shields. As these veterans grew old in service and passed the age of sixty, they demanded of Alexander's successors the benefits and rewards promised to them. Deemed unruly and ungrateful for making such petitions, these worn-out soldiers were sent away to southern Afghanistan where, we are told, they were to be secretly assigned by twos and threes to perilous missions from which they would not return. Betrayed, they still haunt the region of Kandahar.[34]

To be fair, Alexander's empire had begun falling apart during his reign; his death merely accelerated the process. In the eastern reaches of that empire, the king's successes proved especially ephemeral. In spite of his best and most brutal efforts, the conquest of Afghanistan and Pakistan remained incomplete, the occupation unstable. Alexander had known this. In the Indus Valley of Pakistan, he made what has been called "a tactical retreat without parallel in the reign."[35] The king gave up this territory to local rulers because he simply did not have the manpower necessary to garrison it. The army he had left along the Oxus was clearly unreliable, and he did not have another to station along the Indus. Alexander's successors understood this problem as well, especially after the second settlers' revolt in Bactria. Later, when the Macedonian general Seleucus claimed all the conquered provinces east of Babylonia, he acknowledged the inevitable and formally traded away much of modern Pakistan and southeastern Afghanistan to the rajah Chandragupta Maurya in exchange for hundreds of war elephants of more immediate value.[36]

Seleucus deemed these areas uncontrollable and expendable, but he worked hard to hang onto Bactria. He campaigned there between 308 and 305 B.C.E., but we have none of the details. Seleucus may have killed the latest satrap, Stasanor, but we cannot be sure. Among the natives, it could only help that Seleucus was married to Spitamenes's daughter Apama; everyone else among Alexander's old guard had repudiated the foreign wife assigned to him at Susa in 324 B.C.E., but Seleucus gambled wisely on Apama's usefulness. She played an active role in her husband's affairs, for which she received honors from various quarters. For instance, she entertained embassies and granted royal patronage. Apama supported a petition to help a detachment of Greek mercenaries from the city of Miletus, and along with Demodamus— Seleucus's general during the Bactrian campaign—she restored the temple and cult at Didyma.[37] Curiously, this was the original home of the Branchidae, who had been massacred in Apama's native land. What welcome Seleucus received from any survivors of Alexander's garrisons we cannot easily guess. No direct records indicate who they were, how many, or in what condition. Many had been old or unfit when they first settled in Bactria twenty years earlier. Since then, time and two rebellions had devastated their ranks. Seleucus might have done something to reinforce these Greeks, but another decade would pass before he could seriously address the matter.[38]

Seleucus first had to return west, where he joined in the continuous wars that shaped the new world. In 305 B.C.E., after the extermination of Alexander's bloodline, Seleucus and several other generals declared themselves kings. During their struggles, Seleucus put to good use his bartered elephants at the Battle of Ipsus in 301, a conflict that ended all hopes of ever reuniting the empire Alexander had conquered.[39] Twenty years later, the victors of Ipsus turned on each other. Seleucus and Lysimachus, the very last of Alexander's generals, fought at Corupedium for the chance to rule a region that Seleucus had not seen for over fifty years—his homeland of Macedonia. Lysimachus fell dead on the battlefield, and shortly thereafter Seleucus was assassinated.[40] In his tribute to these men, Appian of Alexandria wrote: "Thus perished these two kings, the brawniest and bravest of them all, one at the age of seventy and the other three years older, each one fighting with his own hands until the day he died."[41] Another of history's fateful generations had done its work and gone, this one warring to the end.

Before his death, Seleucus had wisely promoted his son Antiochus to the rank of viceroy. As joint king with his father, Antiochus assumed responsibility for the East—including the important satrapy of Bactria. His job was to restore order in the region and to strengthen the dynasty's hold over it. This proved to be the perfect assignment for a half-Bactrian, half-Macedonian king whose grandfather was Spitamenes.

By this time, however, not many of Alexander's original settlers can have been alive. The peace such men had allegedly won proved illusory, although it cannot be said that anyone of that era really expected much else. Alexander's veterans could remember how pragmatically their forebears had placed limits on peace rather than war. Many Greek treaties and truces had a specified expiration date, since it was foolhardy to think peace could last indefinitely. In 445 B.C.E., Athens and Sparta agreed to a thirty-year cessation of their hostilities; war resumed ahead of schedule in 431. Ten years later, the two sides agreed to live in peace for a half century; they missed that target by about forty-five years.[42]

No sane Greek or Macedonian would plan for anything like peace everlasting; if harmony could endure for thirty or fifty years, that would be all anyone could hope for (but of course even that was too much). Only we in the modern world would dare to think of waging "a war to end all wars." This grand illusion crumbled all too quickly when we added a numeral to that World War and embarked upon its successor. Now we speak readily of a World War III as if it had the force of Greek inevitability behind it. One of the most talked about wars in history has not yet happened, but its place has been reserved.[43]

The patterns in history need not be deterministic, of course. There is always a chance that another World War will not be fought, or that the United States will succeed in Afghanistan where other superpowers have failed, just as there once existed a possibility that Alexander would live long enough to finish the business he started. The king would have been sixty-nine in the year 287 B.C.E., a fact without significance if not for a famous essay by the renowned historian Arnold Toynbee (1889–1975).[44] What might be different, Toynbee wondered, if Alexander had survived to that date? He therefore imagined the king recovering from his illness at Babylon. That occurrence allowed Alexander to devote some time to purely peaceful pursuits before conquering the Mediterranean world all the way to Gibraltar (thus forestalling the rise of the Roman Empire). Next, the king allegedly returned to India and finished his mission there by overwhelming the kingdom of Magadha and annexing the entire subcontinent. His armies ascended the Nile Valley and reached tropical Africa. When word came that the Chinese might establish a superstate as mighty as his own, Alexander marshaled an invasion from his city on the Jaxartes (Alexandria Eschate). In just four years, he conquered the Far East and unified a world-state before becoming bored and feebleminded. When Toynbee's Alexander finally died in 287, his son, Alexander IV, succeeded him without the slightest disturbance. The Great's old generals retired peacefully, and Alexander after Alexander ruled the world right up to the most recent, Alexander LXXXVI (Toynbee never explains why anyone in his scenario should be using Roman numerals). For twenty-three hundred years, Alexander's empire endured without rancor or revolt.

Toynbee's what-if world takes little notice of Bactria, assuming as it does that Alexander had truly pacified the region. There was no second settlers' revolt, no lingering animosity, no frontier isolation. In an empire stretching from the Atlantic to the Pacific, Bactria would be dead center rather than remote and marginalized. His Bactria would never become our Afghanistan, and Alexander LXXXVI would not have to worry that a malevolent Taliban or al-Qaeda might target from there his gleaming Alexandrias on the Hudson and Potomac.

But the contingencies of history, as we have seen, created a very different chronicle. There were wars and rumors of wars, rebellions and reprisals—all *before* Alexander settled upon his sickbed in Babylon. It would ask a lot of the young king to expect him to rise up and somehow solve the hateful problems that had helped put him at death's door. Could he have done it? We'll never know.

CHAPTER SEVEN

The Legacy

LOST AND FOUND

In the historical rather than hypothetical year 287 B.C.E., Alexander the Great was thirty-six years gone and a new generation stood ready to rule the various fragments of his empire. In Bactria, Antiochus, the son of Seleucus and Apama, served his parents' interests by rebuilding and resettling the region as viceroy, from about 295 to 281.[1] The death of Seleucus then inaugurated a twenty-year reign, during which King Antiochus I never returned to his mother's Afghan homeland. Nor apparently did his successor, King Antiochus II (261–246), *his* son King Seleucus II (246–225), or *his* son King Seleucus III (225–223). These monarchs governed the so-called Seleucid realm from their base in Syria, relying heavily upon outlying satraps as the Achaemenids and Alexander had done. We know that the Seleucids kept a satrap on station in Bactria, because a Babylonian clay tablet refers to such an official (though, unfortunately, not by name) in about 275 B.C.E.[2] Otherwise, the same spotlight that followed Alexander also focused on his royal successors, leaving us once more in the dark about people, places, and events elsewhere. Bactria therefore slipped back into the shadows at the edge of the ancient Greek world, waiting more than half a century for the spotlight of history to swing that way again. When it did, a fresh band of rebels found themselves face to face with another great king.

Not until the reign of Antiochus (III) the Great (223–187 B.C.E.) did a Seleucid ruler return in force to the region. A lot had apparently changed in the East, because Antiochus III invaded Bactria in order to reclaim it from renegades. Between 212 and 205, a century after Seleucus's initial conquests there, Antiochus III fought a famous campaign chronicled by the historian Polybius.[3] The troublemakers were Greek settlers who had thrown off their allegiance to the Seleucid dynasty and created local kings of their own. Reprising the familiar roles of Bessus, Athenodorus, Biton, and Philon, a satrap named Diodotus and his son, Diodotus II, seized power in Bactria between 250 and 225, only to be overthrown in turn by another Greek settler, named Euthydemus. It was against this "King Euthydemus I" that Antiochus marched with his mighty army, intending to punish this latest warlord in the land of Afghanistan.

We know almost nothing about the rebel Euthydemus except that his family had originally come from Asia Minor (modern Turkey). What qualified him to usurp power in Bactria, besides the killing of Diodotus's family, we cannot say. No doubt the bottom line was his ability to command, coupled with a fierce, independent, fighting spirit among his followers. Like Bessus and others, Euthydemus had little chance of defeating the massive army coming after him, but he could count on his cavalry to do some damage while he waited out the worst of the invasion. Time always took the side of the Bactrian insurgents, even now that the battle pitted Greek against Greek.

Learning of Antiochus's approach, Euthydemus defended the western frontiers of Bactria by deploying a huge cavalry of ten thousand soldiers along the Arius River (modern Hari-rud, near Herat). Antiochus, however, caught these troops off guard and got his own army across the river before Euthydemus could effectively react. In his finest hour, Antiochus won the ensuing battle, fighting with the bravado of an Alexander; the Seleucid king lost his horse and a few teeth, but he relentlessly drove back the army of Euthydemus. Outmaneuvered and outmatched, the rebel king withdrew to Bactra as Bessus had done, hoping to rally his followers and keep his crown. For two long years (208–206 B.C.E.), the famed walls of old Bactra held back the Seleucid army in one of the greatest sieges of ancient history.[4] The city never fell.

In the end, both sides faced exhaustion and agreed to negotiate. Polybius provides a glimpse into the back-and-forth shuffle of envoys, concluding with the dispatch of Euthydemus's son, Demetrius, to meet Antiochus and finalize the bargain. Both camps saved face. Euthydemus claimed credit for killing the earlier rebels, the Diodotus clan, and therefore insisted on keeping the hard-won throne of Bactria for himself and his son. Antiochus acquiesced, anxious to quit Bactria and move on (like Alexander) to India. He had no interest in facing the nomadic Scythians massing on the Jaxartes frontier, and King Euthydemus made a gratifying show of humility by surrendering his elephant corps and provisions suitable for the needs of the Seleucid army. For the future, Antiochus pledged one of his daughters as a bride for Demetrius.

Whether such a marriage ever took place, we do not know. The historical spotlight followed Antiochus III to India, where he renewed the century-old treaty between the Seleucids and native Mauryas, and then back west to the Mediterranean for an epochal showdown with Rome.[5] All the while, Bactria slipped back into a deeper darkness. Scattered texts record the names of only three Greek rulers in that part of the world after the time of Euthydemus and Demetrius: Kings Menander, Apollodotus, and Eucratides the Great.[6] True to form, these men are described as warriors; Menander died in camp, and Eucratides allegedly waged so many campaigns that he "bled Bactria to death" before being murdered by his own (unnamed) son. The body of Eucratides then suffered such desecration that the miserable deed was still being lamented fifteen hundred years later in the works of the Renaissance writer Boccaccio.[7]

Except for this vague impression that the Greeks in Bactria viciously exterminated each other in the centuries after Alexander and Seleucus first settled them there, the world soon forgot the complex history of ancient Afghanistan. In 1735, however, someone stumbled upon a remarkable record of their long twilight struggle in central Asia. We owe that discovery to Theophilus Siegfried Bayer (1694–1738), a German polymath who excelled in classical studies.[8] His youthful hopes of traveling beyond Germany and the Baltic coast were dashed by bouts of depression and severe hypochondria. In 1716, he defended a doctoral dissertation about the last words spoken by Jesus on the cross. A decade later, Bayer helped found the Imperial Academy of St. Petersburg, Russia. He accepted the chair of Greek and Roman antiquities, but his interests migrated steadily toward sinology. He reportedly learned Arabic, Sanskrit, Tamil, Persian, and Hindi, in addition to Greek and Latin. Bayer, however, never mastered Russian during his dozen years in St. Petersburg; he wrote and conversed in Latin. Credited with authoring the world's first systematic analysis of a coin hoard in 1727, Bayer understood the value of numismatic (coin-based) research.[9]

In 1735, only a few years before his own premature death, Bayer received an unexpected visit from a dying man. Somehow, wrote Bayer, ailing Count Jacob Bruce (1670–1735) got himself to the Imperial Academy and arranged for the bequest of his antiquities collection to the museum.[10] That noble gesture capped a celebrated career of service to science. Bruce, born in Moscow to the family of a Scottish mercenary, traveled widely and studied astronomy with Edmund Halley of comet fame. Back in Russia, Bruce applied his talents to the sundry needs of Peter the Great, whether in establishing schools and observatories or overseeing mines and munitions; it was even Bruce who arranged the czar's grand funeral in 1725.[11]

One busy day, while Bruce was supervising military constructions at either Astrakan or Casan (Bayer could not clearly recall the place reported to him by his dying guest), workers unearthed an aged silver coin bearing in Greek the name "King Eucratides the Great" (ΒΑΣΙΛΕΩΣ ΜΕΓΑΛΟΥ ΕΥΚΡΑΤΙΔΟΥ). The large denomination, called a tetradrachm, showed on one side the bust of the king facing right, wearing a fine cavalry helmet with crest and attached bull's horns; the reverse depicted two horsemen with couched spears, the Dioskouroi (Heavenly Twins) of Greek mythology. This unique coin became part of Bruce's famous collection. Later, this same artifact arrived at the

Imperial Academy, along with Bruce's other treasures, the very day after he died. Theophilus Bayer studied the coin and connected the name on it to the Greek king of Bactria mentioned only briefly by a few ancient authors. He kept searching throughout the corpus of Greek and Latin literature for the names of any other Greek rulers of Bactria, hoping somehow to understand what had finally happened to the soldiers and settlers left there by Alexander the Great. In the end, Bayer found short references to seven kings in all: Diodotus I and his son Diodotus II; Euthydemus and his son Demetrius; a Menander whose (Buddhist?) subjects quarreled over his mortal remains; an Apollodotus who, like Menander, ruled some part of western India; and Eucratides the Great, surely the very king whose silver coin Bayer now held in his hand. The tetradrachm made real the phantom Eucratides, giving a face to the incredible, though abbreviated, story of Bactria gleaned by Bayer from various fragments of ancient texts.

Theophilus Bayer never lived to see whether numismatics might shine some light on the lives of other such kings; he died in the year his work on Bactria was published, at the age of forty-four.[12] Except for a few minor corrections to Bayer's treatise, the rest of the eighteenth century witnessed only slight progress in this new field of Bactrian numismatic studies.[13] In 1762, Joseph Pellerin published details about a second Eucratides coin, this one brought to Paris.[14] Because it showed a portrait of a younger man, Pellerin identified the king as perhaps a second Eucratides. This attribution, false as it would turn out, marked the first attempt to identify on a coin the unnamed son who murdered Eucratides the Great.[15] Sixteen years later, Pellerin published details about another addition to his collection.[16] This specimen, struck in gold, confirmed the existence of "King Euthydemus"

(ΒΑΣΙΛΕΩΣ ΕΥΘΥΔΗΜΟΥ). The coin bore the image of the king on one side, and the hero-god Hercules on the other.

Just before the eighteenth century ended, one more discovery thrilled those in the hunt for relics of Bactria's vanished Greek kings. In 1799, Théodore-Edme Mionnet (conservator of coins in the French royal collection, now the Bibliothèque nationale in Paris) identified the name of a king completely unknown from the written sources.[17] This "King Heliocles the Just" (ΒΑΣΙΛΕΩΣ ΗΛΙΟΚΛΕΟΥΣ ΔΙΚΑΙΟΥ) looked so much like Eucratides that scholars immediately assumed, as most still do, that Heliocles was a close relative—most likely a son or brother—of the ill-fated Eucratides the Great. The coin's reverse featured the god Zeus holding his scepter and thunderbolt.

Thus, as the century closed, experts had uncovered a total of four coins documenting the reigns of three elusive rulers: Euthydemus, Eucratides, and Heliocles. It was an exhilarating if painstaking start. Kings Diodotus I and II, Demetrius, Apollodotus, and Menander remained unaccounted for in the numismatic record. The next century, however, would reveal them all—and many more besides.

What pushed ahead so rapidly the progress of Bactrian studies was primarily the growing concern of nineteenth-century Russia and Britain for the strategic territories of central Asia. The Great Game was afoot. As more and more spies, diplomats, soldiers, and then armies penetrated modern Afghanistan, fresh information trickled and then flooded back to anxious European scholars. One of the earliest explorers was William Moorcroft, a London veterinarian hired by the East India Company to improve its stock of cavalry horses.[18] Moorcroft loved to roam and spy in fabled places such as Tibet, Bukhara, and Afghanistan. He disguised himself by staining his skin with walnut juice, circling his eyes with lamp black, and smearing his face with the ashes of burned cow dung. Between 1812 and 1825, Moorcroft wandered through central Asia collecting valuable information and ancient coins. Captured and released on several occasions, he died under mysterious circumstances and was buried in an unmarked grave outside the fabled walls of Balkh.

Beginning in 1833, the British East India Company financed the explorations of another enigmatic but educated wanderer then living in Kabul.[19] Barefoot and red-bearded, packing only a few books, a map, a compass, and an astrolabe, mild-mannered Charles Masson prowled Afghanistan and avidly collected antiquities of all types. In the area of Begram (the city founded by Alexander and today buried under the principal airbase of the country), Masson discovered and sent to London some sixty-eight thousand coins.[20] Masson took special notice of the fact that many of these coins represented a bilingual currency, with Greek names and titles on one side translated into the Kharoshthi script of ancient India on the other. These coins, each a little Rosetta stone, provided the key to deciphering the early writing systems of South Asia. When first hired to explore Afghanistan, Masson claimed to be an American adventurer who had traveled east from Kentucky. Others assumed that he was an Italian or Frenchman. He turned out to be an English deserter named James Lewis, absent without leave since July 1827 from the Bengal Artillery. In 1835, Masson/Lewis agreed to operate as a British spy (then called a "newswriter") in exchange for an official pardon. Angry over the policies leading inexorably toward the disastrous First Afghan War, he resigned in 1838 and later returned to England, pardoned but nonetheless unpopular and unheralded.

Fate dealt nearly all these pioneers a luckless hand. Alexander "Bukhara" Burnes at first considered himself "the most fortunate man on earth for his years" as he gathered intelligence, accolades, and promotions in service to the British East India Company.[21] He followed in the footsteps of Moorcroft, searching out his hero's grave in Balkh. Accounts of Burnes's many exploits among the Afghans made him a lionized celebrity. For a time, he enjoyed all the acclaim that his contemporary Masson/Lewis could never achieve. Lieutenant Burnes found himself summoned to audiences before the prime minister and king, feted in the most fashionable circles of London, entreated to give speeches and make public appearances, elected a member of learned societies, and awarded medals for his contributions to knowledge. His readers and listeners thrilled to reports of finding ancient coins and other artifacts left behind by Alexander the Great and his lost Greek colonists. But only a few years later, back in Afghanistan, Sir Alexander was hacked to death by a vicious mob. Pieces of his body hung in the trees of his garden for months.[22] This was the brutal assassination that set off the sad train of events ending in the British retreat from Kabul in the First Afghan War.

The daredevil lives of men like Burnes, Masson/Lewis, and Moorcroft made possible an expensive renaissance in Bactrian history, one focusing especially on the period after Alexander's death. This all occurred at a most propitious moment. In 1836, a German scholar named Johann Gustav Droysen (1808–1884) published a book that first made fashionable among leading scholars the study of Alexander's eastern legacy.[23] This ground-breaking achievement challenged an outdated dogma of classical studies. Before Droysen, historians had taken little interest in the three hundred years that followed the reign of Alexander; these centuries, from 323 to 30 B.C.E., fell into a gap between the "glory that was Greece, / And the grandeur that was Rome."[24] The glories of Greece meant to earlier scholars essentially the achievements of classical Athens: its famous playwrights and philosophers, the histories of Herodotus and Thucydides, the incredible Parthenon, and the democracy of Pericles. There allegedly followed a long decline after Alexander's stormy career during which the Greeks produced few notable poets, philosophers, historians, architects, or enlightened political leaders. It was claimed that Alexander and his conquests had exposed the Greeks to unrefined, barbarian influences, allowing debased eastern cultures to contaminate the triumphant West. What eventually saved civilization was the grandeur of Rome, which produced great talents again and protected Europe from Asiatic pollution. Such thinking dismissed everything from Alexander to Cleopatra as beneath the dignity of serious scholarship.

Droysen, however, stood firm in the breach. He argued that Alexander and his wars had actually set in motion something quite wonderful and of signal importance to the world. In this new vision of history, nothing less than the hand of God had guided the invincible Alexander in order to create a distinctive age, without which Christianity, as a universal religion, could never have succeeded. The name that Droysen attached to that new era ("Hellenistic") comes in fact from the Greek New Testament itself. In Acts 6:1 and 9:29, the author traditionally known as Luke used an improvised word to identify those natives who imitated the conquering Greeks and their culture: such people were not actually Greeks (Ελληνες = Hellenes), but rather Greekists (Ελληνισται = Hellenistai) who chose to assimilate.[25] This very act of adopting the Greek language, and then adapting it to suit a new context in the Middle East, is quintessentially Hellenistic; the word defines itself.

The eastward diffusion of Greek culture (Ελληνισμος = Hellenism) was therefore to Droysen part of a divine plan, and those non-Greeks who embraced Hellenism (the Hellenistai) gave the gospel its extraordinary reach far beyond its Jewish roots. From the military talents of Alexander sprang the missionary triumphs of Paul, and the Hellenistic centuries connecting them were a fertile time of religious and cultural preparation no longer to be ignored: Blessed be the fall of Darius and Persia, that the Greek might inherit the earth. Droysen's views gave Alexander a good heart and imperialism a good name, a combination that appealed to many readers in the nineteenth century. After all, the military and colonial processes that had aided the triumph of Christianity in a pagan world might serve God's purpose again, perhaps in modern-day Africa, India, or Afghanistan. Droysen had made the Hellenistic world worthy of study at just the right moment, and in just the right way. As British troops marched to places like Kandahar and Kabul, they followed consciously in the footsteps of Alexander, and many felt that they were fulfilling the same kind of benevolent destiny as described by Droysen and his partisans. The invaders read ancient accounts of the Macedonian campaigns and looked for the cities and forts mentioned in them. They scoured the ground for Hellenistic relics left by the king's colonists and, in the process, found Greek coins in staggering numbers. On the Russian side, too, the search intensified. At Tashkent, Akram Askarov amassed a private collection of over fifteen thousand coins, of which about five hundred were acquired by the Hermitage Museum.[26] A brisk trade in ancient coins livened the shops of Samarkand, and a Russian general used his troops at Merv to gather fifteen hundred coins in just two hours.[27] Much of this money was clearly the currency of later periods, but some of it derived from the reigns of ancient Greek kings, the forgotten descendants of unknown men who had remained at their Bactrian posts.

AND SOMETIMES LOST AGAIN

By the time of the Second Afghan War, busy scholars felt overwhelmed with numismatic evidence. The reigns of dozens of lost kings had come to light, and more kept surfacing as experts sorted out the new finds from Afghanistan. These royal ghosts were but names and faces, but nothing could be more alluring: there was an Agathocles who struck a series of special coins commemorating his forebears in Bactria; an Antimachus shown with an impish Mona Lisa smile; a few queens with names like Calliope and Agathocleia; an Amyntas wearing a Macedonian cap and bearing the same name as Alexander's grandfather.[28] There were so many reigns that it seemed impossible to fit them all into Hellenistic Bactria without inferring a baffling array of "kings and sub-kings" who fought and killed each other constantly.[29] Based on the coinages, no other region appeared as unstable and self-destructive as Bactria. Hellenistic Macedonia was for generations a model of dynastic solidarity. The Seleucids in Syria and Ptolemies in Egypt suffered through some stretches of political disorder but, nonetheless, endured well into the first century B.C.E. before falling to the Romans. Bactria, on the other hand, tore itself apart with a proliferation of warlords among the Greeks who kept their crumbling fiefdoms in chaos.[30] This extreme level of volatility seems, literally, to go with the territory.

Nothing so illustrates the world that was, as opposed to Toynbee's world that might have been, as the profusion of ancient coinages found in Afghanistan. Instead of unity and harmony, there was rending conflict. To the usurpations and assassinations recorded in literary fragments about Diodotus I, Diodotus II, Euthydemus, Demetrius, and Eucratides must be added more generations of strife as revealed on the money. The fighting associated with Alexander's invasion persisted among his settlers and among those of the Seleucids, too. Like Spitamenes, not all these warriors claimed a royal title: coins reveal that a man named Sophytes exercised some independent authority in central Asia before the consolidation of Seleucid power, but he was not a king.[31] The pattern for these Hellenistic leaders was to add over time a growing number of grander titles, from none by a Sophytes to simply King (Basileus) by a Diodotus, Euthydemus, or Demetrius; and then King plus an honorific cult-name such as Megas (the Great), Dikaios (the Just), Soter (the Savior), Aniketos (the Invincible), and even Theos (the God). Thus, we eventually find emblazoned on the Bactrian coins of petty warlords such brash identifiers as "King Strato the God Manifest and Savior" or "King Archebius the Just and Victory-Bearing." Of course, these Greek texts were often repeated on the other side of the coin using a native script such as Kharoshthi: Maharajasa Tratarasa Mahatasa Jayamtasa Hipustratasa (King Hippostratos the Great, Conqueror and Savior).

As portable discs of information technology, ancient coins convey all kinds of data useful to modern historians. Besides names, portraits, and titles, we discover on them a host of tutelary gods and goddesses. Most of those deities are Greek (Athena, Zeus, Poseidon, Apollo, Artemis, etc.), but some are Indian (Vasudeva-Krishna, Samkarshana, etc.). We find animals (elephant, horse, lion, camel, zebu) and other objects (tripod, caduceus, anchor, tree, chakra wheel). Such details can tell a story about the people who made and used this money. Even little things, like the mistakes made when engraving the words on the coin dies, expose the declining levels of Greek literacy among the workers in the mints.[32] Careful study allows us to fill in the huge blanks left in Bactrian history by the loss of literary sources: seven Hellenistic rulers have become forty-five (and still counting) thanks to the numismatic research begun by Bayer in 1735.[33]

Ancient coins found in isolation here or there in Afghanistan speak eloquently of the past, but coins recovered in association with others make the best witnesses. When some poor soul of the Hellenistic era faced danger or uncertainty, he or she most often gathered the household's money and valuables to be buried for safekeeping. Once the threat passed, the trove would naturally be recovered. But if the owner never returned for the hoard, it might remain hidden for centuries until accidentally stumbled upon by a farmer or well digger. This pattern of behavior has at least two important consequences. First, the contents of such a hoard usually reflect the currency circulating at the moment of burial, which can inform us of ancient trade systems and help establish chronologies for coinages otherwise undatable. Second, the discovery of numerous hoards from a given time and place provides a sort of misery index, suggesting that some particularly disastrous circumstance made it impossible for many owners to retrieve their valuables: the more hoards there are to be found today, the more tragic were the times in which they were deposited and left unclaimed.[34] As it turns out, Afghanistan has yielded some of the largest and most extraordinary ancient hoards ever unearthed. These troves confirm that Hellenistic Bactria was plagued by insurrections and invasions, but they also offer a particularly rich documentation of interrelated coins. Out of its misery, Bactria ransomed its own history.

In 1877, for example, a huge hoard washed from the banks of the Amu Darya. This so-called Oxus Treasure contained over a thousand ancient coins, plus gold and silver jewelry, bowls, plaques, and other precious objects. During Britain's Second Afghan War, daring Muslim merchants smuggled parts of this hoard across Afghanistan. Although waylaid by thieves, the merchants and part of their treasure were rescued. The harried merchants then managed to reach Rawalpindi, where they sold the surviving portion of the hoard to eager collectors who later donated much of the great prize to the British Museum.[35] Russian archaeologists now claim that the Oxus Treasure represents some of the rich offerings made to a Zoroastrian temple at Takht-i Sangin (the Throne of Stone). In the face of a nomadic invasion of Bactria circa 150 B.C.E., the priests allegedly grabbed these valuables and hid them nearby. The attack proved devastating, the Greeks who had built and maintained the temple abandoned the area, and so the hoard remained hidden for over two thousand years, until erosion exposed its contents.[36]

On August 23, 1946, frontier guards digging the foundation for a cattle shed beside their barracks at Khisht-Tepe (the Mound of Bricks) struck a buried vase from which two ancient coins emerged. Closer inspection revealed another 626 Greek silver coins, some of them the largest ever minted in the ancient world. Fortunately, this discovery remained intact, quite unlike the Oxus Treasure. Officials carefully shipped the coins to the state museum in Kabul. Buried circa 100 B.C.E., this so-called Qunduz Hoard may have been some person's life savings or a fund from which state payments were drawn, perhaps for an ancient garrison on precisely the same spot as the modern one. The site lies on the left bank of the Amu Darya, about eleven miles west of its confluence with the Qunduz River. A caravan route once passed this way, crossing the Oxus (here about seven hundred yards wide) into Sogdiana.[37]

A year after the recovery of the Qunduz Hoard, a huge ancient treasure turned up at Mir Zakah. Located thirty-three miles northeast of Gardez in the tempestuous Paktiya Province, the village of Mir Zakah straddles another old caravan route. This mountainous region joins the borderlands between modern Afghanistan and Pakistan, where al-Qaeda based its operations far from prying eyes and easy intervention. No state has ever found the people there amenable to supervision, and tribal feuds erupt frequently and quite fiercely. When a local Afghan fished an ancient coin from an open well at Mir Zakah, others flocked to the place and began searching for more treasure. Coins kept coming up, so villagers kept going down. A government official from the Kabul Museum eventually arrived to secure the find, and tried for two weeks to explore the site. Angry, armed locals made it clear that they resented this intrusion into their affairs. Describing his work as more a negotiation than an excavation, the official persevered until the quarrels escalated to an intolerable level. He managed to leave Mir Zakah alive, with about eleven thousand coins plus other artifacts. These finds made it safely to the Kabul Museum, but no one could guess how much had been lost. A rapid influx of ancient coins to the bazaars of Kabul, Gardez, and Ghazni indicated that thousands of pieces had escaped into the marketplace.[38]

When the population around Mir Zakah had simmered down sufficiently, the Afghan government sent another team—under military guard—to explore the site. In 1948, more than four hundred additional coins came to light, plus ancient jewelry and other objects. The wet environment encompassing the hoard added to the despair of experts who had to contend not only with the looting of the site, but also with the loss of coins that simply dissolved or crumbled when handled. Many objects came through the process unscathed, but a regrettable number did not.[39]

A farmer tilling his fields near Balkh in August 1966 discovered a pot full of encrusted coins. He sold part of the hoard to a curio dealer in Kabul. These turned out to be mostly Athenian tetradrachms from the classical period, which naturally sold well. The dealer therefore bought more specimens from the farmer, presumably from the same pot. The total could never be ascertained since the farmer apparently supplied coins to different dealers, but at least 150 specimens were seen. This Greek money must have circulated in Bactria as bullion before the time of Alexander's invasion. A similar hoard had been found on the east side of Kabul in 1933. Its contents may have included a thousand coins of the Greek city-states. The Kabul Museum obtained over 100 pieces, but the remainder disappeared.[40]

More fortunate were the ancient finds from Ai Khanoum made in the 1960s and 1970s. In addition to 274 individual coins recovered at the site (plus 10 unminted flans), two important hoards were scientifically excavated. In 1970, a cache of 677 coins (some of them unique) emerged from the administrative district of the ancient city. Most of these coins apparently came to Ai Khanoum from the Indian Punjab, perhaps as booty from a successful Greek raid into India. Curiously, the hoard had been plundered from the treasury of Ai Khanoum after the Greeks abandoned the city circa 150 B.C.E., apparently by local squatters in the context of the same nomadic invasions that compelled the burial of the nearby Oxus Treasure. Another Ai Khanoum hoard surfaced in 1973, this one containing 63 silver coins hidden in the kitchen of a house located just outside the ramparts of Ai Khanoum. This hoard, too, was stashed in about 150 B.C.E. during the reign of Eucratides the Great. The coins themselves, along with all the other artifacts from Ai Khanoum, entered the Kabul Museum for study and safekeeping. Less fortunately, a hoard from Ai Khanoum appeared on the world market in 1974. A local farmer stumbled upon it and quickly hustled its contents to the lucrative bazaar of Kabul, where merchants bought portions and shipped them to connoisseurs in Europe and the United States. The treasure originally included at least 142 Greek coins before it dispersed.[41] A deposit ten times larger was found somewhere around Ai Khanoum in 1993. It followed the other along the money trail through Pakistan to London and New York.[42]

At another Afghan site also excavated in the 1970s, a series of ancient tombs yielded about 20,600 gold artifacts (jewelry, bowls, weapons, etc.) plus some coins.[43] Appropriately named Tillya-Tepe (the Golden Mound), the necropolis included an eclectic mix of Persian, Greek, Indian, Chinese, and even Roman treasures. Its contents were carefully transported over the Hindu Kush Mountains to the Kabul Museum in February 1979, just months ahead of the Soviet invasion.

In the countries bordering Afghanistan, many additional Bactrian hoards have been found. Thousands of ancient coins have been recovered from irrigation canals, farmlands, brickworks, and other locales. Wherever people disturb the soil of central Asia, Greek coins are liable to appear. In recent years, many important new coins have been identified in these hoards, including those of previously unknown kings.[44]

It is, of course, a travesty that so many hoards vanish before experts can study them adequately. Losing such information is like burning the pages from the last known copy of a priceless manuscript. Imagine, then, the frustration of receiving a telephone call in the middle of the night from a coin dealer in England announcing a major new hoard from Afghanistan being sold by nine or more Pakistani merchants. One seller alone had already pocketed hundreds of millions of dollars from just the gold jewelry and silver plate. The remaining coins were being offered at a million dollars *per ton!* Indeed, an incredible six thousand pounds of ancient coinage was still available from the hoard, surely the largest ancient treasure ever found. The historical value of the find had been compromised the moment it scattered, unrecorded, to surreptitious buyers. Though still important, the greatest hoard in history had already lost much of its value as evidence.

As it happened, the treasure came from a familiar site—Mir Zakah. In 1992, a villager allegedly dredged up a gold coin in her water jug, setting off a frenzied and deadly search of the well's inexhaustible waters. The story of the woman at the well suspiciously repeats details of the discovery of the first Mir Zakah hoard. This time, with no viable government in Kabul to intervene, the fighting ran its bloody course. Eventually, the locals created a twelve-member committee to oversee the looting, negotiate with Pakistan dealers, and share out the profits. They even arranged for the purchase of a generator and water pump. Somehow, tribal investors claim, the profits of this enterprise never reached Mir Zakah, and the whole operation collapsed for want of funds. Even so, an estimated 550,000 coins made the journey from Mir Zakah to Japan, Europe, and America.[45] This single hoard from a tiny village in Afghanistan is almost six times larger than the total of all ancient hoards recorded throughout the territories of Greece and Macedonia.[46] Mir Zakah might have been the most important archaeological and numismatic discovery of modern times; instead, it is the black hole of Bactrian studies.

We should at least be grateful that much of the first hoard from Mir Zakah had reached the state museum in Kabul, where the large Qunduz Hoard, part of the Kabul Hoard, and most of the treasures from Ai Khanoum also found shelter. But that is another story, equally horrible. At the time of the Soviet invasion, this museum held the best of Afghanistan's extraordinary cultural patrimony, a rich historical and artistic record stretching all the way back to the beginnings of the brilliant Bronze Age of central Asia. Naturally, concerned Afghans protected their national treasures as best they could. Anticipating chaos, curators and volunteers crated the collection with hopes of a better day to come. Those hopes were eventually dashed. After 1989, the civil war among rival Afghan warlords drove away most of the museum's staff. Those who remained kept secret the fact that some artifacts had been transferred to a bank vault in the city. Such hidden treasures, including all the Tillya-Tepe gold, survived; elsewhere, the museum itself and its remaining contents offered criminals an easy target.[47]

On May 12, 1993, rockets crashed into the museum during a battle between rival factions of the mujahideen. Looters then systematically plundered the building, including thousands of ancient coins. The Ai Khanoum Hoards, the Qunduz Hoard, the first Mir Zakah Treasure, and others cascaded onto the illicit antiquities market. Some larger antiquities were spared, but in 1995, more rockets hit the museum as the Taliban moved against Kabul. Soldiers occupied the premises and set up a military post. In the end, much that had ever been scientifically excavated in Afghanistan vanished in these criminal acts of cultural genocide: sculptures, inscriptions, ceramics, jewelry, glassware, frescoes, and of course the world's most important collection of Bactrian coins.[48]

Little could be done to stop the pillaging of museums and plundering of archaeological sites in Afghanistan. Paul Bucherer-Dietschi of the Foundation Bibliotheca Afghanica established a museum-in-exile at Bubendorf, Switzerland. This rescue operation housed items donated by well-meaning patrons hoping that at least a core of artifacts could be safely returned to Kabul someday. A few items actually are pieces from the looted national museum, but many are substitutes garnered from collections around the world. According to Bucherer, the Taliban might have cooperated in the preservation of many Afghan artifacts had al-Qaeda not exerted its hard-line, destructive influence. Eventually, the Taliban condemned in the name of religion Afghanistan's pre-Muslim past. Not content to sell off Bactrian and Buddhist artworks, the Taliban pounded offending museum objects into powder. Claims Bucherer, "The Taliban came in the morning, hammered until prayer time, paused, hammered again, paused for tea, then hammered for the rest of the day."[49]

Another group active through this crisis has been the Society for the Preservation of Afghanistan's Cultural Heritage (SPACH). One hero of this organization, Nancy Hatch Dupree, is the widow of the renowned expert Louis Dupree, who dominated Afghan studies until his death in March 1989. A scholar in her own right, Nancy Dupree has documented the years of hardship inflicted on the Kabul Museum and its collections. SPACH has maintained a newsletter and other publications to keep the world informed. The group has purchased some of the stolen artifacts to be held in trust, but most items command prices far beyond SPACH's budget. Too many greedy private collectors with deep pockets have proved willing to buy the stolen artworks. Antiquities traders from London, New York, Tokyo, and Hong Kong flocked to hotels in Peshawar to arrange major sales. Millions of dollars worth of merchandise moved through the darkened backrooms of bazaars. Not only did this activity devastate a nation's cultural heritage, but it also funded arms deals for the Taliban and al-Qaeda.[50] Many people participated in this tragedy without even realizing it. Those buying Bactrian coins through Internet auctions have often been shocked when informed that the goods being sold were actually stolen from the Kabul Museum.[51] Imagine the shameless public auction of items looted from, say, the Museum of American History. That is precisely what happened to the coins on which our histories of Hellenistic Bactria must be based. To all the hazards that our invaluable data have endured, we now must add e-plunder to the list.

And what if collectors from, say, Japan drove into Colonial Williamsburg with heavy equipment, scraped up everything of value, loaded it onto trucks, and shipped it to Tokyo? Not only have the museums of Afghanistan been stripped and their contents sold abroad, but also raiding parties have systematically gone to the source and plundered the archaeological sites themselves. At Balkh, the regional headquarters of Alexander the Great, modern warlords have used pickaxes, bulldozers, and explosives to crater the ground in search of saleable antiquities.[52] Elsewhere, reports from Herat, Tillya-Tepe, Hadda, and Qaisar speak of looted sites that have yielded ancient figurines, coins, and a unique golden crown. The impressive remains at the religious complex of Surkh Kotal may have been destroyed. Just outside Kabul, the Buddhist pillar at Minar-i Chakri (once mistakenly attributed to Alexander) fell during a mortar attack in 1998.[53] Then, on February 26, 2001, the Taliban leader Mullah Omar called for the annihilation of all pre-Islamic statues and figural art in Afghanistan.[54] Within days, one of history's most reprehensible cultural crimes had been committed. The gigantic Buddhas of Bamian, carved into the sheer cliffs of the Hindu Kush, had watched over this beautiful valley for fifteen centuries. Standing amid rock-cut monastic caves, these soaring figures awed the seventh century Chinese pilgrim Hieun-Tsang. They survived the scramblings and scribblings of countless travelers, including Moorcroft and Masson/Lewis. The latter left as his mark, high above the head of the tallest Buddha, an arrogant little rhyme to taunt later explorers:

> If any fool this high *samootch* explore,
> Know Charles Masson has been here before.

It took a century for archaeologists to discover this calling card, but no one will ever overlook the mark left by the Taliban—gaping, empty niches where dynamite and artillery blasted to bits the peaceful Buddhas.[55]

There is still no end in sight. Every new step, good or bad, has consequences for Afghanistan's ancient heritage. Take, for example, the wholly commendable effort by the world community to help rid the region of land mines. Somewhere between five and seven million mines remain to be cleared from Afghanistan. These devices, a terrifying legacy of the last twenty-five years of fighting, still kill about fifteen Afghans every day. Throughout the country, danger lurks along roadways, irrigation canals, pastures, farmlands, and mountain footpaths. Scampering children are especially vulnerable, as are refugees returning to abandoned homesteads still surrounded by old mines. One key to Afghanistan's future is the eradication of these explosives, an expensive and perilous task to which numerous humanitarian organizations are dedicated.

To restate the obvious, the world owes these groups much gratitude for running grave risks. It is all the more heinous, therefore, that some professional looters have taken the metal detectors intended for mine clearance and used them to scavenge known archaeological sites.[56] As mine-clearing agencies necessarily import more sophisticated technologies such as ground-penetrating radar, these too will be turned by some criminals into a high-tech means to dig the grave of Bactrian history.

CHAPTER EIGHT

Conclusion

Lend an ear to Plato where he says,
That men like soldiers may not quit the post
Allotted by the Gods.

Tennyson

PLATO WHO?

When Lord Tennyson's lines from "Lucretius" first appeared in
Macmillan's Magazine (May 1868), the public never asked which
Plato the poet meant.[1] Readers thought only of *the* Plato, one of
the greatest figures in the history of philosophy. A disciple of
Socrates and mentor of Aristotle, this Plato (ca. 429–347 B.C.E.)
founded the Academy in Athens and wrote such classic texts as
The Republic and *The Laws*. His works gave the world the elaborate legend of lost Atlantis, and his name became the very by-
word for spiritual love. Plato's thoughts weighed on the minds of
other greats, including Copernicus, Luther, Macchiavelli, More,
Galileo, Kepler, and Leibniz. No one was ever likely to confuse

this heavyweight with the handful of other ancients who bore the same name, an obscure rhetorician here or a minor playwright there whose very existence would not be known outside a gathering of degreed classicists.[2] What reader of Tennyson would think for a moment of Plato the physician (cited once by Galen), Plato the Theban cavalry commander (mentioned once by Plutarch), or even Gemistos Plethon (ca. 1355–1452 C.E.), called by Marsilio Ficino "a second Plato" at the time of the Council of Ferrara?[3] No, there was for all practical purposes but one Plato in the vocabulary of the poets and the pantheon of the philosophers.

And yet, there once lived a royal Plato, a king so grandiose that he called himself "the God Manifest," and who kept at their posts some of the last Greek soldiers to serve in Afghanistan. When Tennyson composed his poem, not a person alive had yet heard of this highborn Bactrian Plato. No extant texts recorded his reign; no known statues preserved his image; no surviving monuments bore witness to a single moment in his forgotten life. As with so many other rulers, only a chance discovery (made somewhere in the Afghan district of Hazara) brought this Plato back into the light of history. In 1871, on the eve of the Second Afghan War, an itinerant goldsmith from Shakhan-Dheri came upon a curious silver coin.[4] A well-known antiquities dealer, Chandra Mall, obtained the prize and showed it to a British resident of Rawalpindi, who in turn posted a notice of the discovery to the Asiatic Society of Bengal. Everyone marveled that an ancient Greek coin from Afghanistan bore the astonishing name and title of "King Plato, the God Manifest."

The curious coin eventually passed into the collection of the British Museum, where it received special attention from leading experts.[5] The first of them published an interesting theory. In 1875, W. S. W. Vaux noted that at least one other arcane Plato had served in Alexander's army.[6] This soldier, an Athenian, brought some reinforcements to the king in 330 B.C.E. Vaux therefore surmised "that the royal personage on the coin under consideration may have been a descendant of this officer." As Vaux explained, the Athenian soldier named Plato had probably been settled in Bactria where, generations later, one of his distant scions became a local king and minted the silver coin. It was a charming (and as even Vaux admitted, rather fanciful) theory true to the times in which it was conceived. In the nineteenth century, persistent rumors that descendants of Alexander's original settlers still inhabited the hills of Afghanistan made it seem likely that King Plato was but an early link in that long chain. Before his brutal murder, Alexander "Bukhara" Burnes had reported to his startled countrymen:

> I heard from these people [Tadjiks from Badakhshan] a variety
> of particulars regarding the reputed descendants of Alexander
> the Great, which are yet said to exist in this neighborhood, and
> the valley of the Oxus, as well as the countries near the head of
> the Indus. The subject had occupied much of my attention, and
> a tea merchant of our small caravan had amused me on the
> road from Khooloom, with the received lineage of these Mace-
> donians. He was a priest, and believed Alexander the Great to
> be a prophet, which, in his eyes satisfactorily accounted for the
> uninterrupted progeny of Greeks, since no human being could
> injure so holy a race.[7]

In the area of Samarkand, a later traveler recorded, "The exploits of Alexander . . . in this region have been preserved by legend, and are known to every inhabitant. Many of the petty princes in the mountain countries of the Upper Oxus claim to be descended from him."[8] Such legends, of course, inspired Rudyard Kipling's magical tale "The Man Who Would Be King," in which a roguish English adventurer convinces the Kafirs (infidels) of Afghanistan that he is a son of Alexander the Great and, thus, a god to be obeyed.[9]

The search for the lost world of Hellenistic Afghanistan escalated at times into a romantic fantasy pursued in the context of Johann Gustav Droysen's ideas and buttressed by the ideals of British imperialism. It culminated in that famous claim by Sir William Woodthorpe Tarn, made on the bicentennial of Theophilus Siegfried Bayer's work, that Alexander's invasion not only punished the local warlords but also produced a Hellenistic kingdom in Bactria that became a genuine paradise in which Greeks and non-Greeks, Hellenes and Hellenistai, lived together as equals and embraced one another in Law and Love.[10] Tarn connected the elusive kings discovered on Bactrian coins to the high-minded ideals he attributed to Alexander, making Afghanistan the one place where his hero's ideas took hold. This was a tantalizing thesis, but one that has since been thoroughly challenged.

The strongest response came from A. K. Narain, a fine Indian scholar whose book *The Indo-Greeks* first appeared in 1957, the year of Tarn's death. Narain's counterblast emphasized the other side of the coins—namely, the obvious Indian influences in language, religion, and philosophy that transformed the Graeco-Bactrians into Indo-Greeks. Narain downplayed the effect of a benevolent Hellenism in the East, soberly assessing the legacy of Alexander and his settlers from a different perspective: "Their history is part of the history of India and not of the Hellenistic states: they came, they saw, but India conquered."[11]

Perhaps reflecting a larger debate on the repercussions of British imperialism and colonialism, the modern world has indeed taken a second look at Alexander, Bactria, and the Hellenistic age. Few scholars would now entertain seriously Droysen's view that God sent Alexander to prepare the way for Jesus; Tarn's optimistic theory that in Afghanistan the invading Greeks came to accept the conquered natives as full and equal partners has few supporters left.

Experts now describe the Hellenistic age as a glass half empty, containing the dregs of a disappointing brew whose taste we know all too well. It was the one ancient era in which modern societies can recognize themselves.[12] Colonial powers exploited large native populations. Big Government sponsored Big Science, especially for technological spin-offs that might help the military. A costly arms race strained state budgets. Utopianism appealed to many who felt alienated and powerless; established religions lost out to fads, magic, mysticism, and agnosticism. Religious strife shook Palestine and surrounding regions. Acts of terrorism killed thousands, including one incident in Asia Minor (modern Turkey) that claimed upward of eighty thousand victims. In spite of improved general education, people turned in droves to astrology, bourgeois kitsch, and the escapism provided by situation comedies crammed with stock characters, silly plots, and lots of sex. The world shrank into a global village, or rather a global city-state (cosmopolis), as the Greeks liked to put it in their own language.

Greek culture self-consciously (and self-righteously, some

would complain) intruded everywhere. The disappearance of Persia's ruling elite transformed the balance of power and marginalized many peoples. The conquerors' language thrust itself even upon cities as ancient as Babylon, which had already flourished a thousand years before the first Greek ever uttered the first Greek word somewhere out in the Balkans. The New Testament would be written not in Hebrew or Aramaic, but rather in Greek because a king, his army, and its colonial administration had passed that way and decreed a new world order.

In what sort of world, then, did "King Plato the God Manifest" actually reign? Was he a harmless dreamer, as Tarn proposed, a man who adopted the name of a famous philosopher and tried to create a little utopian state out of a few towns in Bactria?[13] Or was he a vicious assassin, one of many warlords in Bactria, who betrayed and killed his father, Eucratides, and then desecrated the body, as argued by Narain?[14] Coins alone cannot tell us—we need other evidence about the Bactrians, such as the archaeological remains of the cities in which they lived, worked, worshiped, and died. But finding and excavating just one of the "thousand cities of Bactria" proved to be the greatest challenge yet.[15]

LADY MOON

Archaeology now confirms that the lost world of Hellenistic Bactria was no utopia. The sharp edge of Alexander's wars never dulled in the centuries after his death. Bitterness prevailed, and the resentful Greeks never opened their arms to the indigenous peoples in the way that some have imagined. We see this best at Ai Khanoum, a Greek colony on the site, mentioned in chapter 1, where the Northern Alliance anchored its defenses against the Taliban. Ai Khanoum is known thanks to archaeological excavations conducted there by the Délégation Archéologique Française en Afghanistan (DAFA).[16] For many years, members of the DAFA had searched for the remains of ancient Greek settlements in Afghanistan, but with disappointing results. Even at Balkh, where Alexander and his successors certainly based their main operations, archaeologists could find no strong evidence of the missing Greeks. When Tarn died in 1957, the DAFA still had not discovered the ruins of any of Alexander's Afghan colonies. Then quite unexpectedly, in 1961, Afghanistan's King Muhammad Zahir Shah stumbled upon an extraordinary Greek site on the northern borders of his nation.[17] Near the village of Ai Khanoum (meaning "Lady Moon" in Uzbek), the king and his hunting party paused to examine some unusual stone objects, including the ornate capital of a building column carved in the Corinthian style of ancient Greece. In November of that year, the king brought these discoveries to the attention of the DAFA and commissioned an archaeological inspection of the site. Explorations had to be undertaken with caution, since Ai Khanoum lay in a sensitive border region watched closely by Soviet troops. The arrival there of foreigners and their equipment could easily alarm trigger-happy patrols. The intrepid archaeologists found an entire city shrouded by dust, with the outlines of ancient streets and buildings clearly visible. Until the Soviet invasion of Afghanistan shut down the excavations in 1979, the renowned French archaeologist Paul Bernard led a team of experts that patiently unearthed key sections of the city. It ranks among the greatest discoveries in modern archaeology.[18]

The large site occupies the strategic confluence of the Oxus and Kokcha Rivers, with a level terrace along the left bank of the Oxus backed by a natural acropolis rising up to the south (see Map 4). On the high ground, a citadel looks out over the countryside. Here, the Northern Alliance aimed its guns against the Taliban. In fact, the soldiers of Commander Ahmad Shah Massoud exposed an important ancient structure—perhaps a Greek temple—while entrenching their battery on these heights.[19] The heart of the ancient city stretched over the terrace below, protected on its exposed northeast corner by a particularly strong wall and defensive ditch. There the ramparts stood nearly thirty-three feet high, with a thickness of twenty to twenty-six feet; rectangular towers jutted out another thirty-three feet. Every precaution had been taken to safeguard the citizenry from attack, underscoring the ongoing military role of the site.

A main gateway through the ramparts opened onto a grand avenue running the length of the lower city. To the left of this thoroughfare lay a fine Greek theater—the largest in the East, exceeding even the capacity of the theater in Babylon. Approximately five thousand patrons could attend performances at the theater at Ai Khanoum, with its thirty-five tiers of seats rising up toward the acropolis. The Greek devotion to drama could be seen elsewhere in the city, where a fountain spout took the familiar form of a theater mask. In the terribly decomposed remnants of a royal library, archaeologists uncovered literary scraps perhaps belonging to a play by Sophocles. Further down the main street of Ai Khanoum, a large armory and arsenal stood on the left. Its shelves held all the requisite military gear of the time: spears, shields, uniforms, harnesses, and even a spiked *khasak* used to wound the feet of elephants. This impressive site clearly provided a garrison that guarded the Oxus frontier.

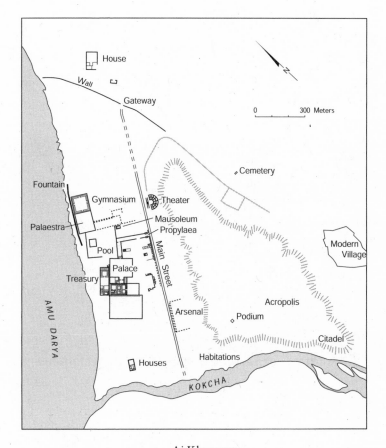

4. Ai Khanoum

Most of the other buildings of the city covered the area to the right of the main thoroughfare. Access to them seems to have been controlled by a monumental gatehouse (propylaea). Archaeologists suggest that this gateway served as a checkpoint to protect the downtown civic center from outsiders. This posh section of town held the finest private homes and a number of quintessentially Greek structures, where, the archaeologists have surmised, most non-Greeks were not welcome. This evidence of elitist, colonialist snobbery smacks of our modern gated communities and systems of apartheid.

Those granted entry into this exclusive part of town could stroll up to an amazing monument, where Kineas, one of the Greek founders of the city, lay buried in a fine mausoleum. Whether this man had been one of Alexander's settlers, or Seleucus's, cannot be determined. What most intrigues us is the Greek inscription carved in stone at the front of the tomb.[20] The surviving portion reads:

> These wise sayings of earlier men, the words of well-known
> men, are enshrined in the holy Pytho. There Klearchos copied
> them faithfully, and set them up here in the sanctuary of
> Kineas, blazing from afar—

> > As a child, be well-behaved.
> > As a youth, be self-controlled.
> > As an adult, be just.
> > As an elder, be wise.
> > As one dying, be without pain.

To help safeguard the Greekness of the settlers at Ai Khanoum, Klearchos (perhaps the same well-known philosopher of that name) undertook the mission commemorated in this text. He traveled to Delphi in central Greece, where a shrine (the holy Pytho) was dedicated to the god Apollo. The Greeks believed that Apollo gave oracular responses to important questions, and that the god also issued various other pronouncements in the form of maxims or proverbs. These included "Know thyself," the first step toward true knowledge. For this reason, the

Greek priests at Delphi maintained a record of all the wise and useful utterances of Apollo and others; the total eventually reached 150 or so "Delphic Maxims," which served as a primer of Hellenism. Alexander's veterans had feared it impossible to remain Greek in the remoteness of Bactria, but later inhabitants could find solace in the Delphic Maxims "blazing from afar."[21]

Just past the mausoleum, on the western edge of the city, a privileged citizen might enter the sprawling gymnasium complex with associated pool and wrestling ground (palaestra). No Greek male could easily manage without these facilities, because they furnished a hallowed precinct for the physical and mental training of a citizen. Young men prepared their bodies for battle and listened to lectures on history, art, and philosophy. Archaeologists found at Ai Khanoum evidence of imported olive oil and the implements called strigils used to scrape off oil, sweat, and dirt after exercise. The gymnasium provided an entrance into public life, where its devotees might maintain a practiced air of superiority over all outsiders. Even had an unwelcome Bactrian managed to get past the guardhouse and wander into the gymnasium, he could not have participated in its activities. Like at a private school or club today, there was an examination of all candidates and certainly a waiting list. Greek boys from good families got in and guarded the privilege against the hoi polloi. For native peoples to "go Greek" and become one of the Hellenistai required more than a desire to do so: they had to somehow gain access to the gymnasium, where youngsters probably recited some ancient version of Kipling's poem:

> Father, Mother, and Me,
> Sister and Auntie say
> All the people like us are We,
> And everyone else is They.[22]

The Greeks who controlled the gymnasium at Ai Khanoum probably enjoyed, by and large, the fifty or so mansions that formed the elite residential district on the southwest side of the city. These were luxurious homes on generous lots, neatly spaced along parallel streets. All the mansions faced north and had the same design, a testament to the planned community of the Greek settlers. Special attention was devoted to the construction of fine bathrooms with mosaic floors and heated water. Such amenities took the edge off what was otherwise a hardship post.

And then there was the palace built by the Greek kings who later ruled Bactria as an independent Hellenistic state. A visitor able to pass beyond the monumental propylaea into the administrative center of the city would follow along a broad avenue that eventually turned south and approached the royal quarter. A gateway led into a vast formal courtyard flanked on its four sides by a portico of 118 columns with ornate Corinthian capitals. Nearly seven temples the size of the famous Athenian Parthenon could be parked inside this sprawling courtyard. On the south side, a colonnaded vestibule carried the visitor into a series of corridors that opened onto audience halls, chancery offices, royal living quarters, and yet another courtyard. Fine mosaic floors adorned some of the bathrooms in the king's apartments.

A treasure house occupied the west flank of the palace complex. The Greeks were in the process of adding more storerooms to accommodate the volume of luxury goods acquired through trade and conquest, but parts of the treasury remained unfinished and unused at the time of the city's death. Parchment and papyrus copies of precious literary texts were archived there. Some rooms contained stores of pearls, coral, lapis lazuli, garnet, agate, turquoise, sapphire, onyx, crystal, beryl, and carnelian.

Artworks from India, including parts of an elaborate inlaid throne or couch, were probably brought back as the spoils of recent wars.[23] Some storerooms contained ceramic vases filled with luxury goods, their contents neatly marked in ink. Stores of imported olive oil and incense were noted on jars, along with such pertinent information as the year, remaining quantity, and the names of palace officials in charge of the items. A number of vessels also contained silver coins that had been carefully counted and sealed inside, as vouched by various officials. One pitcher held five hundred Greek coins, and another ten thousand Indian *karshapana* coins from Taxila. The latter was probably loot from military campaigns into India or payment exacted from a vassal prince.

These labeled treasury deposits allow us to witness the administrative system at work in the busy palace. A pragmatic bureaucracy borrowed from the traditions of both Greece and Persia, and the Ai Khanoum functionaries likewise bore Greek and indigenous names.[24] We find treasury supervisors with Greek names (Zeno, Timodemos, Philiskos) and their subordinates with mixed nomenclature (Greek: Hermaios, Hippias, Theophrastus; indigenous: Oxyboakes, Oxybazos). There is no evidence anywhere that non-Greeks shared equally in the wealth, prestige, or power of the palace. The best an Oxyboakes could do was land a lower-level civil service job, working under Greek bosses.

As a whole, these non-Greeks are hard to find in the archaeological record at Ai Khanoum. Perhaps this is because the city belonged mainly to the Greeks, and the countryside to the farmers, pastoralists, and nomads of the indigenous population. To some extent, many natives may have ignored the Greeks and gone about their lives as if nothing had really changed. To the average herdsman up in the hills, what did it matter if the king was called Darius or Eucratides? Why should he want to visit a segregated city, sit through a play he could not understand, or strip naked to wrestle in the city's gymnasium? Still, some of the architecture at Ai Khanoum, especially the temples, shows strong local influence. Aramaic, the administrative language of the old Persian Empire, remained in use among some of the people in the city; presumably they never became completely comfortable with Greek. The excavators of Ai Khanoum argue that the cramped, single-room shanties found high on the acropolis hillside—away from the exclusive sectors of town—probably housed the non-Greek residents. Even the Hellenistai were walled off from the true Hellenes.

Ai Khanoum tells another story, equally sad. It has been the casualty of wars ancient and modern, its ruinations a recurring proof that peace seldom visits long in Afghanistan. Most recently, the results of the painstaking excavations by the French have been obliterated by callous looters and careless warlords.[25] Nearly everything stored in the Kabul Museum, of course, has been stolen. At Ai Khanoum itself, a local "commander" named Mahbuhbullah claims to have pilfered three hundred pounds of ancient silver and gold artifacts, mostly coins and jewelry.[26] He allegedly organized labor gangs to dig up the ruins and established an on-site bazaar for foreign antiquities dealers. One Hellenistic glass bowl with gilt decorations sold for eighty thousand dollars in Afghanistan, and for millions abroad. Other looted artifacts include a gold bracelet in the form of a cobra, the faience bust of a Greek king, votive sculptures, a bronze Hercules, a larger-than-life-size statue of Athena, and an ivory plaque depicting Aphrodite attended by Eros.

In the process of stealing these items, diggers have churned up the ground so frantically that the whole city now resembles a cratered lunar landscape. Broken pottery lies everywhere, alongside expended ammunition from the Northern Alliance gun emplacement on the acropolis. Looters' tunnels have been cut deep into the heart of the Hellenistic city. Bulldozers and heavy trucks have carried off to area teahouses and private homes the Greek columns that once were the pride of Bactria's kings.

These depredations repeat an ageless pattern. In antiquity, too, during the lifetime of King Plato, the Greek city at Ai Khanoum suffered abandonment and looting. Eucratides the Great was apparently the last to govern there, and his assassination plunged Bactria into such chaos that the Greeks quickly pulled out of Ai Khanoum. As Alexander's settlers had tried to do, these colonists fled the frontier. Some probably stayed around Bactra, to be ruled for a while by Eucratides's sons, Heliocles and Plato, while others streamed over the mountains toward India. In their wake, the omnipresent Scythian nomads thrust down into the territory surrounding Ai Khanoum. Resurgent, too, were the native Bactrians. They slowly emerged from the shadows for the first time since the Greeks had colonized the site over a century and a half earlier. Those persons long denied access to the center of the Greek city now wandered freely among the elite buildings, avenues, and monuments. Squatters occupied the abandoned palace. Some took residence in the treasury itself and helped themselves to what remained. They smashed the coinage jars, the contents of which were scattered; some of the coins were carried off and buried elsewhere in the city, where archaeologists later found them. Fires were set, and many treasures were melted into ingots on which an unknown language was etched. Scavengers began eventually to strip the dead city of its stone and bricks. Ceilings and walls collapsed. Hundreds of towering Greek columns fell at the hands of later inhabitants searching for the bronze fittings inside. The once sumptuous palace became a debris field where looters then, as looters now, ransacked an irreplaceable archaeological treasure.

Not in the palace, but in the theater, there appeared the most significant sign that the first European attempt to transform Afghanistan had ultimately failed. Where once Alexander's and Seleucus's settlers had assembled by the thousands to keep alive their ancestral arts, where practiced actors had donned their masks and recited the lines of classical poets, a new kind of tragedy now unfolded on a stage littered with the human wreckage of an awakened population. The natives needed no Greek theater, so they piled upon its stage and front row seats the scattered remains of their unburied dead, whose bodies were otherwise in the way. As if the Greeks had never come, the Devourer dogs were growling again over the bones of the Bactrians.[27]

ANCIENT SOURCES

The awesome figure of Alexander the Great cannot be seen in ordinary light. He is a creature of nightfall and shadows, phosphorus and flickers, not of the noonday sun. Our sources hide him from us in all but veiled, ethereal visions of a man once flesh and blood. We see him three times removed. First, he deliberately cloaked himself in mystery. He encouraged only chosen artists to paint or sculpt his image.[1] He authorized a single official history of his reign, and even then killed the writer (Callisthenes) halfway through the campaign.[2] He did not hesitate to show his displeasure at others who tried to chronicle the events of his life.[3] Determined to manipulate his own mythology, Alexander was an effective and relentless censor throughout his career.

Second, after Alexander's death in 323 B.C.E., dozens of his former compatriots took up their pens and papyrus to recount the hero's deeds. These men included his chamberlain (Chares), members of his fleet (Nearchus and Onesicritus), a general (Ptolemy), and an engineering specialist (Aristobulus).[4] They wrote from memory and, at times, consulted available documents, such as the king's correspondence and official journal.[5] One influential early writer (Cleitarchus) may have relied entirely on information provided by others. The works of these men were shaped and shaded by powerful new forces, particularly the heated politics that attended the birth of the Hellenistic age. People had axes to grind, and the sparks give us only a flickering impression of the real Alexander at the center of these self-serving narratives. Ptolemy provides a notable example. A major player in Alexander's wars, beginning with the one in Bactria, he later competed for authority and eventually won control of Egypt. When Ptolemy declared himself to be the king of Egypt, he established a dynasty that culminated, centuries later, in the celebrated reign of Cleopatra VII. Such ambitious rulers knew the value of propaganda, and Ptolemy dared even to steal Alexander's body to bolster his position (see chapter 6). He also took the time to write a history of Alexander's campaigns, in which Ptolemy featured himself as a hero and castigated his rivals (such as Perdiccas) as incompetents. Through innuendo and omission, Ptolemy's memoirs further distorted the events of his time.[6]

But sad to say, not one of the sources mentioned thus far survives intact for us to read. Our third problem is that the earliest extant narratives of Alexander's reign were written three hundred to five hundred years after the events they describe; they are no more firsthand, primary accounts of Alexander's wars than we are eyewitnesses to Newton's "discovery" of gravity or Columbus's voyages to the New World. The first of these available histories was the work of Diodorus of Sicily, a Greek who lived in the latter half of the first century B.C.E. He compiled a

History of the World, in which Alexander's reign occupies the seventeenth volume.[7] Unfortunately, a long lacuna, or textual gap, falls right in the midst of the Bactrian campaigns. Thus, we do not get the full benefit of Diodorus's work when researching the affairs of Alexander in Afghanistan.

Next, a Roman named Quintus Curtius Rufus produced a ten-volume history of Alexander in the first century C.E.[8] The first two volumes do not survive, but those devoted to the Bactrian wars are available. This is extremely important, because Curtius introduces a great deal of evidence not available otherwise (such as geographical details), and his is the only narrative that fully treats the Bactrian campaigns in a chronological (rather than topical) fashion. Curtius, however, displays a great love for rhetorical flourishes, which he interjects at every opportunity. He also wrote under the impression that Alexander's career followed the stock pattern of great men ruined by success. Curtius believed that excessive good fortune corrupted Alexander's noble character, beginning with the death of Darius. Other moralistic treatments of Alexander's career were written by Plutarch of Chaeronea early in the second century C.E. In fact, he crafted the famous essay *On the Fortune or Virtue of Alexander* as part of his collected *Moralia.*[9] Plutarch also wrote a series of Greek and Roman biographies, the *Parallel Lives,* one of which was devoted to Alexander.[10] In it, Plutarch duly notes that his work was never intended to be comprehensive; he elected to sketch Alexander's life as a portraitist might do, highlighting only those things that reveal some interesting aspect of the king's character. Thus, his biography is anecdotal rather than analytical.

Writing in the mid–second century C.E., Arrian of Nicomedia penned a history of Alexander's campaigns in seven volumes; a related treatise on India also survives, but his account of Alexander's successors does not.[11] Arrian expresses a laudatory view of Alexander that omits many of the negative episodes recorded in other sources. He is therefore far less critical of the king than, say, Curtius or Diodorus is; some scholars accuse Arrian of a deliberate whitewash. This naturally affects Arrian's reliability on some important matters, such as the massacres and conspiracies that occurred in and around Bactria. More frustrating is the decision by Arrian to abandon his normal chronological approach when writing about the Bactrian campaigns. He interrupts his narrative to treat as a moralistic whole the series of disturbing events associated with this war: the mutilation of Bessus, the murder of Cleitus, the *proskynesis* fiasco, the pages' conspiracy, and the fall of Callisthenes.[12] Otherwise, his narrative is a compelling military chronicle rich in tactical detail.

Sometime in the third century c.e., a Roman author named Justin decided to produce a condensed Latin version (an epitome) of a much larger work written by Pompeius Trogus late in the first century b.c.e.[13] Justin has often been criticized for doing a slipshod job of summarizing Trogus's account, for inevitably a great deal of important information and useful context were lost. What is worse, Justin's abridgement supplanted Trogus's original, so that now we have access only to a dim reflection of the much fuller (and presumably more worthwhile) forerunner. This is the basic problem lying behind all these extant sources: their success made obsolete the histories upon which they were based. Over time, we end up with the derivative accounts, all far removed from the events and persons they describe.

Still, scholars must be grateful for the later, secondary sources that do exist, since they are our last link to one of the most significant rulers in history.[14] As a bonus, we can sometimes glimpse the lost primary sources where they are embedded as either quotations or paraphrases in the accounts of later authors.[15] Arrian, for example, states plainly at the beginning of his history that he relied most upon the memoirs of Ptolemy and Aristobulus (now lost). This is useful to know. Furthermore, Arrian actually cites on occasion one or both of his main sources directly: "Alexander captured the seventh Sogdian city at the first assault. Ptolemy says that the men there surrendered, but while Aristobulus agrees that the town fell by storm, he claims that Alexander killed all the captives. Ptolemy says that Alexander distributed the prisoners among his troops and ordered that they be kept bound and under guard." This passage (Arrian 4.3.5) reveals to us two so-called fragments of the lost sources: a piece of Ptolemy's history and a piece of Aristobulus's. Arrian notes that his sources do not agree on the fate of the captives. Such information gives us a chance to see beyond Arrian's account and to appreciate the contradictions he encountered while researching materials unavailable to us. From this picture, we may decide that one of the eyewitnesses was simply mistaken, or that one (Ptolemy) has covered up an atrocity, or that the other (Aristobulus) invented one through exaggeration.

Scholars look closely for definitive patterns among these fragments, but the task is never that easy. In another case, Arrian (4.14.3) writes: "Regarding Callisthenes, Aristobulus says that he was shackled and hauled around with the army until he died of a disease. Ptolemy reports that Callisthenes was tortured on the rack and then hanged." Here, Ptolemy gives the more damning version. Arrian's own frustration is palpable in the next lines of the same passage: "Thus, not even the most trustworthy narra-

tives by actual eyewitnesses can agree on events that were quite
public and well known." We can determine what some other
contemporaries had to say about the fate of Callisthenes.
Plutarch records in his *Alexander* (55.9), among other things, a
fragment from Chares (Alexander's chamberlain): "About Callisthenes's death, some say that he was hanged on Alexander's orders, others that he was bound hand and foot and died of disease.
Chares writes that Callisthenes was kept in chains for seven
months awaiting trial . . . but died in India of obesity and lice."

This passage adds to the versions of Ptolemy and Aristobulus
(unnamed) the additional details supplied in Chares's work. Curtius (8.8.21) cites no source, but remarks that Callisthenes was
tortured to death. Did he get this directly or indirectly from
Ptolemy, or from some other witness? Does this lend any cre-
dence to Ptolemy's version? We do not know what Diodorus had
to say because, as noted, this part of his work is lost. Justin's epitome of Trogus (15.33–37) offers a bizarre twist: "Alexander cru-
elly mangled Callisthenes's limbs and cut off his ears, nose, and
lips to render him a shocking and miserable sight. Callisthenes
was carried around in a cage along with a dog to terrify onlook-
ers. . . . Lysimachus pitied Callisthenes, and slipped him some
poison to put an end to his agony." We may wonder whether
Justin has accurately summarized what he read in Trogus's history or confused the manner of Callisthenes's torture with that of
Bessus. Is the dog an invented detail? Does it suggest that
Alexander used the Greeks' aversion to Bactria's Devourer dogs
as a psychological weapon against traitors? These are not idle
speculations. Knowing the answers would go a long way toward
telling us what sort of man Alexander had become in Bactria.

These examples illuminate the nature of our evidence and the wispy trails we must follow in order to get even a sense of what the eyewitnesses originally reported. We are so far removed from the Alexander who arrested Callisthenes that we may never know for sure what happened. Even so, these troublesome histories provide our best evidence about ancient Afghanistan—we know very little about the region before Alexander's arrival in Bactria; after his departure, the curtain crashes down again. The kinds of written sources that would allow us to track Alexander year by year simply did not survive the centuries that followed.[16] Some notable Hellenistic historians, Polybius and Appian in particular, chose to focus on Western events; their overriding interest in Rome's military expansion into the Hellenistic world precluded much writing about places as far east as Bactria—except in the one special case of Antiochus III on the eve of his war with Rome (see chapter 7). Ancient biographers selected a few figures from the earliest Hellenistic period, such as Alexander, Demetrius, and Eumenes, while ignoring important men like Seleucus, Ptolemy, and Lysimachus and their successors in the East. Other writers took a larger view. Diodorus, for example, continued his comprehensive history, but, unfortunately, the sections about Hellenistic Bactria are among the long stretches now missing from the work. The last complete copy of Diodorus's history vanished in 1453 C.E., when the Ottoman Turks sacked Constantinople. The world history published in Greek by Pompeius Trogus exists only in the later, condensed version in Latin by Justin. This includes an abbreviated account of Eucratides's reign, but the surviving details are sometimes vague or unbelievable (such as the claim that Eucratides with three hundred men withstood a siege against sixty thousand enemies).[17] A history specifically devoted to the Hellenistic East, written by Apollodorus of Artemita, has been lost except for a few extracts copied into volumes such as the geographical treatises of Strabo. By horrible accident rather than insidious design, a wealth of material once available about Hellenistic Bactria has dropped from sight. Without these sources, we stumble in the dark. That is why the material evidence from archaeology and numismatics has proved essential to historians' efforts (see chapters 6–8).

NOTES

CHAPTER ONE. INTRODUCTION

1. For a concise, up-to-date introduction to Afghan history, see William Vogelsang, *The Afghans* (Oxford: Blackwell, 2002).

2. On the First Afghan War, see Patrick Macrory, *The Fierce Pawns* (Philadelphia: Lippincott, 1966); James Norris, *The First Afghan War, 1838–1842* (Cambridge: Cambridge University Press, 1967); John Waller, *Beyond the Khyber Pass* (New York: Random House, 1990).

3. James Lunt, *Bokhara Burnes* (London: Faber and Faber, 1969), p. 191.

4. Peter Hopkirk, *The Great Game: The Struggle for Empire in Central Asia* (New York: Kodansha International, 1992), pp. 192–93; Karl Meyer and Shareen Brysac, *Tournament of Shadows: The Great Game and the Race for Empire in Central Asia* (Washington, D.C.: Counterpoint, 1999), p. 64; Stephen Tanner, *Afghanistan: A Military History from Alexander the Great to the Fall of the Taliban* (New York: Da Capo Press, 2002), p. 136. On the sheepskins and camels, see Macrory, *The Fierce Pawns,* pp. 101 and 107.

5. Some captured Europeans did not make this ill-fated march and

were later rescued, among them the fiery Lady Sale, whose diary has been published: Patrick Macrory, ed., *Lady Sale: The First Afghan War* (Hamden, Conn.: Archon Books, 1969), to which is appended the account of Dr. William Brydon, the lone survivor of the military retreat. A slightly different version of Brydon's memoir appears in Louis Dupree, *Afghanistan* (Princeton: Princeton University Press, 1980), pp. 390–93; Dupree argues that Brydon deserted his men.

    6. Dost Muhammed finally gained control of Afghanistan's three main cities (Kabul, Kandahar, and Herat) only weeks before his death; even then some important areas remained outside his power: J. L. Lee, *The "Ancient Supremacy": Bukhara, Afghanistan, and the Battle for Balkh, 1731–1901* (Leiden: Brill, 1996), pp. 286–88.

    7. See, for example, Brian Robson, *The Road to Kabul: The Second Afghan War, 1878–1881* (London: Arms and Armour Press, 1986); and William Trousdale, ed., *War in Afghanistan, 1879–1880: The Personal Diary of Major General Sir Charles Metcalfe MacGregor* (Detroit: Wayne State University Press, 1985).

    8. The quotation is drawn from the poem "Lord Roberts" by Rudyard Kipling (1914); the lines continue, "Whom neither ease nor honours moved / An hair's-breadth from his aim."

    9. Quoted by Tanner, *Afghanistan,* p. 217; and by Meyer and Brysac, *Tournament of Shadows,* p. 199. In spite of Roberts's plea, the British did fight a third war in Afghanistan, which lasted only a month, in 1919. It did, however, occasion the first use of military aircraft there and saw the first aerial bombardment of Kabul.

    10. On this conflict, see Antonio Giustozzi, *War, Politics, and Society in Afghanistan, 1978–1991* (Washington, D.C.: Georgetown University Press, 2000); John Keegan, "The Ordeal of Afghanistan," *Atlantic Monthly* (November 1985): 94–105; Anthony Arnold, *The Fateful Pebble: Afghanistan's Role in the Fall of the Soviet Empire* (Novato, Calif.: Presidio Press, 1993); Henry Bradsher, *Afghanistan and the Soviet Union* (Durham, N.C.: Duke University Press, 1983); Nancy and Richard Newell, *The Struggle for Afghanistan* (Ithaca: Cornell University Press, 1981); Barnett Rubin, *The Fragmentation of Afghanistan,* 2nd ed. (New

Haven: Yale University Press, 2002); and Rosanne Klass, ed., *Afghanistan: The Great Game Revisited* (New York: Freedom House, 1987).

11. Quoted in Karl Meyer, *The Dust of Empire: The Race for Mastery in the Asian Heartland* (New York: Century Foundation, 2003), p. 131.

12. K. Wafadar, "Afghanistan in 1980: The Struggle Continues," *Asian Survey* 21 (1981): 172–80.

13. Zbigniew Brzezinski repeated the comment in an interview for *Le Nouvel Observateur* (January 15–21, 1998): 76. The Vietnam analogy became very popular: Mohammad Yousaf and Mark Adkin, *Afghanistan—the Bear Trap: The Defeat of a Superpower* (Havertown, Pa.: Casemate, 2001), pp. 62–77.

14. On the weapons and tactics of the mujahideen, consult Ali Ahmad Jalali and Lester Grau, *Afghan Guerilla Warfare: In the Words of the Mujahideen Fighters* (St. Paul, Minn.: MBI, 2001). For an excellent description of the mujahideen warriors, see Yousaf and Adkin, *Bear Trap,* pp. 32–37.

15. Testimony before the Senate Select Committee on Intelligence (September 26, 1984) admonished that "the most glaring deficiency continues to be the lack of any effective means [for the mujahideen] to combat Soviet jets and helicopters": Alex Alexiev, *The War in Afghanistan: Soviet Strategy and the State of the Resistance* (Santa Monica, Calif.: Rand Corporation, 1984), p. 5. According to Richard Clarke in his controversial book *Against All Enemies: Inside America's War on Terror* (New York: Free Press, 2004), pp. 48–49, he himself initiated this policy change in direct response to the success of the Soviet Hind-D helicopter. Caspar Weinberger opposed the deployment: James Mann, *Rise of the Vulcans: The History of Bush's War Cabinet* (New York: Viking, 2004), p. 123. On the use of these "wonder weapons" in the field, see Yousaf and Adkin, *Bear Trap,* pp. 174–88.

16. John Griffiths, *Afghanistan: A History of Conflict,* 2nd ed. (London: Carlton Books, 2001), p. 182. Clarke, *Against All Enemies,* p. 50, cites the rapid success of the Stinger deployment and naturally insists that there was no long-term threat posed by these weapons (pp. 51–52).

For a slightly different perspective stressing the expensive buyback of these weapons, see Steve Coll, *Ghost Wars: The Secret History of the CIA, Afghanistan, and Bin Laden, from the Soviet Invasion to September 10, 2001* (New York: Penguin Press, 2004), pp. 11–13, 149–51, 336–40, and 346–47.

17. The actual number of Soviet deaths may be considerably higher, perhaps forty thousand to fifty thousand. See Arnold, *The Fateful Pebble,* pp. 188–91. Whether the Soviet war represented another *Western* invasion or not is a matter of perspective. As one writer notes, "The Soviets in Afghanistan could be presented as the latest in a series of Western invaders": Norman Friedman, *Terrorism, Afghanistan, and America's New Way of War* (Annapolis: U.S. Naval Institute, 2003), p. 48.

18. Gulbuddin Hekmatyar, the chief recipient of U.S. military aid, became prime minister under the Islamabad Accord in 1993 and attacked Kabul from 1994 to early 1995: Michael Griffin, *Reaping the Whirlwind: The Taliban Movement in Afghanistan* (London: Pluto Press, 2001), pp. 76–77.

19. For more on the general background, see Ahmed Rashid, *Jihad: The Rise of Militant Islam in Central Asia* (New Haven: Yale University Press, 2002), and his earlier work, *Taliban: Islam, Oil, and Fundamentalism in Central Asia* (New Haven: Yale University Press, 2000); Kamal Matinuddin, *The Taliban Phenomenon: Afghanistan, 1994–1997* (Oxford: Oxford University Press, 1999); Neamatollah Nojumi, *The Rise of the Taliban* (New York: Palgrave, 2002).

20. For a useful account, see Peter Bergen, *Holy War, Inc.: Inside the Secret World of Osama bin Laden* (New York: Touchstone, 2001).

21. On the air campaign, see Mark Bowden, "The Kabul-ki Dance," *Atlantic Monthly* (November 2002): 65–87; and Friedman, *America's New Way of War,* pp. 166–71. General Tommy Franks locates some of the Predator pilots in Langley, Virginia: *American Soldier* (New York: Regan Books, 2004), pp. 289–90.

22. Michael O'Hanlon, "A Flawed Masterpiece," *Foreign Affairs* 81.3 (2002): 47–63.

23. Donald Rumsfeld, "Transforming the Military," *Foreign Affairs* 81.3 (2002): 21.

24. Franks, *American Soldier,* pp. 306–7.

25. Some *preliminary* accounts, however, have already reached an eager public: Robin Moore, *The Hunt for bin Laden: Task Force Dagger* (New York: Random House, 2003); Jon Lee Anderson, *The Lion's Grave: Dispatches from Afghanistan* (New York: Grove Press, 2002); Harlan Ullman, *Unfinished Business* (New York: Citadel Press, 2003); Friedman, *America's New Way of War;* Anthony Cordesman, *The Lessons of Afghanistan: War Fighting, Intelligence, and Force Transformation* (Washington, D.C.: Center for Strategic and International Studies, 2002); Andrew Exum, *This Man's Army: A Soldier's Story from the Front Lines of the War on Terrorism* (New York: Gotham Books, 2004); Philip Smucker, *Al Qaeda's Great Escape: The Military and the Media on Terror's Trail* (Washington, D.C.: Brassey's, 2004); and a particularly grim assessment in *Imperial Hubris: Why the West Is Losing the War on Terror* (Washington, D.C.: Brassey's, 2004).

26. *Imperial Hubris,* p. 177.

27. Franks, *American Soldier,* p. 381.

28. On the humanitarian crisis, see Arthur Helton, "Rescuing the Refugees," *Foreign Affairs* 81.2 (2002): 71–82.

29. On the relapse of Afghanistan into the perilous status quo ante, and the dangerous policy of allying with warlords, see Kathy Gannon, "Afghanistan Unbound," *Foreign* Affairs 83.3 (2004): 35–46. On the helicopters, see Tim McGirk, "A Dearth of Troops," *Time* 162.22 (December 1, 2003): 17.

30. Mark Thompson and Michael Duffy, "Is the Army Stretched Too Thin?" *Time* 162.9 (September 1, 2003): 36–43.

31. The phrase comes from Louis Dupree, *Afghanistan,* p. 316.

32. Max Cary, *The Geographic Background of Greek and Roman History* (Oxford: Clarendon Press, 1949), p. 200.

33. Griffiths, *Afghanistan,* p. 19.

34. President Bush used the phrase within hours of the 9–11 attacks, as widely reported by CBS News and other organizations; ad-

ministration officials have followed suit—e.g., Rumsfeld, "Transforming the Military," p. 21: "Here we were, in 2002, fighting the first war of the twenty-first century . . ." I use the word *Western* in its modern sense, inasmuch as historians consider Greece and Macedonia to be the founders of Western civilization. In the fourth century B.C.E., this terminology would have been meaningless.

35. On the reign of Philip II, see Nicholas Hammond, *Philip of Macedon* (Baltimore: Johns Hopkins University Press, 1994); and Eugene Borza, *In the Shadow of Olympus: The Emergence of Macedon* (Princeton: Princeton University Press, 1990). On the motivations for war (both revenge and conquest), see the analysis of Edmund Bloedow, "Why Did Philip and Alexander Launch a War against the Persian Empire?" *L'Antiquité Classique* 72 (2003): 261–74.

36. On Persia, see Pierre Briant, *Histoire de l'empire perse de Cyrus à Alexandre,* 2 vols. (Leiden: Nederlands Instituut voor het Nabije Oosten, 1996).

37. On the League of Corinth and Panhellenism, see Michael Flower, "Alexander the Great and Panhellenism," in *Alexander the Great in Fact and Fiction,* ed. A. B. Bosworth and E. J. Baynham (Oxford: Oxford University Press, 2000), pp. 96–135; and W. Lindsay Adams, "Philip II, the League of Corinth, and the Governance of Greece," *Ancient Macedonia* 6 (1998): 15–22.

38. Arrian 2.14.4–9.

39. For example, Alexander destroyed the city of Thebes: Arrian 1.7–8; Diodorus 17.8.2–14.1; Justin 11.2.7; Plutarch, *Alexander* 11.7–12.

40. On Alexander's campaigns in general, consult J. F. C. Fuller, *The Generalship of Alexander the Great* (New Brunswick, N.J.: Rutgers University Press, 1960; reprint, New York: Da Capo Press, 1989); N. G. L. Hammond, *Alexander the Great: King, Commander, and Statesman,* 2nd ed. (Bristol: Bristol Press, 1989); and Donald Engels, *Alexander the Great and the Logistics of the Macedonian Army* (Berkeley: University of California Press, 1978).

41. Carl Nylander, "Darius III—the Coward King: Point and

Counterpoint," in *Alexander the Great,* ed. Jesper Carlsen et al. (Rome: "L'Erma" di Bretschneider, 1993), pp. 145–59; and now, Pierre Briant, *Darius dans l'ombre d'Alexandre* (Paris: Fayard, 2003).

42. The evolving image of Alexander has been traced by A. S. Shahbazi, "Iranians and Alexander," *American Journal of Ancient History* 2.1 (2003): 5–38.

43. Ibid., p. 13, citing a Persian oracle.

44. Ibid., pp. 24–25.

45. Like Donald Rumsfeld, Alexander preferred dead over alive. See Friedman, *America's New Way of War,* p. 154.

46. Compare the basic sentiments of Alexander's speech, as reported by the later Roman author Curtius 6.3.1–18, and Bush's "Address to a Joint Session of Congress and the American People," September 20, 2001.

47. See, for examples, the front-page photograph of the September 25, 2001, edition of the *Houston Chronicle,* and the two-page spread on pp. 92–93 accompanying Lois Raimondo's "Long Road Home: A Story of War and Revelation in Afghanistan," *National Geographic* 201.6 (June 2002): 82–105. Among the stones in Raimondo's photograph can be seen a Greek architectural fragment.

48. W. W. Tarn, *Alexander the Great,* 2 vols. (Cambridge: Cambridge University Press, 1948). See also his famous essay, "Alexander the Great and the Unity of Mankind," *Proceedings of the British Academy* 19 (1933): 123–66.

49. Tarn, "Unity of Mankind," p. 127.

50. Richard Todd, "W. W. Tarn and the Alexander Ideal," *Historian* 37 (1964): 48–55.

51. A. B. Bosworth, "The Impossible Dream: W. W. Tarn's *Alexander* in Retrospect," *Ancient Society* 13 (1983): 131–50.

52. P. M. Fraser, *Cities of Alexander the Great* (Oxford: Clarendon Press, 1996), p. 190.

53. There is much useful data to be found in Matinuddin, *Taliban Phenomenon;* note, however, that the claim (p. 118) that Alexander introduced the poppy into Afghanistan cannot be substantiated.

CHAPTER TWO. HUNTING THE ENEMY

1. On this region, see Frank Holt, *Alexander the Great and Bactria: The Formation of a Greek Frontier in Central Asia* (Leiden: Brill, 1988), pp. 28–29. An interesting survey also exists in Robert Byron, *The Road to Oxiana* (1937; reprint, New York: Oxford University Press, 1982), pp. 245–57. It is not certain whether ancient Zariaspa-Bactra lies directly beneath modern Balkh or perhaps a little south, nearer the mountains: J. L. Lee, *The "Ancient Supremacy": Bukhara, Afghanistan, and the Battle for Balkh, 1731–1901* (Leiden: Brill, 1996), p. 2, n. 3. See also Rodney Young, "The South Wall of Balkh-Bactra," *American Journal of Archaeology* 59 (1955): 267–76.

2. Ronald Latham, trans. and ed., *The Travels of Marco Polo* (London: Penguin Books, 1958), p. 74.

3. F. R. Allchin and Norman Hammond, *The Archaeology of Afghanistan* (London: Academic Press, 1978), pp. 390–91.

4. Robin Moore, *The Hunt for bin Laden: Task Force Dagger* (New York: Random House, 2003), pp. 82–83.

5. Arnold Toynbee, *Between Oxus and Jumna* (Oxford: Oxford University Press, 1961), p. 96.

6. Mary Boyce, *A History of Zoroastrianism* (Leiden: Brill, 1975), 1:275–76.

7. Clement of Alexandria, *Protreptikos* 5.65.3, citing Berossos. Anahita was sometimes identified with Ishtar in Mesopotamia and Artemis in Greece.

8. William Hanaway Jr., "Anahita and Alexander," *Journal of the American Oriental Society* 102 (1982): 285–95.

9. Strabo 11.11.3. See also Frantz Grenet, *Les pratiques funéraires dans l'Asie centrale sédentaire de la conquête grecque à l'Islamisation* (Paris: CNRS, 1984), pp. 74–75; and Frank Holt, *Thundering Zeus: The Making of Hellenistic Bactria* (Berkeley: University of California Press, 1999), pp. 122–23.

10. Alexander is said to have honored the Apis cult in Egypt: Arrian 3.1.4; Diodorus 17.49.1; Curtius 4.7.5. The king's accommodation of

local customs must not, however, be pushed too far: note the cautions of Stanley Burstein, "Alexander in Egypt: Continuity or Change," and "Pharaoh Alexander: A Scholarly Myth," in the collection of his articles titled *Graeco-Africana: Studies in the History of Greek Relations with Egypt and Nubia* (New Rochelle: Aristide Caratzas, 1995), pp. 43–61.

11. Arrian 7.3.1–6; Plutarch, *Alexander* 69.6–8; Diodorus 17.107.4–5; Strabo 15.1.64.

12. Arrian 6.29.4–11; Plutarch, *Alexander* 69.3–4; Curtius 10.1.22–38; Strabo 15.3.7.

13. Strabo 11.11.3.

14. Extant sources from the Roman period lead us to believe that one of the attendees, Gobares (or Bagodaras) the Mede, fled to Alexander: Curtius 7.4.1–19; Diodorus 17.83.7–8. Curtius provides a summary of Bessus's words but quotes those of Gobares at length, as if the latter were recounting the tale.

15. Irbil (ancient Arbela) served briefly in the 1990s as the capital of semi-independent Iraqi Kurdistan; Kurds rejoiced openly there when U.S. forces drove Saddam Hussein from power.

16. See Holt, *Alexander and Bactria,* pp. 44–45.

17. E. W. Marsden, *The Campaign of Gaugamela* (Liverpool: Liverpool University Press, 1964), p. 44.

18. Ibid., p. 59.

19. Even the Greeks said of Darius that "no man exhibited less valor or sense in war," and that "his life was one long series of disasters": Arrian 3.22.2–3. Modern experts are still dealing with these accusations: Barry Strauss and Josiah Ober, *The Anatomy of Error: Ancient Military Disasters and Their Lessons for Modern Strategists* (New York: St. Martin's Press, 1990), pp. 103–31; Carl Nylander, "Darius III—the Coward King, Point and Counterpoint," in *Alexander the Great: Reality and Myth,* ed. Jesper Carlsen et al. (Rome: "L'Erma" di Bretschneider, 1993), pp. 145–59.

20. The sad story of Darius's demise comes down to us from a few Persian loyalists who fled to Alexander rather than join Bessus: Arrian 3.21.1–10; Curtius 5.9.2–13.25.

21. Holt, *Alexander and Bactria,* pp. 46–49.

22. For the background, see A. B. Bosworth, "Alexander and the Iranians," *Journal of Hellenic Studies* 100 (1980): 1–21.

23. Arrian 3.25; Curtius 6.6.13–35; Diodorus 17.78.

24. The careers of these men are conveniently summarized in Waldemar Heckel, *The Marshals of Alexander's Empire* (London: Routledge, 1992).

25. Arrian 3.25.8; Barsaentes was not apprehended until 326 B.C.E., according to Curtius 8.13.3–4.

26. On this (and other) Alexandrias founded by Alexander, see P. M. Fraser, *Cities of Alexander the Great* (Oxford: Clarendon Press, 1996), pp. 133–40.

27. Alexander left as settlers in this new city and its environs about seven thousand locals and three thousand soldiers (mercenary volunteers and others unfit for further duty): Arrian 3.28.4; Diodorus 17.83.2; Curtius 7.3.23.

28. Donald Engels, *Alexander the Great and the Logistics of the Macedonian Army* (Berkeley: University of California Press, 1978), p. 91; cf. David Buchbinder, "The Other Enemy in Afghanistan: Creepy-Crawlies," *Christian Science Monitor,* June 24, 2002.

29. Engels, *Logistics,* pp. 18–25 and 144–45.

30. Frank Holt, "Imperium Macedonicum and the East: The Problem of Logistics," *Ancient Macedonia* 5 (1993): 585–92. The observations of a Pakistani brigadier involved in the Afghan war against the Soviets from 1983 to 1986 are cogent: "My major headache was logistics." See Mohammad Yousaf and Mark Adkin, *Afghanistan—the Bear Trap: The Defeat of a Superpower* (Havertown, Pa.: Casemate, 2001), pp. 97–112, esp. p. 98.

31. The Salang Tunnel, completed in August 1964, sits at 11,100 feet above sea level. It is still subject to closure due to heavy snowstorms and deadly avalanches.

32. Alexander later took a shorter route, presumably the Shibar Pass, on his way back to the Kabul Valley; this suggests that he favored the Khawak in 329 B.C.E. See Strabo 15.1.26.

33. Holt, "Imperium Macedonicum," pp. 586–88.

34. Håkan Grudd et al., "A 7400-Year Tree Ring Chronology in Northern Swedish Lapland: Natural Climate Variability Expressed on Annual to Millennial Timescales," *Holocene* 12.6 (2002): 657–65; Samuli Helama et al., "The Supra-Long Scots Pine Tree-Ring Record for Finnish Lapland: Part 2, Interannual to Centennial Variability in Summer Temperatures for 7500 Years," *Holocene* 12.6 (2002): 681–87, esp. Table 4.

35. See, e.g., Christian Habicht, *Athens from Alexander to Antony* (Cambridge: Harvard University Press, 1997), p. 26.

36. Arrian 3.29.1; Strabo 15.2.10. There is still some dispute about the locations of these ancient sites. See Edvard Rtveladze, *Makedoniya-lik Aleksandr i Baqtria va So'g'diyonada* (Tashkent: Academy of Fine Arts of the Republic of Uzbekistan, 2002); Paul Bernard, "Greek Geography and Literary Fiction from Bactria to India: The Case of the Aornoi and Taxila," in *Coins, Art, and Chronology: Essays on the Pre-Islamic History of the Indo-Iranian Borderlands*, ed. Michael Alram and Deborah Klimburg-Salter (Vienna: Verlag der österreichischen Akademie der Wissenschaften, 1999), pp. 51–98; and Janos Harmatta, "Alexander the Great in Central Asia," *Acta Antiqua Academiae Scientiarum Hungaricae* 39 (1999): 129–36.

37. Curtius 7.3.2 and 7.4.33–40; Diodorus 17.83.4–6; Arrian 3.28.3. Curtius 7.4.3 speaks of Bessus's "ferox verbis" and even questions the Bactrian's sanity; the fear is noted at 7.4.1.

38. Engels, *Logistics,* pp. 95–96 calculates that sixty-four thousand soldiers, thirty-six thousand noncombatants, and ten thousand cavalry horses crossed the Hindu Kush with Alexander.

39. Curtius 7.4.13. See Elizabeth Baynham, *Alexander the Great: The Unique History of Quintus Curtius* (Ann Arbor: University of Michigan Press, 1998), pp. 52–54.

40. Curtius 7.3.2 and 7.4.33–40; Diodorus 17.83.4–6; Arrian 3.28.3.

41. This business of trophy heads, both here and later in the Bactrian campaign, brings to mind some modern parallels. The reporter Geraldo Rivera expressed his desire to bash bin Laden's head and then

bronze it as a trophy; this echoed the earlier sentiment of the CIA's Cofer Black, who wanted the terrorist's head brought to him in a box to show the president. Allegedly, an order was placed for dry ice and special containers to convey the head: Bob Woodward, *Bush at War* (New York: Simon and Schuster, 2002), pp. 103, 141, and 143; and Philip Smucker, *Al Qaeda's Great Escape: The Military and the Media on Terror's Trail* (Washington, D.C.: Brassey's, 2004), pp. 66–67 and 126.

42. Arrian 3.28.10; Curtius 7.4.20.

43. Arrian 3.29.1; Curtius 7.5.1.

44. Holt, "Imperium Macedonicum," pp. 588–92.

45. Rtveladze, *Makedoniyalik Aleksandr,* pp. 28–66.

46. Arrian 3.29.2–4; Curtius 7.5.17–18. Aristobulus, a member of Alexander's entourage, kept meticulous records on rivers and other natural phenomena; he is the ultimate source behind some of these details. A long-overdue study of the problem has been published by Edmund Bloedow, "On the Crossing of Rivers: Alexander's Διφθέραι," *Klio* 84 (2002): 57–75.

47. John Griffiths, *Afghanistan: A History of Conflict,* 2nd ed. (London: Carlton Books, 2001), p. 262.

48. Holt, *Alexander and Bactria,* pp. 49–50.

49. There is no real reason to dismiss the story, although ardent admirers of Alexander (such as W. W. Tarn) would rather it not be true. See Holt, *Alexander and Bactria,* pp. 74–75.

50. Curtius 7.5.26 and 36–7; Arrian 3.30.5 (citing Aristobulus as the eyewitness for this version).

51. On Ptolemy, see Heckel, *Marshals,* pp. 222–27 and Walter Ellis, *Ptolemy of Egypt* (London: Routledge, 1994).

52. Arrian 3.29.7–30.3 (based on Ptolemy's history).

53. Arrian 3.30.4; Curtius 7.5.38–9.

54. The Afghan Loya Jirga, or Great Assembly, is a gathering of representatives from all parts of the country. Delegates are summoned to confirm the legitimacy of a ruler, affirm governmental changes, or decide other issues of national importance.

55. Plutarch, *Alexander* 21.6. See also Diodorus 17.27.5; Curtius

3.12.16–17; and Pierre Briant, *Histoire de l'empire perse de Cyrus à Alexandre* (Leiden: Nederlands Instituut voor het Nabije Oosten, 1996), 1:237.

56. Alexander's appearance: Plutarch, *Alexander* 4.1–7; Diodorus 17.66.3; Curtius 5.2.13–15; Aelian, *Varia Historia* 12.14.

57. Plutarch, *Moralia* 329F–330A; Diodorus 17.77.5; Curtius 6.6.4–5. Alexander no doubt wore the Persian royal costume at the ceremonial punishment of his rival; he preferred to forego such foreign garments as trousers and jacket.

58. Byron, "Ode to Napoleon Bonaparte."

59. Arrian 4.7.3; Curtius 7.5.40, 43, and 7.10.10; Diodorus 17.83.9; Plutarch, *Alexander* 43.6.

60. E.g., Arrian 4.7.4 at the start of a famous digression.

61. The photograph appears in Griffiths, *Afghanistan.*

CHAPTER THREE. A DESPERATE STRUGGLE

1. Frank Holt, *Alexander the Great and Bactria: The Formation of a Greek Frontier in Central Asia* (Leiden: Brill, 1988), pp. 52–53.

2. For example, Alexander offered sacrifices at the Danube River in 335 B.C.E. (Arrian 1.4.5), the Jaxartes River in 329 (Pliny, *Natural History* 6.18), and the Hyphasis River in 326 (Arrian 5.29.1–2; Plutarch, *Alexander* 62.7–8; Curtius 9.3.19; Diodorus 17. 95.1–2).

3. On the geography of these regions, see Holt, *Alexander and Bactria,* pp. 11–32. These Scythians included groups variously called the Dahae, Massagetae, Sacae, and so forth. Curtius 4.6.3 describes the Bactrians as warlike, valiant, uncouth, and plain-living, like the Scythians. Arrian 4.17.5 stresses their poverty and love of war.

4. Arrian 1.4. A. B. Bosworth, *Conquest and Empire: The Reign of Alexander the Great* (Cambridge: Cambridge University Press, 1988), p. 30, says, "It was a gratuitous act of terrorism on a helpless people."

5. Arrian 3.30.6; cf. Curtius 7.6.10 and 4.5.2. On the air base, dubbed K-2, see Tommy Franks, *American Soldier* (New York: Regan Books, 2004), pp. 256 and 286–87.

6. On this important site, consult Paul Bernard, "Maracanda-Afrasiab colonie grecque," *Atti dei Convegni Lincei* 127 (1996): 331–65.

7. Arrian 4.1.3; Curtius 7.6.13. On this city, see P. M. Fraser, *Cities of Alexander the Great* (Oxford: Clarendon Press, 1996), pp. 151–53.

8. Holt, *Alexander and Bactria,* pp. 55–58; and "Alexander's Settlements in Central Asia," *Ancient Macedonia* 4 (1986): 315–23.

9. Arrian 4.1.5; Curtius 7.6.13.

10. Curtius 7.6.1–2; Arrian 3.30.10–11 says thirty thousand. Since we must be cautious of the large, rounded numbers in our sources, the smaller figure is given here. This is a timeless problem; cf. Philip Smucker, *Al Qaeda's Great Escape: The Military and the Media on Terror's Trail* (Washington, D.C.: Brassey's, 2004), pp. 193–94.

11. Arrian 3.30.11 says twenty-two thousand died; Curtius 7.6.4–9 claims that the rebels repented and surrendered.

12. Arrian 4.2.1–3.5; Curtius 7.6.16–23.

13. John Lascaratos, "The Wounding of Alexander the Great in Cyropolis (329 B.C.): The First Reported Case of the Syndrome of Transient Cortical Blindness?" *History of Ophthalmology* 42.3 (1997): 283–87.

14. Quoted in Brian Robson, *The Road to Kabul: The Second Afghan War, 1878–1881* (London: Arms and Armour Press, 1986), p. 158.

15. Arrian 4.1.5; Curtius 7.6.13–14.

16. See Ali Ahmad Jalali and Lester Grau, *Afghan Guerilla Warfare: In the Words of the Mujahideen Fighters* (St. Paul, Minn.: MBI, 2001). Some mujahideen operations involved one "commander" and a dozen or so men (pp. 23–25); others combined thousands of fighters under dozens of warlords (pp. 174–95). For a sympathetic portrait of one such warlord (Ahmad Shah Massoud, the "Lion of Panshir"), see Sebastian Junger, *Fire* (New York: W. W. Norton, 2001), pp. 199–222.

17. Grenville Byford, "The Wrong War," *Foreign Affairs* 81.4 (2002): 34–43.

18. This question of whether both sides in a struggle should be considered terrorists is still cogent today: Norman Friedman, *Terrorism, Afghanistan, and America's New Way of War* (Annapolis: U.S. Naval Institute Press, 2003), pp. 88–91. Or we may approach the issue from the

opposite direction and avoid treating *any* of the combatants as terrorists, as one author advises even in the case of Osama bin Laden: *Imperial Hubris: Why the West Is Losing the War on Terror* (Washington, D.C.: Brassey's, 2004), pp. 246–47.

19. Valerii Nikonorov, *The Armies of Bactria, 700 B.C.–450 A.D.* (Stockport: Montvert Publications, 1997), 1:21.

20. An incredible collection of ancient weaponry, both Greek and central Asian, has been excavated in the territory of Bactria: Boris Litvinsky and Igor Pichikyan, *Ellinisticheskiy khram Oksa v Baktrii (Iuzhnyi Tadzhikistan)* (Moscow: Vostochnaya Literatura, 2000), 2:25–383.

21. Curtius 4.13.4–5. By contrast, the Macedonians tended to be clean shaven in order to keep the enemy from grabbing their beards in battle: Plutarch, *Moralia* 180B.

22. On the Macedonian army, consult the following works: Nicholas Hammond, *The Macedonian State* (Oxford: Clarendon Press, 1989), pp. 100–136; Robert Milns, "The Army of Alexander the Great," in *Alexandre le Grand: Image et Réalité,* ed. Ernst Badian (Geneva: Fondation Hardt, 1976), pp. 87–130; and Nick Sekunda, *The Army of Alexander the Great* (London: Osprey, 1984).

23. N. G. L. Hammond, "Training in the Use of the Sarissa and Its Effect in Battle, 359–333 B.C.," *Antichthon* 14 (1980): 53–63.

24. Arrian 3.27.4: Alexander appointed Hephaestion and Cleitus.

25. Arrian 4.17.3. Consult Ernst Badian, "Orientals in Alexander's Army," *Journal of Hellenic Studies* 85 (1965): 160–61; A. B. Bosworth, *Conquest and Empire,* pp. 271–73.

26. Arrian 4.3.6–4.3; Curtius 7.6.25–7.29.

27. Arrian 4.4.4–8; Curtius 7.8.1–9.16. See also Edmund Bloedow, "On the Crossing of Rivers: Alexander's Διφθεραι," *Klio* 84 (2002): 61–63.

28. J. F. C. Fuller, *The Generalship of Alexander the Great* (New Brunswick, N. J.: Rutgers University Press, 1960; reprint, New York: Da Capo Press, 1989), p. 237.

29. Arrian 4.4.9.

30. Arrian 4.5.2–6.2; Curtius 7.7.30–39. One analysis of the disaster: N. G. L. Hammond, "The Macedonian Defeat Near Samarcand," *Ancient World* 22.2 (1991): 41–47, which favors the account of Arrian.

31. Compare the ambush set by the mujahideen near Abdullah-e Burj in 1980. There, too, the attackers chose to hit while the enemy troops were tired. The Soviet command disintegrated in confusion, and some soldiers tried to swim the river to safety: Jalali and Grau, *Afghan Guerilla Warfare,* pp. 31–33.

32. This is obvious in the versions reported in Arrian 4.5.1–6.2.

33. Donald Engels, *Alexander the Great and the Logistics of the Macedonian Army* (Berkeley: University of California Press, 1978), pp. 153–56.

34. Arrian 4.6.3–7; Curtius 7.9.20–21. Curtius 7.9.22 says that every native of military age was killed. A few who impressed the king might have been spared: 7.10.4–9.

35. Ian Worthington, *Alexander the Great: Man and God* (New York: Pearson Longman, 2004), p. 134, deriving the figure from Diodorus (Contents of Book 17).

36. John Griffiths, *Afghanistan: A History of Conflict,* 2nd ed. (London: Carlton Books, 2001), p. 32.

37. A stark account of such tactics may be found in Barnett Rubin, "Human Rights in Afghanistan," in *Afghanistan: The Great Game Revisited*, ed. Rosanne Klass (New York: Freedom House, 1987), pp. 340–44. See also Junger, *Fire,* p. 24; and Mohammad Yousaf and Mark Adkin, *Afghanistan—the Bear Trap: The Defeat of a Superpower* (Havertown, Pa.: Casemate, 2001), pp. 179–80 (the attack on Rugyan Village).

38. In the Kremlin, mujahideen were labeled terrorists, bandits, and gangsters.

39. Henry Bradsher, *Afghanistan and the Soviet Union* (Durham, N.C.: Duke University Press, 1983), p. 14.

40. Arrian 4.7.1–3; Curtius 7.10.10–12.

41. Frank Holt, "Spitamenes against Alexander," *Historikogeographika* 4 (1994): 51–55. See also the accounts of modern warlords in Afghanistan: Jalali and Grau, *Afghan Guerilla Warfare,* pp. 147–95.

42. W. Lindsay Adams, "Antipater and Cassander: Generalship on Restricted Resources in the Fourth Century," *Ancient World* 10 (1984): 79–88; Ernst Badian, "Agis III: Revisions and Reflections," in *Ventures into Greek History,* ed. Ian Worthington (Oxford: Clarendon Press, 1994), pp. 258–92.

43. Plutarch, *Moralia* 329B.

44. Plutarch, *Moralia* 328E.

45. Tarn, *Hellenistic Civilisation,* 3rd ed. (New York: Meridian Books, 1961), p. 5.

46. The sentiment goes back at least as far as the Clinton administration: Stephen Tanner, *Afghanistan: A Military History from Alexander the Great to the Fall of the Taliban* (New York: Da Capo Press, 2002), p. 293.

47. As argued more fully in Holt, *Alexander and Bactria,* pp. 25–33.

48. Curtius 8.2.16: "They were accustomed to brigandage even in peacetime."

CHAPTER FOUR. THE HYDRA
HEADS OF BACTRIA

1. The Macedonian hammer-and-anvil tactic has been highlighted in the West Point history curriculum: Elmer May et al., *Ancient and Medieval Warfare* (Wayne, N.J.: Avery, 1984), p. 22.

2. Sebastian Junger, *Fire* (New York: W. W. Norton, 2001), p. 214.

3. Quoted in Philip Smucker, *Al Qaeda's Great Escape: The Military and the Media on Terror's Trail* (Washington, D.C.: Brassey's, 2004), p. 126.

4. Ibid., pp. 144–97, esp. 179 and 191. See Tommy Franks, *American Soldier* (New York: Regan Books, 2004), pp. 379–81, for a more positive assessment.

5. The Soviets experienced a similar trend: Yossef Bodansky, "Soviet Military Involvement in Afghanistan," in *Afghanistan: The Great Game Revisited,* ed. Rosanne Klass (New York: Freedom House, 1987), pp. 252–53.

6. On the problematic chronology and geography of this campaign season, see Edvard Rtveladze, *Makedoniyalik Aleksandr i Baqtria va So'g'diyonada* (Tashkent: Academy of Fine Arts of the Republic of Uzbekistan, 2002); Frantz Grenet and Claude Rapin, "Alexander, Ai Khanum, Termez: Remarks on the Spring Campaign of 328," *Bulletin of the Asia Institute* 12 (1998): 79–89; Frank Holt, *Alexander the Great and Bactria* (Leiden: Brill, 1988), pp. 60–64; Paul Bernard, "Alexandre et Ai Khanoum," *Journal des Savants* (1982): 125–38; and A. B. Bosworth, "A Missing Year in the History of Alexander the Great," *Journal of Hellenic Studies* 101 (1981): 17–37.

7. Arrian 4.16.1 and 4.17.1; Curtius 8.1.6.

8. Arrian 4.15.7–8; Plutarch, *Alexander* 57.5–9; Strabo 11.11.5; Curtius 7.10.13–14.

9. Plutarch, *Alexander* 57.4–8, tells us that the king had recently received a grave portent: a lamb born with testicles on its head. The oil omen gave him greater hopes for the future.

10. Arrian 4.16.2 mentions the detached units, which may have peeled off from the main force one by one. See the remarks in A. B. Bosworth, *A Historical Commentary on Arrian's History of Alexander* (Oxford: Clarendon Press, 1995), 2:113.

11. Curtius 7.11.1–29; Strabo 11.11.4; Polyaenus 4.3.29; and the *Metz Epitome* 15–28. Arrian 4.18.4–19.4 follows a different tradition that may be corrupted and confused: see Holt, *Alexander and Bactria,* p. 61; Bosworth, *Historical Commentary,* 2:124–27; and Elizabeth Baynham, *Alexander the Great: The Unique History of Quintus Curtius* (Ann Arbor: University of Michigan Press, 1998), pp. 92–95.

12. Three hundred mountaineers volunteered to climb the rock, said by Curtius (7.11.2) to reach thirty stadia (about 3.7 miles) in height. This must be an exaggeration, or perhaps an inclined measurement from the foot of the mountain to its peak.

13. Although Arrian fails to report the punishment of Ariamazes and his followers, the atrocity is not to be doubted: Bosworth, *Historical Commentary,* 2:130.

14. Curtius 7.11.29; see also Pierre Briant, *L'Asie centrale et les roy-*

aumes proche-orientaux du premier millénaire (c. VIIIe-IVe siècles avant notre ère) (Paris: Éditions Recherche sur les Civilisations, 1984), p. 82.

15. Curtius 8.1.1–3; Arrian 4.16.3.

16. Eugene Schuyler, *Turkistan: Notes of a Journey in Russian Turkistan, Khokand, Bukhara, and Kuldja* (New York: Scribner, Armstrong, and Company, 1876), pp. 276–78 and 281–83; Michael Wood, *In the Footsteps of Alexander the Great* (Berkeley: University of California Press, 1997), p. 166.

17. Frank Holt, *Thundering Zeus: The Making of Hellenistic Bactria* (Berkeley: University of California Press, 1999), pp. 37–47. See chapter 8.

18. Curtius 8.1.3–5; Arrian 4.16.4–5. See Holt, "Spitamenes against Alexander," *Historikogeographika* 4 (1994): 51–58.

19. The site of the captured garrison is unknown. According to Arrian 4.16.4, Spitamenes was reinforced with six hundred Massagetan Scythians; Curtius 8.1.3 says eight hundred.

20. The mujahideen attack on Urgun in 1983 provides an instructive example of the limitations of siege craft by guerilla forces. About eight hundred insurgents participated in the operation. They were successful in capturing an outlying fort, but the city itself could not be taken. It was impossible for the attackers to maintain their supplies. See Ali Ahmad Jalali and Lester Grau, *Afghan Guerilla Warfare: In The Words of the Mujahideen Fighters* (St. Paul, Minn.: MBI, 2001), pp. 197–204.

21. Curtius 8.1.3–5. Attinas is otherwise unknown in the Alexander sources.

22. Arrian 4.16.6–7.

23. Arrian 4.16.6. Polyaenus 5.44.1 reports that, prior to his service with the Macedonian kings, the Olynthian Aristonicus had toured on behalf of Memnon of Rhodes.

24. Plutarch, *Moralia* 334F. The bronze statue showed the brave musician holding a spear and kithara.

25. Curtius 8.1.7–10; Arrian 4.15.1–6 (misattributed to Bactra).

26. Curtius 8.1.10–19. Diodorus locates the game park at Basista in the table of contents for his (lost) narrative.

27. Curtius 8.1.19; Arrian 4.17.3.

28. Curtius 6.5.3 reports that Artabazus was ninety-five years old in 330 B.C.E. Bosworth, *Historical Commentary,* 2:118, calculates that he was "under sixty when he abdicated his satrapy."

29. For background, see Robert Kebric, "Old Age, the Ancient Military, and Alexander's Army: Positive Examples for a Graying America," *Gerontologist* 28 (1985): 298–302.

30. Curtius 8.1.21; cf. 5.10.3.

31. Curtius 8.2.13.

32. W. W. Tarn, *Alexander the Great* (Cambridge: Cambridge University Press, 1948), p. 123. Arrian, too, blamed Cleitus and sympathized with Alexander: 4.9.1–2.

33. Curtius 8.1.35.

34. Plutarch, *Moralia* 341F.

35. Victor Hanson, *The Western Way of War* (New York: Knopf, 1989).

36. On Macedonian banquets (symposia), see Eugene Borza, "The Symposium at Alexander's Court," *Ancient Macedonia* 3 (1983): 45–55. For details on the archaeological remains at Maracanda where the fateful banquet occurred, consult Paul Bernard, "Fouilles de la mission franco-soviétique à l'ancienne Samarkand (Afrasiab): Première campagne, 1989," *Comptes Rendus de l'Académie des Inscriptions et Belles-Lettres* (1990): 356–80, and "Maracanda-Afrasiab colonie grecque," *Atti dei Convegni Lincei* 127 (1996): 331–65.

37. On the somewhat amusing class of ancient professional flatterers, see the anecdotes in Athenaeus, *Deipnosophistae* 234C–261E.

38. Plutarch, *Alexander* 29.6, and *Moralia* 334E and 331E.

39. There are some variations among our sources, as one might expect given the rowdy and poorly remembered circumstances: Arrian 4.8.1–9.6; Plutarch, *Alexander* 50.1–52.2; Curtius 8.1.20–2.12; and Justin 12.6.

40. Desa Philadelphia, "The Perils of Protest," *Time* (April 14, 2003): 24; Jennifer Harper, "Jab at Bush a Flap for Dixie Chicks," *Washington Times,* March 16, 2003.

41. A. B. Bosworth, *Conquest and Empire: The Reign of Alexander the Great* (Cambridge: Cambridge University Press, 1988), p. 114. Elizabeth Carney, "The Death of Clitus," *Greek, Roman, and Byzantine Studies* 22 (1981): 149–60, looks for a personal affront to Cleitus.

42. A good analysis of the sources may be found in A. B. Bosworth, "The Tumult and the Shouting: Two Interpretations of the Cleitus Episode," *Ancient History Bulletin* 10.1 (1996): 19–30. A forceful case has been made that Alexander and his men were suffering from posttraumatic stress disorder, brought on by the violence of the campaign and manifested in Alexander's explosive anger, abuse of alcohol, lack of trustworthy perception, and loss of social trust: Lawrence Tritle, "Alexander the Great and the Killing of Cleitus the Black," in *Crossroads of History: The Age of Alexander,* ed. Waldemar Heckel and Lawrence Tritle (Claremont, Calif.: Regina Books, 2003), pp. 127–46.

43. Alexander's wrath, like that of his avowed ancestor Achilles, was atoned in Homeric style: Elizabeth Carney, "Artifice and Alexander History," in *Alexander the Great in Fact and Fiction,* ed. A. B. Bosworth and E. J. Baynham (Oxford: Oxford University Press, 2000), pp. 278–81.

44. Arrian 4.17.3; Curtius 8.2.14–15. The king made it clear for the meantime that Coenus held overall command in Sogdiana lest another disaster arise over confused rank and responsibility.

45. Curtius 8.2.14–18.

46. Curtius 8.2.19.

47. Arrian 4.17.4–7. Old Erigyius, who had so proudly displayed Satibarzanes's head, died at about this time. Alexander honored him with a splendid funeral: Curtius 8.2.40.

48. Curtius 8.3.1–15; Arrian 4.17.7 (crediting the Scythians); *Metz Epitome* 20–23.

49. Arrian 7.4.6. She may be the source for this version of her father's death, crediting her mother for siding with the Greeks and Macedonians.

50. Some scholars have detected a strong religious element to the resistance against Alexander: A. S. Shahbazi, "Iranians and Alexander," *American Journal of Ancient History* 2.1 (2003): 19–29.

51. J. F. C. Fuller, *The Generalship of Alexander the Great* (New Brunswick, N.J.: Rutgers University Press, 1960; reprint, New York: Da Capo Press, 1989), p. 122; cf. Tarn, *Alexander,* p. 73.

52. See Barnett Rubin, "Human Rights in Afghanistan," in *Afghanistan: The Great Game Revisited,* ed. Rosanne Klass (New York: Freedom House, 1987), p. 343.

53. Curtius 8.2.19–33; Arrian 4.21.1–10; Plutarch, *Alexander* 58; Strabo 11.11.4. See Holt, *Alexander and Bactria,* p. 66; and Bosworth, *Historical Commentary,* 2:134–39.

54. Curtius 8.2.28–33; *Metz Epitome* 19 adds three daughters.

55. Curtius 8.2.22 and 25.

56. Frantz Grenet, "Old Samarkand: Nexus of the Ancient World," *Archaeology Odyssey* 6.5 (September–October 2003): 31–32.

57. Holt, *Alexander and Bactria,* pp. 66–70.

58. Jalali and Grau, *Afghan Guerilla Warfare,* p. 225.

CHAPTER FIVE. LOVE AND WAR

1. Curtius 8.3.16; *Metz Epitome* 23; Plutarch, *Alexander* 57.3.

2. Arrian 4.18.1–3; Curtius 8.3.16–17.

3. On the life and legacy of Roxane, see Frank Holt, "Alexander the Great's Little Star," *History Today* 38 (September 1988): 31–39; Elizabeth Carney, *Women and Monarchy in Macedonia* (Norman: University of Oklahoma Press, 2000), pp. 106–7 and 146–48.

4. Arrian 4.18.4, 19.4–20.4; Curtius 8.4.21–30; Plutarch, *Alexander* 47.7–8, *Moralia* 332E and 338D; *Metz Epitome* 28–31; Strabo 11.11.4.

5. Lucian, *Herodotus* 4–6.

6. This famous film starred Richard Burton, Fredric March, and Claire Bloom. See Peter Green, "The Movies Make Hay with the Classic World," *Horizon* 3.5 (1961): 52–57.

7. The photo by Steve McCurry accompanied the feature story by Debra Denker, "Along Afghanistan's War-Torn Frontier," *National Geographic* 167.6 (June 1985): 772–97.

8. Cathy Newman, "A Life Revealed," *National Geographic* 201.4 (April 2002), with photographs and commentary by Steve McCurry.

9. Helmut Berve, *Das Alexanderreich auf prosopographischer Grundlage* (Munich: C. H. Beck'sche, 1926; reprint, Salem, N.H.: Ayer, 1988), 2:346–47 (no. 688).

10. Artaxerxes III was murdered in 338 B.C.E. and his successor, Artaxerxes IV, was killed in 336. The next king, Darius III, was of course later slain by Bessus and his compatriots.

11. Curtius 8.4.27; see also Marcel Renard and Jean Servais, "A propos du marriage d'Alexandre et de Roxane," *L'Antiquité Classique* 24 (1955): 29–50.

12. Diodorus 17.16.2.

13. Athenaeus 10.435A; Plutarch, *Alexander* 21.4–22.3; Diodorus 17.77.7; Curtius 6.6.8. Modern commentaries include Carney, *Women,* pp. 97–100; W. W. Tarn, "Alexander's Attitude to Sex," pp. 319–26 in his *Alexander the Great,* vol. 2 (Cambridge: Cambridge University Press, 1948).

14. Carney, *Women,* p. 107.

15. Curtius 8.4.30; Arrian 7.6.5.

16. Not even Darius's daughters knew Greek when they were captured: Diodorus 17.67.1. The same is true of Bessus, satrap of Bactria (Curtius 5.11.7), in spite of modern arguments that his province had been heavily colonized by Greeks before Alexander's reign: A. K. Narain, *The Indo-Greeks* (Oxford: Clarendon Press, 1957), pp. 1–6, weakly restated in "The Greeks of Bactria and India," in *The Cambridge Ancient History,* ed. A. Astin et al. (Cambridge: Cambridge University Press, 1989), 8:389, n. 8. Roxane would have had no experience with her husband's language or culture, since even the Branchidae had lost these traits.

17. Again, it is possible that the seasons were affected in these years by a rare cooling trend: see chapter 2.

18. Curtius 8.4.1–17; *Metz Epitome* 24–27. Ice brought down an MH-60 helicopter loaded with Green Berets early in Operation Enduring Freedom, nearly causing the first coalition casualties: Tommy Franks, *American Soldier* (New York: Regan Books, 2004), pp. 298–99.

19. Curtius 8.4.18–20; cf. Arrian 4.21.10 and A. B. Bosworth, *A Historical Commentary on Arrian's History of Alexander* (Oxford: Clarendon Press, 1995), 2:139.

20. Curtius 8.5.2; Arrian 4.22.1–2.

21. According to Curtius 8.4.30, the king's companions were ashamed that Oxyartes had become Alexander's father-in-law, but they kept silent on the matter out of fear.

22. Pierre Briant, *Histoire de l'empire perse de Cyrus à Alexandre* (Leiden: Nederlands Instituut voor het Nabije Oosten, 1996), 1:234–35.

23. Arrian 4.9.9–12.5; Curtius 8.5.5–24; Plutarch, *Alexander* 54; Justin 12.7.1–3. Note also Bosworth, *Historical Commentary,* 2:68–90.

24. Plutarch, *Alexander* 54.1–2; Arrian 4.10.1 and 4.12.7. For balance, see David Golan, "The Fate of a Court Historian, Callisthenes," *Athenaeum* 66 (1988): 99–120.

25. Plutarch, *Alexander* 55.1–2; Curtius 8.6.1; Arrian 4.12.6–7.

26. Arrian 4.13.1–14.2; Curtius 8.6.2–8.20; Plutarch, *Alexander* 55.3–8. See also Elizabeth Carney, "The Conspiracy of Hermolaus," *Classical Journal* 76 (1981): 223–31.

27. For details, consult Ernst Badian, "Conspiracies," in *Alexander the Great in Fact and Fiction,* ed. A. B. Bosworth and E. J. Baynham (Oxford: Oxford University Press, 2000), pp. 50–95. Philotas's case reminded everyone of the dire charges easily leveled under questionable circumstances.

28. The demise of Callisthenes was variously reported: Curtius 8.8.21–23; Arrian 4.14.3–4; Plutarch, *Alexander* 55.9. Justin 15.3.3–7 curiously reports that Callisthenes was tortured, had his ears, nose, and lips cut off, and was then hauled about in a cage with a dog to terrorize others. These details call to mind the treatment of Bessus and the scourge of the Devourer dogs. See appendix.

29. Johnson, "The Vanity of Human Wishes," 1.157–60.

30. Arrian 4.22.3. Many of these troops were probably mercenaries.

31. See, for example, the figures in Tables 4 and 5 of Donald Engels, *Alexander the Great and the Logistics of the Macedonian Army* (Berkeley: University of California Press, 1978), pp. 146–49. By contrast, in August

2003 the United States had 10,000 troops in Afghanistan, but 140,000 in Iraq.

32. When Alexander died in 323 B.C.E., there were more than 23,000 Greeks and Macedonians in Bactria: Diodorus 18.7.2.

33. Plutarch, *Alexander* 57.3.

34. Barsaentes was eventually turned in by the Indians: Arrian 3.25.8; Curtius 8.13.3–4 (including the rebel prince Damaraxus). Sisicottus was by this time reconciled to Alexander's regime, but he reminds us how readily the Afghan borderlands harbor fresh warlords: Arrian 4.30.4.

35. Arrian 4.22.4; Strabo 15.1.26.

36. Arrian 4.22.5.

37. Curtius 8.10.1–4; Arrian 4.22.6–7, with Bosworth, *Historical Commentary*, pp. 146–53.

38. Brian Robson, *The Road to Kabul: The Second Afghan War, 1878–1881* (London: Arms and Armour Press, 1986), p. 90.

39. Arrian 4.22.8; cf. Ernst Badian, "Alexander at Peucelaotis," *Classical Quarterly* 37 (1987): 117–28.

40. Curtius 8.10.4–12.4; Arrian 4.23–30; Justin 12.7.4–13; Plutarch, *Alexander* 58.6–9; *Metz Epitome* 35–48; Strabo 15.1.7–8; Diodorus 17.84.1–86.3 (resuming after a long lacuna). This operation closely resembles a rare Soviet winter offensive up the same valleys in 1985 (minus, of course, the air-assault regiment): Mohammad Yousaf and Mark Adkin, *Afghanistan—the Bear Trap: The Defeat of a Superpower* (Havertown, Pa.: Casemate, 2001), pp. 132–34.

41. Badian, "Alexander at Peucelaotis," p. 126. Of fundamental importance is A. B. Bosworth, *Alexander and the East: The Tragedy of Triumph* (Oxford: Oxford University Press, 1996), which emphasizes the theme of terror.

42. Curtius 8.10.17; Arrian 5.1.1–3.4; with Bosworth, *Historical Commentary*, pp. 197–219.

43. Arrian 4.25.4.

44. Sir Marc Aurel Stein, *On Alexander's Track to the Indus: Personal Narrative of Explorations on the North-West Frontier of India* (London,

1929; reprint, Edison, N.J.: Castle Books, 2004). See also Paul Bernard, "Greek Geography and Literary Fiction from Bactria to India: The Case of the Aornoi and Taxila," in *Coins, Art, and Chronology: Essays on the Pre-Islamic History of the Indo-Iranian Borderlands,* ed. Michael Alram and Deborah Klimburg-Salter (Vienna: Verlag der österreichischen Akademie der Wissenschaften, 1999), pp. 51–98.

45. The king had recently been hit in the shoulder by an arrow (Curtius 8.10.6; Arrian 4.23.3; Plutarch, *Moralia* 327B) and this time took an arrow in the ankle or calf: Arrian 4.26.4; Curtius 8.10.28–29; *Metz Epitome* 40; Plutarch, *Alexander* 28.2.

46. Bosworth, *Historical Commentary,* 2:172–73.

47. Stein, *Alexander's Track,* p. 45.

48. Diodorus 17.84.2–6; *Metz Epitome* 43–45; Arrian 4.27.3–4; Plutarch, *Alexander* 59.6–7.

49. Curtius 8.11.2–25; Diodorus 17.85.1–86.1; Arrian 4.28.1–30.4; *Metz Epitome* 46–47; Plutarch, *Alexander* 58.5; Justin 12.7.12–13; Strabo 15.1.8. This Aornus is not to be confused with the city of the same name north of the Hindu Kush.

50. Diodorus 17.86.1; Curtius 8.12.1–3.

51. Diodorus 17.86.3; Curtius 8.12.4; Arrian 4.30.9.

CHAPTER SIX. DARK SHADOWS

1. Yossef Bodansky, "Soviet Military Involvement in Afghanistan," in *Afghanistan: The Great Game Revisited,* ed. Rosanne Klass (New York: Freedom House, 1987), p. 234.

2. N. G. L. Hammond, *The Genius of Alexander the Great* (Chapel Hill: University of North Carolina Press, 1997), pp. 136 and 159.

3. Arrian 5.20.7; cf. A. B. Bosworth, *A Historical Commentary on Arrian's History of Alexander* (Oxford: Clarendon Press, 1995), 2:320–22.

4. For the sources and discussion, see Frank Holt, "The Hyphasis 'Mutiny': A Source Study," *Ancient World* 5 (1982): 33–59.

5. As, for example, at Alexandria/Begram: Arrian 4.22.5. Coenus

himself was probably ill at the time of the speech: Frank Holt, "The Death of Coenus: Another Study in Method," *Ancient History Bulletin* 14.1–2 (2000): 54–55.

6. Ian Worthington, "How 'Great' was Alexander?" *Ancient History Bulletin* 13.2 (1999): 44, answered by Frank Holt, "Alexander the Great Today: In the Interests of Historical Accuracy?" *Ancient History Bulletin* 13.3 (1999): 112–13, answered by Worthington, "Alexander and 'the Interests of Historical Accuracy': A Reply," *Ancient History Bulletin* 13.4 (1999): 136–39, answered by Holt, "Death of Coenus," pp. 49–55.

7. Arrian 6.2.3. On Philip, see Waldemar Heckel, *The Marshals of Alexander's Empire* (London: Routledge, 1992), pp. 331–32.

8. Arrian 6.15.3; Curtius 9.8.9–10.

9. Curtius 9.4.26–5.30; Arrian 6.11.1–8; Diodorus 17.98–99; *Metz Epitome* 75–77. On this terrifying campaign, see A. B. Bosworth, *Alexander and the East: The Tragedy of Triumph* (Oxford: Oxford University Press, 1996), pp. 133–43.

10. According to Justin 12.5.13, Alexander had singled out the malcontents in his army to become settlers in Bactria and Sogdiana. Whether these soldiers were already seditious when left behind, or whether they earned that distinction later in this (and a second) rebellion, is uncertain.

11. Diodorus 17.99.5–6; Curtius 9.7.1–11; Frank Holt, *Alexander the Great and Bactria: The Formation of a Greek Frontier in Central Asia* (Leiden: Brill, 1988), pp. 82–85.

12. Philip Smucker, *Al Qaeda's Great Escape: The Military and the Media on Terror's Trail* (Washington, D.C.: Brassey's, 2004), esp. pp. 110 and 126–27.

13. Curtius 9.7.10–11.

14. Diodorus 18.7.1.

15. Diodorus 18.3.3.

16. Arrian 6.27.2; Curtius 10.1.20.

17. Ernst Badian, "Alexander the Great and the Loneliness of Power," *Journal of the Australasian Universities Language and Literature Association* 17 (1962): 80–91, and "Harpalus," *Journal of Hellenic Stud-*

ies 81 (1961): 16–43, especially pp. 21–24, where the phrase *reign of terror* is used prominently.

18. Badian, "Harpalus," pp. 16–43; and for more recent bibliography, Christopher Blackwell, *In the Absence of Alexander: Harpalus and the Failure of Macedonian Authority* (New York: Peter Lang, 1999).

19. Curtius 10.2.8–3.14; Diodorus 17.109.1–3; Arrian 7.8.1–11.9; Plutarch, *Alexander* 71.

20. Arrian 7.6.5. We have no data about the other two sons of Oxyartes mentioned in Curtius 8.4.22.

21. For example, A. B. Bosworth, "The Death of Alexander the Great: Rumour and Propaganda," *Classical Quarterly* 21 (1971): 112–36; Eugene Borza and J. Reames-Zimmerman, "Some New Thoughts on the Death of Alexander the Great," *Ancient World* 31.1 (2000): 22–30; Donald Engels, "A Note on Alexander's Death," *Classical Philology* 73 (1978): 224–28; David Oldach et al., "A Mysterious Death," *New England Journal of Medicine* 338 (1998): 1764–68; and C. N. Sbarounis, "Did Alexander the Great Die of Acute Pancreatitis?" *Journal of Clinical Gastroenterology* 24.4 (1997): 294–96.

22. Plutarch, *Alexander* 77.6.

23. Curtius 10.5.5–9.21; Diodorus 18.2.1–4; Justin 13.1–3; cf. Plutarch, *Alexander* 77.5.

24. Curtius 10.10.1–8; Diodorus 18.3.1–5; Justin 13.4. On Perdiccas's fascinating role, consult Heckel, *Marshals,* pp. 143–63. For the period in general, see A. B. Bosworth, *The Legacy of Alexander: Politics, Warfare, and Propaganda under the Successors* (Oxford: Oxford University Press, 2002).

25. Diodorus 18.4.8 and 7.1–5.

26. Paul Bernard, "Nouvelle contribution de l'épigraphie cunéiforme à l'histoire hellénistique," *Bulletin de Correspondance Hellenique* 114 (1990): 513–41.

27. Diodorus 18.7.5–9.

28. Holt, *Alexander and Bactria,* pp. 88–90, where the numbers are discussed.

29. Diodorus 18.36.5.

30. The date has been recently clarified by Edward Anson, "The Dating of Perdiccas' Death and the Assembly at Triparadeisos," *Greek, Roman, and Byzantine Studies* 43 (2003): 373–90.

31. Diodorus 19.11.3–9.

32. Helmut Berve, *Das Alexanderreich auf prosopographischer Grundlage,* vol. 2 (Munich: C. H. Beck'sche, 1926; reprint, Salem, N.H.: Ayer, 1988).

33. About an equal number of nameless women can be rooted out of the sources, but their anonymity also tells us something. See Waldemar Heckel, "Fifty-Two Anonymae in the History of Alexander," *Historia* 36.1 (1987): 114–19.

34. Diodorus 19.41.2; Plutarch, *Eumenes* 16.4 and 19.2. See N. G. L. Hammond, "Alexander's Veterans after His Death," *Greek, Roman, and Byzantine Studies* 25 (1984): 51–61; and Bosworth, *Legacy,* pp. 164–66.

35. A. B. Bosworth, "The Indian Satrapies under Alexander the Great," *Antichthon* 17 (1983): 45.

36. Holt, *Alexander and Bactria,* pp. 99–100, and "Response," in *Hellenistic History and Culture,* ed. Peter Green (Berkeley: University of California Press, 1993), pp. 54–64.

37. Susan Sherwin-White and Amélie Kuhrt, *From Samarkhand to Sardis: A New Approach to the Seleucid Empire* (Berkeley: University of California Press, 1993), pp. 25–27.

38. Frank Holt, *Thundering Zeus: The Making of Hellenistic Bactria* (Berkeley: University of California Press, 1999), pp. 24–29.

39. At Ipsus in Phrygia, Seleucus and Lysimachus defeated Antigonus the One-Eyed and his son Demetrius, the last to try to unify the empire: Diodorus 21.1.2; Plutarch, *Demetrius* 28.9. Antigonus, at the age of eighty-one, died fighting on the field of battle; on his career, see Richard Billows, *Antigonus the One-Eyed and the Creation of the Hellenistic State* (Berkeley: University of California Press, 1990).

40. Appian, *Syrian Wars* 62–63. See also Sherwin-White and Kuhrt, *Samarkhand to Sardis,* pp. 21–22.

41. Appian, *Syrian Wars* 64.

42. Thucydides 5.17–19. On the ancient anomaly of peacetime, see John Rich and Graham Shipley, eds., *War and Society in the Greek World* (London: Routledge, 1993), pp. 18–22.

43. Unless, of course, World War III has already begun: Thomas Friedman, *Longitudes and Attitudes: Exploring the World after September 11* (New York: Farrar, Straus, and Giroux, 2002), pp. 45–51 and 112.

44. Arnold Toynbee, *Some Problems in Greek History* (London: Oxford University Press, 1969), pp. 441–86.

CHAPTER SEVEN. THE LEGACY

1. Frank Holt, *Thundering Zeus: The Making of Hellenistic Bactria* (Berkeley: University of California Press, 1999), pp. 24–46.

2. For the inscription, see ibid., pp. 174–75.

3. Ibid., pp. 126–33 and 181–82.

4. Polybius 29.12.8. For a cautionary note, see Stanislaw Kalita, "Oblezenie, którego nie bylo? Uwagi na marginesie historii wojny Antiocha III z Eurtydemosem królem Baktrii," in *Studia Classica et Byzantina Alexandro Krawczuk Oblata,* ed. Maciej Salamon and Zdzislaw Kapera (Krakow: Uniwersytet Jagiellónski, 1996), pp. 47–55.

5. H. H. Schmitt, *Untersuchungen zur Geschichte Antiochos des Grossen und seiner Zeit* (Wiesbaden: Historia Einzelschriften, 1964); Susan Sherwin-White and Amélie Kuhrt, *From Samarkhand to Sardis: A New Approach to the Seleucid Empire* (Berkeley: University of California Press, 1993), pp. 188–216; Paul Bernard, "L'Asie Centrale et l'Empire séleucide," *Topoi* 4 (1994): 477–80; J. D. Lerner, *The Impact of Seleucid Decline on the Eastern Iranian Plateau* (Stuttgart: Franz Steiner Verlag, 1999), pp. 45–61.

6. Holt, *Thundering Zeus,* pp. 178–84.

7. Boccaccio, *De Casibus Illustrium Virorum* 6.6; see also Laurent de Premierfait's expanded French edition of 1409; and A. D. H. Bivar, "The Death of Eucratides in Medieval Tradition," *Journal of the Royal Asiatic Society* (1950): 7–13.

8. On Bayer's life, see the "Mémoire historique sur la vie et les ouvrages de Mr. Bayer," *Bibliothèque Germanique* 50 (1741): 99–113; and Knud Lunbaek, *T. S. Bayer (1694–1738): Pioneer Sinologist* (London: Curzon Press, 1986).

9. See Philip Kinns, "Two Eighteenth-Century Studies of Greek Coin Hoards: Bayer and Pellerin," in *Medals and Coins from Budé to Mommsen,* ed. Michael Crawford, C. Ligota, and J. Trapp (London: Warburg Institute, 1990), pp. 101–14.

10. Bayer, *Historia Regni Graecorum Bactriani* (St. Petersburg: Academia Scientiarum, 1738), pp. 99–100.

11. For the historical and intellectual context of Bruce's career, see Lindsey Hughes, *Russia in the Age of Peter the Great* (New Haven: Yale University Press, 1998).

12. Bayer did illustrate in *Historia Regni Graecorum Bactriani* a small coin that he thought might be attributable to Diodotus, but this was a mistaken attribution. See Holt, *Thundering Zeus,* pp. 72–73.

13. Marie-Thérèse Allouche-LePage, *L'Art monétaire des royaumes bactriens* (Paris: Didier, 1956), p. 198.

14. Joseph Pellerin, *Recueil de médailles de rois* (Paris: H. L. Guerin and L. F. Delatour, 1762), pp. 130–31.

15. Pellerin's coin has since been attributed to the same Eucratides who minted the tetradrachm published by Bayer. Pellerin's tetradrachm is now in the Bibliothèque nationale in Paris: Dominique Gerin, "Becker et les monnaies bactriennes du Cabinet de France," pt. 1, *Bulletin de la Société Francaise de Numismatique* 38.4 (1983): 305–9.

16. Pellerin, *Additions aux neuf volumes de Recueils de médailles de rois* (Paris: Desaint, 1778), pp. 95–106. This coin is also now part of the Bibliothèque nationale: Osmund Bopearachchi, *Monnaies gréco-bactriennes et indo-grecques: Catalogue raisonné* (Paris: Bibliothèque nationale, 1991), p. 154; cf. p. 205.

17. On the history of this coin, see D. Gerin, "Becker et les monnaies bactriennes du Cabinet de France," pt. 4, *Bulletin de la Société Française de Numismatique* 38.5 (1983): 321–22. It was actually acquired by the

Bibliothèque nationale in 1788, but not until 1799 was it classified as Bactrian. See Bopearachchi, *Monnaies,* p. 224.

18. On Moorcroft, see Garry Alder, *Beyond Bokhara: The Life of William Moorcroft, Asian Explorer and Pioneer Veterinary Surgeon* (London: Century, 1985); and Karl Meyer and Shareen Brysac, *Tournament of Shadows: The Great Game and the Race for Empire in Central Asia* (Washington, D.C.: Counterpoint, 1999), pp. 3–51.

19. Gordon Whitteridge, *Charles Masson of Afghanistan* (Warminster: Aris and Phillips, 1986); Elizabeth Errington, "Rediscovering the Collections of Charles Masson," in *Coins, Art, and Chronology: Essays on the Pre-Islamic History of the Indo-Iranian Borderlands,* ed. Michael Alram and Deborah Klimburg-Salter (Vienna: Verlag der österreichischen Akademie der Wissenschaften, 1999), pp. 207–37, and "Discovering Ancient Afghanistan: The Masson Collection," *Minerva* 13.6 (2002): 53–55, introducing a new exhibition at the British Museum.

20. Masson, "Second Memoir on the Ancient Coins Found at Beghram, in the Kohistan of Kabul," *Journal of the Asiatic Society* 49 (1836): 20.

21. James Lunt, *Bokhara Burnes* (London: Faber and Faber, 1969), pp. 26–27.

22. As recorded in the diary of Lady Sale: Patrick Macrory, ed., *Lady Sale: The First Afghan War* (Hamden, Conn.: Archon Books, 1969), p. 87. She also collected Bactrian coins: Alexander Cunningham, *Coins of Alexander's Successors in the East* (London, 1844; reprint, Chicago: Argonaut, 1969), pp. 100, 166, and 177.

23. J. G. Droysen, *Geschichte der Diadochen* (Gotha, Germany: n.p., 1836). On Droysen himself, see Arnaldo Momigliano, "J. G. Droysen between Greeks and Jews," in *Essays in Ancient and Modern Historiography* (Middletown, Conn.: Wesleyan University Press, 1977), pp. 307–24; and Robert Southard, *Droysen and the Prussian School of History* (Lexington: University of Kentucky Press, 1995).

24. These famous phrases are quoted from the poem "To Helen" by Edgar Allan Poe. For a stimulating review of approaches to Hellenistic history, see Stanley Burstein, "The Legacy of Alexander: New Ways

of Being Greek in the Hellenistic Period," in *Crossroads of History: The Age of Alexander,* ed. Waldemar Heckel and Lawrence Tritle (Claremont, Calif.: Regina Books, 2003), pp. 217–42.

25. See also 2 Maccabees 4:13.

26. B. V. Lunin, "Uzbekskii arkheolog-liubitel' i sobiratel' drevnostei Akram-Palvan Askarov," *Obscestvennye Nauki v Uzbekistane* 6 (1960): 74.

27. At Merv, General Komarov, early in the twentieth century, employed a force of about one hundred Cossacks to collect the coins. Ibid.

28. The finds of this period are discussed in Cunningham, *Coins;* the author was one of the most active collectors of the time.

29. The existence of subkings, long inferred from the coinage, has been confirmed by a rare document: J. R. Rea, R. C. Senior, and A. S. Hollis, "A Tax Receipt from Hellenistic Bactria," *Zeitschrift fur Papyrologie und Epigraphik* 104 (1994): 261–80. This parchment shows that Antimachus I Theos ruled with two junior partners, Antimachus II and Eumenes.

30. Holt, *Thundering Zeus,* pp. 19–20 and 137.

31. R. B. Whitehead, "The Eastern Satrap Sophytes," *Numismatic Chronicle* (1943): 60–72; and Osmund Bopearachchi, "Sophytes, the Enigmatic Ruler of Central Asia" (in English and Greek), *Nomismatika Chronika* 15 (1996): 19–39.

32. Frank Holt, "Mimesis in Metal: The Fate of Greek Culture on Bactrian Coins," in *The Eye Expanded: Life and the Arts in Greco-Roman Antiquity,* ed. Frances Titchener and Richard Moorton Jr. (Berkeley: University of California Press, 1999), pp. 93–104.

33. An excellent presentation of these coins may be found in Osmund Bopearachchi, *Monnaies,* devoted to the French national collection. Other important resources include: Frank Holt, "The So-Called Pedigree Coins of the Bactrian Greeks," in *Ancient Coins of the Graeco-Roman World,* ed. W. Heckel and R. Sullivan (Waterloo, Ontario: Wilfrid Laurier University Press, 1984), pp. 69–91; A. N. Lahiri, *Corpus of Indo-Greek Coins* (Calcutta: Poddar Publications, 1965); and Michael Mitchiner, *Indo-Greek and Indo-Scythian Coinage,* vol. 1 (London: Hawkins, 1975).

34. Frank Holt, "Alexander the Great and the Spoils of War," *Ancient Macedonia* 6 (1999): 499–506; and P. J. Casey, *Understanding Ancient Coins* (Norman: University of Oklahoma Press, 1986), pp. 51–53 and 61–62.

35. For further details, see Frank Holt, *Alexander the Great and the Mystery of the Elephant Medallions* (Berkeley: University of California Press, 2003), pp. 27–41.

36. Fully elaborated in the Russian publication of Boris Litvinsky and Igor Pichikyan, *Ellinisticheskiy khram Oksa v Baktrii (Iuzhnyi Tadzhikistan),* 2 vols. (Moscow: Vostochnaya Literatura, 2000).

37. Raoul Curiel and Gerard Fussman, *Le trésor monétaire de Qunduz* (Paris: Klincksieck, 1965).

38. Raoul Curiel and Daniel Schlumberger, *Trésors monétaires d'Afghanistan* (Paris: Klincksieck, 1953), pp. 65–91; and T. N. Ramachandran and Y. D. Sharma, *Archaeological Reconnaissance in Afghanistan: Preliminary Report of the Indian Archaeological Delegation* (New Delhi: Department of Archaeology, 1956).

39. Curiel and Schlumberger, *Trésors monétaires,* pp. 92–99.

40. Hyla Troxell and William Spengler, "A Hoard of Early Greek Coins from Afghanistan," *American Numismatic Society Museum Notes* 15 (1969): 1–19.

41. Olivier Guillaume, ed., *Graeco-Bactrian and Indian Coins from Afghanistan* (Delhi: Oxford University Press, 1991); and Frank Holt, "The Euthydemid Coinage of Bactria: Further Hoard Evidence from Ai Khanoum," *Revue Numismatique* 23 (1981): 7–44.

42. Osmund Bopearachchi, "Découvertes récentes de trésors indogrecs: Nouvelles données historiques," *Comptes Rendus de l'Académie des Inscriptions et Belles-Lettres* (1995): 616–20.

43. Victor Sarianidi, *The Golden Hoard of Bactria* (St. Petersburg: Aurora Art Publishers, 1985).

44. For examples, Osmund Bopearachchi, "Recent Coin Hoard Evidence on Pre-Kushana Chronology," in *Coins, Art, and Chronology: Essays on the Pre-Islamic History of the Indo Iranian Borderlands,* ed. Michael Alram and Deborah Klimburg-Salter (Vienna: Verlag der

österreichischen Akademie der Wissenschaften, 1999), pp. 99–149; Edvard Rtveladze, "La circulation monétaire au nord de l'Oxus à l'époque gréco-bactrienne," *Revue Numismatique* 26 (1984): 61–76.

45. The estimate has risen steadily: see Osmund Bopearachchi, "La circulation et la production monétaires en Asie centrale et dans l'Inde du nord-ouest (avant et après la conquete d'Alexandre," *Indologica Taurinensia* 25 (1999–2001): 61. See also Bopearachchi, "Le dépôt de Mir Zakah," *Dossiers d'Archéologie* 248 (1999): 36–43.

46. Data derived from Margaret Thompson, Otto Mørkholm, and Colin Kraay, eds., *An Inventory of Greek Coin Hoards* (New York: American Numismatic Society, 1973) and the periodical *Coin Hoards*.

47. Emmanuel de Roux and Roland-Pierre Paringaux, *Razzia sur l'art* (Paris: Fayard, 1999), pp. 211–30; Nancy Dupree, "Museum under Siege," *Archaeology* 49 (March–April 1996): 42–51; Carlotta Gall, "A Hoard of Gold That Afghanistan Quietly Saved," *New York Times,* Thursday, June 24, 2004.

48. Kristin Romey, "The Race to Save Afghan Culture," *Archaeology* 55 (May–June 2002): 18–25; Robert Knox, "Afghanistan's Archaeological Heritage: The Long Road Ahead," *Minerva* 14.4 (2003): 51–52; Osmund Bopearachchi, "Vandalized Afghanistan," *Nomismatika Chronika* 21 (2002): 91–96. I have recently been informed by experts on the scene that at least some of the coins have been found, contrary to earlier reports.

49. Romey, "Race to Save Afghan Culture," pp. 22 and 24.

50. John Burns, "In Kabul's Museum, the Past Finds Its Ruin in the Present," *New York Times,* November 30, 1996; and Celestine Bohlen, "Afghan Art Dispersed by the Winds of War," *New York Times,* November 1, 2001.

51. I have personally notified a number of buyers and sellers on eBay that coins listed there were looted from the Kabul Museum, such as Qunduz Hoard nos. 539, 323, 145, 573, 589, and 372.

52. Burns, "Kabul's Museum."

53. Bopearachchi, "Vandalized Afghanistan," p. 92.

54. On Mullah Omar's decision to destroy the Buddhas, see Steve Coll, *Ghost Wars: The Secret History of the CIA, Afghanistan, and Bin*

Laden, from the Soviet Invasion to September 10, 2001 (New York: Penguin Press, 2004), pp. 348–50; and Philippe Flandrin, *Afghanistan: Les trésors sataniques* (Monaco: Éditions du Rocher, 2002).

55. On salvage efforts, see Kristin Romey, "Rebuilding the Bamiyan Buddhas," *Archaeology* 55 (2002): 23.

56. Metal detectors have been used, among other places, at Ai Khanoum: Paul Bernard, "Afghanistan: L'Abolition d'une mémoire," *International Numismatic Newsletter* 26 (1995): 8.

CHAPTER EIGHT. CONCLUSION

1. Tennyson's lines (146–48) refer to *Phaedo,* where Plato argues that suicide violates our duty to the gods.

2. Among standard reference works, *The Oxford Classical Dictionary,* 3rd ed., lists only two Platos: the philosopher and a poorly attested comic playwright. The mammoth eighty-four-volume *Real-Encyclopaedie der classischen Altertumswissenschaft* devotes 195 columns to *the* Plato, and just 7 to all the others combined.

3. Marsilio Ficino, *Opera Omnia,* 2 vols. (1576; reprint, Turin: Bottega d'Erasmo, 1962), 2:1557.

4. J. Delmerick, Letter to the editor, *Proceedings of the Asiatic Society of Bengal* (February 1872): 34–35.

5. W. S. W. Vaux, "On an Unique Coin of Plato, a King of Bactria," *Numismatic Chronicle* 15 (1875): 2–3.

6. Ibid., pp. 18–19. The Athenian soldier is mentioned in Curtius 5.7.12.

7. Alexander Burnes, *Travels into Bokhara* (London: John Murray, 1834), 1:222.

8. Eugene Schuyler, *Turkistan: Notes of a Journey in Russian Turkistan, Khokand, Bukhara, and Kuldja* (New York: Scribner, Armstrong, and Company, 1876), p. 237.

9. The rumors persist amid current fighting: Philip Smucker, *Al Qaeda's Great Escape: The Military and the Media on Terror's Trail* (Wash-

ington, D.C.: Brassey's, 2004), p. 18. Attempts to find the descendants of Alexander's Greek settlers include folklore studies and, now, DNA testing. See Gail Trail, "Tsyam Revisited: A Study of Kalasha Origins," in *Proceedings of the Second International Hindu Kush Cultural Conference,* ed. Elena Bashir and Israr-ud-Din (Oxford: Oxford University Press, 1996), pp. 559–76.

10. Some uncritical scholars carried Tarn's thesis to the extreme. Whereas Tarn acknowledged the eventual collapse of Alexander's dream in Bactria, others moved in the direction of fairy tales: see the remarks on this subject by Frank Holt, *Thundering Zeus: The Making of Hellenistic Bactria* (Berkeley: University of California Press, 1999), p. 11.

11. A. K. Narain, *The Indo-Greeks* (Oxford: Clarendon Press, 1957), p. 11.

12. Expressed by Peter Green, *Alexander to Actium: The Historical Evolution of the Hellenistic Age* (Berkeley: University of California Press, 1990), p. xxi. See also the very useful volume, Andrew Erskin, ed., *A Companion to the Hellenistic World* (Oxford: Blackwell, 2003).

13. W. W. Tarn, *The Greeks in Bactria and India,* 3rd ed. (Chicago: Ares Press, 1984), pp. 209–10.

14. Narain, *Indo-Greeks,* pp. 71–72.

15. Strabo 15.1.3 reports from an earlier source (Apollodorus of Artemita) that Eucratides ruled a thousand cities; see also Justin 41.4.5.

16. To date, eight volumes of *Fouilles d'Aï Khanoum* have appeared, each devoted to a key aspect of the site (coins, temple, ramparts, gymnasium, treasury, etc.). For an English summary, see Paul Bernard, "An Ancient Greek City in Central Asia," *Scientific American* 246 (1982): 148–59. A comprehensive list of the chief excavator's publications may be found in *Bulletin of the Asia Institute* 12 (1998): 3–8, in a volume honoring his work.

17. On the discovery, see Paul Bernard, "Aï Khanoum en Afghanistan hier (1964–1978) et aujourd'hui (2001): Un site en péril, perspectives d'avenir," *Comptes Rendus de l'Académie des Inscriptions et Belles-Lettres* (2001): 971–77.

18. Ibid., pp. 977–90.

19. Ibid., p. 1019.

20. Louis Robert, "De Delphes à l'Oxus," *Comptes Rendus de l'Académie des Inscriptions et Belles-Lettres* (1968): 416–57.

21. Holt, *Thundering Zeus,* pp. 37–46.

22. Kipling, "We and They."

23. Claude Rapin, *Indian Art from Afghanistan: The Legend of Sakuntala and the Indian Treasure of Eucratides at Ai Khanoum* (New Delhi: Manohar, 1996).

24. Frantz Grenet, "L'Onomastique iranienne à Ai Khanoum," *Bulletin de Correspondance Hellénique* 107 (1983): 373–81.

25. On the destruction of Ai Khanoum, see Bernard, "Ai Khanoum en Afghanistan," pp. 991–1027.

26. Anna Badkhen, "War Gives Cover to Antiquities Looter," *San Francisco Chronicle,* Saturday, November 3, 2001.

27. Frantz Grenet, *Les pratiques funéraires dans l'Asie centrale sédentaire de la conquête grecque à l'Islamisation* (Paris: CNRS, 1984), pp. 73–75.

APPENDIX. ANCIENT SOURCES

1. Arrian 1.16.4; Plutarch, *Alexander* 4.1; Cicero, *Epistulae ad Familiares* 5.12.7; Pliny, *Natural History* 7.125. The edict cited by Apuleius, *Florida* 7, is surely an exaggeration. See the important study by Andrew Stewart, *Faces of Power: Alexander's Image and Hellenistic Politics* (Berkeley: University of California Press, 1993).

2. On this and other lost Alexander sources, see the classic work of Lionel Pearson, *The Lost Histories of Alexander the Great* (London: American Philological Association, 1960).

3. For instance, the king issued a stern rebuke and tossed the manuscript of Aristobulus into the Hydaspes River: Lucian, *Quomodo historia conscribenda sit* 12.

4. Pearson, *Lost Histories,* examines each of these sources. What remains of their work was gathered into Felix Jacoby's multivolume Ger-

man collection, *Die Fragmente der griechischen Historiker* (Leiden: Brill, 1926–1958). A new English edition of this indispensable reference is now being prepared by Brill. Meanwhile, some convenient translations are available in Charles A. Robinson Jr., *The History of Alexander the Great,* vol. 1 (Providence: Brown University Press, 1953; reprint, Chicago: Ares Press, 1996); Ian Worthington, ed., *Alexander the Great: A Reader* (London: Routledge, 2003); and Waldemar Heckel and J. C. Yardley, *Alexander the Great: Historical Sources in Translation* (Oxford: Blackwell, 2004).

5. The correspondence and royal journal *(ephemerides)* of Alexander are subjects of much speculation and debate: Edward Anson, "The Ephemerides of Alexander the Great," *Historia* 45.4 (1996): 501–4; Ernst Badian, "The Ring and the Book," in *Zu Alexander der Grosse,* ed. W. Will and J. Heinrichs (Amsterdam: Hakkert, 1987), 1:605–25; J. R. Hamilton, "The Letters in Plutarch's *Alexander,"* *Proceedings of the African Classical Association* 4 (1961): 9–20.

6. R. M. Errington, "Bias in Ptolemy's History of Alexander," *Classical Quarterly* 63 (1969): 233–42; contra, Joseph Roisman, "Ptolemy and His Rivals in His Alexander History," *Classical Quarterly* 34 (1984): 373–85.

7. Translated into English by C. Bradford Welles, *Diodorus of Sicily* (Cambridge: Harvard University Press, 1963), vol. 8 in the Loeb Classical Library series.

8. English translations include: J. C. Rolfe, *Quintus Curtius, History of Alexander,* 2 vols. (Cambridge: Harvard University Press, 1971); John Yardley, *Quintus Curtius Rufus, the History of Alexander* (Harmondsworth: Penguin, 1984), which includes notes by Waldemar Heckel. See also Elizabeth Baynham, *Alexander the Great: The Unique History of Quintus Curtius* (Ann Arbor: University of Michigan Press, 1998).

9. Translated in the Loeb series by F. C. Babbitt, Plutarch, *Moralia* (Cambridge: Harvard University Press, 1936), vol. 4.

10. English translations include: Bernadotte Perrin, *Plutarch's Lives* (Cambridge: Harvard University Press, 1919), vol. 7 in the Loeb series; Ian Scott-Kilvert, *The Age of Alexander: Nine Greek Lives by Plutarch*

(Harmondsworth: Penguin, 1973). See also, J. R. Hamilton, *Plutarch, "Alexander": A Commentary* (Oxford: Clarendon Press, 1969).

11. Translations: P. A. Brunt, *Arrian, History of Alexander and Indica,* 2 vols. (Cambridge: Harvard University Press, 1976) in the Loeb series; Aubrey de Sélincourt, *Arrian, the Campaigns of Alexander* (Harmondsworth: Penguin, 1971), which includes notes by J. R. Hamilton. See also Philip Stadter, *Arrian of Nicomedia* (Chapel Hill: University of North Carolina Press, 1980); and A. B. Bosworth, *From Arrian to Alexander: Studies in Historical Interpretation* (Oxford: Clarendon Press, 1988).

12. This so-called Great Digression (Arrian 4.7.4–14.4) falls precisely at the center of Arrian's history.

13. English translation: J. C. Yardley, *Justin, Epitome of the Philippic History of Pompeius Trogus* (Oxford: Clarendon Press, 1997), vol. 1, with commentary by Waldemar Heckel.

14. A few other ancient authors include incidental references to Alexander, most notably the geographer Strabo and the gossipy Athenaeus. A collection of exotic tales called the *Alexander Romance* also survives, but it is more fiction than fact. A brief synopsis of Alexander's career once existed in Metz (the *Metz Epitome*), but it was lost in the bombing of World War II. Fortunately, a transcription survives. Nonliterary sources such as coins, art, and archaeology fill in some major gaps. See, for example, Frank Holt, *Alexander the Great and the Mystery of the Elephant Medallions* (Berkeley: University of California Press, 2003).

15. These direct citations are called fragments of the lost works. Jacoby, *Die Fragmente,* numbers each one. Scholars refer to them as, say, *FGrH* 134 F5, which means fragment number 5 of the writer Onesicritus (historian number 134 in Jacoby's list). This fragment (about the Devourer dogs) is preserved in the *Geography* of Strabo (11.11.3).

16. On this problem, see Frank Holt, *Thundering Zeus: The Making of Hellenistic Bactria* (Berkeley: University of California Press, 1999), pp. 48–66; the main sources are translated there in appendix D (pp. 174–84).

17. Justin 41.6.

SELECT BIBLIOGRAPHY

Listed below are the major publications cited in the text and notes, with the exception of standard reference works, classical sources such as Plutarch and Arrian, other well-known literary works by such authors as Kipling and Tennyson, and brief newspaper items.

Adams, W. Lindsay. "Antipater and Cassander: Generalship on Restricted Resources in the Fourth Century." *Ancient World* 10 (1984): 79–88.

———. "Philip II, the League of Corinth, and the Governance of Greece." *Ancient Macedonia* 6 (1998): 15–22.

Alder, Garry. *Beyond Bokhara: The Life of William Moorcroft, Asian Explorer and Pioneer Veterinary Surgeon.* London: Century, 1985.

Alexiev, Alex. *The War in Afghanistan: Soviet Strategy and the State of the Resistance.* Santa Monica, Calif.: Rand Corporation, 1984.

Allchin, F. R., and Norman Hammond. *The Archaeology of Afghanistan.* London: Academic Press, 1978.

Allouche-LePage, Marie-Thérèse. *L'Art monétaire des royaumes bactriens.* Paris: Didier, 1956.

Anderson, Jon Lee. *The Lion's Grave: Dispatches from Afghanistan.* New York: Grove Press, 2002.

Anson, Edward. "The Ephemerides of Alexander the Great." *Historia* 45.4 (1996): 501–4.

———. "The Dating of Perdiccas' Death and the Assembly at Triparadeisos." *Greek, Roman, and Byzantine Studies* 43 (2003): 373–90.

Arnold, Anthony. *The Fateful Pebble: Afghanistan's Role in the Fall of the Soviet Empire.* Novato, Calif.: Presidio Press, 1993.

Badian, Ernst. "Harpalus." *Journal of Hellenic Studies* 81 (1961): 16–43.

———. "Alexander the Great and the Loneliness of Power." *Journal of the Australasian Universities Language and Literature Association* 17 (1962): 80–91.

———. "Orientals in Alexander's Army." *Journal of Hellenic Studies* 85 (1965): 160–61.

———. "Alexander at Peucelaotis." *Classical Quarterly* 37 (1987): 117–28.

———. "The Ring and the Book." In *Zu Alexander der Grosse,* ed. W. Will and J. Heinrichs, 1:605–25. 2 vols. Amsterdam: Hakkert, 1987.

———. "Agis III: Revisions and Reflections." In *Ventures into Greek History,* ed. Ian Worthington, pp. 258–92. Oxford: Clarendon Press, 1994.

———. "Conspiracies." In *Alexander the Great in Fact and Fiction,* ed. A. B. Bosworth and E. J. Baynham, pp. 50–95. Oxford: Oxford University Press, 2000.

Bayer, Theophilus. *Historia Regni Graecorum Bactriani.* St. Petersburg: Academia Scientiarum, 1738.

Baynham, Elizabeth. *Alexander the Great: The Unique History of Quintus Curtius.* Ann Arbor: University of Michigan Press, 1998.

Bergen, Peter. *Holy War, Inc.: Inside the Secret World of Osama bin Laden.* New York: Touchstone, 2001.

Bernard, Paul. "Alexander et Ai Khanoum." *Journal des Savants* (1982): 125–38.

———. "An Ancient Greek City in Central Asia." *Scientific American* 246 (1982): 148–59.

———. "Fouilles de la mission franco-soviétique à l'ancienne Samarkand (Afrasiab): Première campagne, 1989." *Comptes Rendus de l'Académie des Inscriptions et Belles-Lettres* (1990): 356–80.

———. "Nouvelle contribution de l'épigraphie cunéiforme à l'histoire hellénistique." *Bulletin de Correspondance Hellenique* 114 (1990): 513–41.

———. "L'Asie centrale et l'Empire séleucide." *Topoi* 4 (1994): 473–511.

———. "Afghanistan: L'Abolition d'une mémoire." *International Numismatic Newsletter* 26 (1995): 6–8.

———. "Maracanda-Afrasiab colonie grecque." *Atti dei Convegni Lincei* 127 (1996): 331–65.

———. "Greek Geography and Literary Fiction from Bactria to India: The Case of the Aornoi and Taxila." In *Coins, Art, and Chronology: Essays on the Pre-Islamic History of the Indo-Iranian Borderlands,* ed. Michael Alram and Deborah Klimburg-Salter, pp. 51–98. Vienna: Verlag der österreichischen Akademie der Wissenschaften, 1999.

———. "Ai Khanoum en Afghanistan hier (1964–1976) et aujourd'hui (2001): Un site en péril, perspectives d'avenir." *Comptes Rendus de l'Académie des Inscriptions et Belles-Lettres* (2001): 971–1029.

Berve, Helmut. *Das Alexanderreich auf prosopographischer Grundlage.* 2 vols. Munich: C. H. Beck'sche, 1926; reprint, Salem, N.H.: Ayer, 1988.

Billows, Richard A. *Antigonos the One-Eyed and the Creation of the Hellenistic State.* Berkeley: University of California Press, 1990.

Bivar, A. D. H. "The Death of Eucratides in Medieval Tradition." *Journal of the Royal Asiatic Society* (1950): 7–13.

Blackwell, Christopher. *In the Absence of Alexander: Harpalus and the Failure of Macedonian Authority.* New York: Peter Lang, 1999.

Bloedow, Edmund. "On the Crossing of Rivers: Alexander's Διφθεραι." *Klio* 84 (2002): 57–75.

———. "Why Did Philip and Alexander Launch a War against the Persian Empire?" *L'Antiquité Classique* 72 (2003): 261–74.

Bodansky, Yossef. "Soviet Military Involvement in Afghanistan." In *Afghanistan: The Great Game Revisited,* ed. Rosanne Klass, pp. 229–85. New York: Freedom House, 1987.

Bopearachchi, Osmund. *Monnaies gréco-bactriennes et indo-grecques: Catalogue raisonné.* Paris: Bibliothèque nationale, 1991.

———. "Découvertes récentes de trésors indo-grecs: Nouvelles données historiques." *Comptes Rendus de l'Académie des Inscriptions et Belles-Lettres* (1995): 611–29.

———. "Sophytes, the Enigmatic Ruler of Central Asia" (in English and Greek). *Nomismatika Chronika* 15 (1996): 19–39.

———. "Le dépôt de Mir Zakah." *Dossiers d'Archéologie* 248 (1999): 36–43.

———. "Recent Coin Hoard Evidence on Pre-Kushana Chronology." In *Coins, Art, and Chronology: Essays on the Pre-Islamic History of the Indo Iranian Borderlands,* ed. Michael Alram and Deborah Klimburg-Salter, pp. 99–149. Vienna: Verlag der österreichischen Akademie der Wissenschaften, 1999.

———. "La circulation et la production monétaires en Asie centrale et dans l'Inde du nord-ouest (avant et après la conquête d'Alexandre)." *Indologica Taurinensia* 25 (1999–2001): 15–121.

———. "Vandalized Afghanistan." *Nomismatika Chronika* 21 (2002): 91–96.

Borza, Eugene. "The Symposium at Alexander's Court." *Ancient Macedonia* 3 (1983): 45–55.

———. *In the Shadow of Olympus: The Emergence of Macedon.* Princeton: Princeton University Press, 1990.

Borza, Eugene, and J. Reames-Zimmerman. "Some New Thoughts on the Death of Alexander the Great." *Ancient World* 31.1 (2000): 22–30.

Bosworth, A. B. "The Death of Alexander the Great: Rumour and Propaganda." *Classical Quarterly* 21 (1971): 112–36.

———. "Alexander and the Iranians." *Journal of Hellenic Studies* 100 (1980): 1–21.

———. *A Historical Commentary on Arrian's History of Alexander.* Vols. 1 and 2. Oxford: Clarendon Press, 1980, 1995.

———. "A Missing Year in the History of Alexander the Great." *Journal of Hellenic Studies* 101 (1981): 17–37.

———. "The Impossible Dream: W. W. Tarn's *Alexander* in Retrospect." *Ancient Society* 13 (1983): 131–50.

————. "The Indian Satrapies under Alexander the Great." *Antichthon* 17 (1983): 37–46.

————. *Conquest and Empire: The Reign of Alexander the Great.* Cambridge: Cambridge University Press, 1988.

————. *From Arrian to Alexander: Studies in Historical Interpretation.* Oxford: Clarendon Press, 1988.

————. *Alexander and the East: The Tragedy of Triumph.* Oxford: Oxford University Press, 1996.

————. "The Tumult and the Shouting: Two Interpretations of the Cleitus Episode." *Ancient History Bulletin* 10.1 (1996): 19–30.

————. *The Legacy of Alexander: Politics, Warfare, and Propaganda under the Successors.* Oxford: Oxford University Press, 2002.

Bowden, Mark. "The Kabul-ki Dance." *Atlantic Monthly* (November 2002): 65–87.

Boyce, Mary. *A History of Zoroastrianism.* 3 vols. Leiden: Brill, 1975.

Bradsher, Henry. *Afghanistan and the Soviet Union.* Durham, N.C.: Duke University Press, 1983.

Briant, Pierre. *L'Asie centrale et les royaumes proche-orientaux du premier millénaire (c. VIIIe–IVe siècles avant notre ère).* Paris: Èditions Recherche sur les Civilisations, 1984.

————. *Histoire de l'empire perse de Cyrus à Alexandre.* 2 vols. Leiden: Nederlands Instituut voor het Nabije Oosten, 1996.

————. *Darius dans l'ombre d'Alexandre.* Paris: Fayard, 2003.

Burnes, Alexander. *Travels into Bokhara.* 3 vols. London: John Murray, 1834.

Burstein, Stanley. *Graeco-Africana: Studies in the History of Greek Relations with Egypt and Nubia.* New Rochelle: Aristide Caratzas, 1995.

————. "The Legacy of Alexander: New Ways of Being Greek in the Hellenistic Period." In *Crossroads of History: The Age of Alexander,* ed. Waldemar Heckel and Lawrence Tritle, pp. 217–42. Claremont, Calif.: Regina Books, 2003.

Byford, Grenville. "The Wrong War." *Foreign Affairs* 81.4 (2002): 34–43.

Byron, Robert. *The Road to Oxiana.* 1937. Reprint, New York: Oxford University Press, 1982.

Carney, Elizabeth. "The Conspiracy of Hermolaus." *Classical Journal* 76 (1981): 223–31.

———. "The Death of Clitus." *Greek, Roman, and Byzantine Studies* 22 (1981): 149–60.

———. "Artifice and Alexander History." In *Alexander the Great in Fact and Fiction,* ed. A. B. Bosworth and E. J. Baynham, pp. 263–85. Oxford: Oxford University Press, 2000.

———. *Women and Monarchy in Macedonia.* Norman: University of Oklahoma Press, 2000.

Cary, Max. *The Geographic Background of Greek and Roman History.* Oxford: Clarendon Press, 1949.

Casey, P. J. *Understanding Ancient Coins.* Norman: University of Oklahoma Press, 1986.

Clarke, Richard. *Against All Enemies: Inside America's War on Terror.* New York: Free Press, 2004.

Coin Hoards. 8 vols. London: Royal Numismatic Society, 1975–1994.

Coll, Steve. *Ghost Wars: The Secret History of the CIA, Afghanistan, and Bin Laden, from the Soviet Invasion to September 10, 2001.* New York: Penguin Press, 2004.

Cordesman, Anthony. *The Lessons of Afghanistan: War Fighting, Intelligence, and Force Transformation.* Washington, D.C.: Center for Strategic and International Studies, 2002.

Cunningham, Alexander. *Coins of Alexander's Successors in the East.* London, 1844. Reprint, Chicago: Argonaut, 1969.

Curiel, Raoul, and Gerard Fussman. *Le trésor monétaire de Qunduz.* Paris: Klincksieck, 1965.

Curiel, Raoul, and Daniel Schlumberger. *Trésors monétaires d'Afghanistan.* Paris: Klincksieck, 1953.

Delmerick, J. Letter to the editor. *Proceedings of the Asiatic Society of Bengal* (February 1872): 34–35.

Denker, Debra. "Along Afghanistan's War-Torn Frontier." *National Geographic* 167.6 (1985): 772–97.

Droysen, J. G. *Geschichte der Diadochen.* Gotha, Germany: n.p., 1836.

Dupree, Louis. *Afghanistan.* Princeton: Princeton University Press, 1980.

Dupree, Nancy. "Museum under Siege." *Archaeology* 49 (March–April 1996): 42–51.

Ellis, Walter. *Ptolemy of Egypt.* London: Routledge, 1994.

Engels, Donald. *Alexander the Great and the Logistics of the Macedonian Army.* Berkeley: University of California Press, 1978.

———. "A Note on Alexander's Death." *Classical Philology* 73 (1978): 224–28.

Errington, Elizabeth. "Rediscovering the Collections of Charles Masson." In *Coins, Art, and Chronology: Essays on the Pre-Islamic History of the Indo-Iranian Borderlands,* ed. Michael Alram and Deborah Klimburg-Salter, pp. 207–37. Vienna: Verlag der österreichischen Akademie der Wissenschaften, 1999.

———. "Discovering Ancient Afghanistan: The Masson Collection." *Minerva* 13.6 (2002): 53–55.

Errington, R. M. "Bias in Ptolemy's History of Alexander." *Classical Quarterly* 63 (1969): 233–42.

Erskine, Andrew, ed. *A Companion to the Hellenistic World.* Oxford: Blackwell, 2003.

Exum, Andrew. *This Man's Army: A Soldier's Story from the Front Lines of the War on Terrorism.* New York: Gotham Books, 2004.

Ficino, Marsilio. *Opera Omnia.* 2 vols. 1576. Reprint, Turin: Bottega d'Erasmo, 1962.

Flandrin, Philippe. *Afghanistan: Les trésors sataniques.* Monaco: Éditions du Rocher, 2002.

Flower, Michael. "Alexander the Great and Panhellenism." In *Alexander the Great in Fact and Fiction,* ed. A. B. Bosworth and E. J. Baynham, pp. 96–135. Oxford: Oxford University Press, 2000.

Franks, Tommy. *American Soldier.* New York: Regan Books, 2004.

Fraser, P. M. *Cities of Alexander the Great.* Oxford: Clarendon Press, 1996.

Friedman, Norman. *Terrorism, Afghanistan, and America's New Way of War.* Annapolis: U.S. Naval Institute, 2003.

Friedman, Thomas. *Longitudes and Attitudes: Exploring the World after September 11.* New York: Farrar, Straus, and Giroux, 2002.

Fuller, J. F. C. *The Generalship of Alexander the Great.* New Brunswick, N.J.: Rutgers University Press, 1960; reprint, New York: Da Capo Press, 1989.

Gannon, Kathy. "Afghanistan Unbound." *Foreign Affairs* 83.3 (2004): 35–46.

Gerin, Dominique. "Becker et les monnaies bactriennes du Cabinet de France." Pts. 1, 4. *Bulletin de la Société Française de Numismatique* 38.4 and 5 (1983): 305–9, 321–22.

Giustozzi, Antonio. *War, Politics, and Society in Afghanistan, 1978–1991.* Washington, D.C.: Georgetown University Press, 2000.

Golan, David. "The Fate of a Court Historian, Callisthenes." *Athenaeum* 66 (1988): 99–120.

Green, Peter. "The Movies Make Hay with the Classic World." *Horizon* 3.5 (1961): 52–57.

———. *Alexander to Actium: The Historical Evolution of the Hellenistic Age.* Berkeley: University of California Press, 1990.

Grenet, Frantz. "L'Onomastique iranienne à Ai Khanoum." *Bulletin de Correspondance Hellénique* 107 (1983): 373–81.

———. *Les pratiques funéraires dans l'Asie centrale sédentaire de la conquête grecque à l'Islamisation.* Paris: CNRS, 1984.

———. "Old Samarkand: Nexus of the Ancient World." *Archaeology Odyssey* 6.5 (September–October 2003): 26–37.

Grenet, Frantz, and Claude Rapin. "Alexander, Ai Khanum, Termez: Remarks on the Spring Campaign of 328." *Bulletin of the Asia Institute* 12 (1998): 79–89.

Griffin, Michael. *Reaping the Whirlwind: The Taliban Movement in Afghanistan.* London: Pluto Press, 2001.

Griffiths, John. *Afghanistan: A History of Conflict.* 2nd ed. London: Carlton Books, 2001.

Grudd, Håkan, et al. "A 7400-Year Tree Ring Chronology in Northern Swedish Lapland: Natural Climate Variability Expressed on Annual to Millennial Timescales." *Holocene* 12.6 (2002): 657–65.

Guillaume, Olivier, ed. *Graeco-Bactrian and Indian Coins from Afghanistan.* Delhi: Oxford University Press, 1991.

Habicht, Christian. *Athens from Alexander to Antony.* Cambridge: Harvard University Press, 1997.

Hamilton, J. R. "The Letters in Plutarch's *Alexander." Proceedings of the African Classical Association* 4 (1961): 9–20.

———. *Plutarch, "Alexander": A Commentary.* Oxford: Clarendon Press, 1969.

Hammond, N. G. L. "Training in the Use of the Sarissa and Its Effect in Battle, 359–333 B.C." *Antichthon* 14 (1980): 53–63.

———. "Alexander's Veterans after His Death." *Greek, Roman, and Byzantine Studies* 25 (1984): 51–61.

———. *Alexander the Great: King, Commander, and Statesman.* 2nd ed. Bristol: Bristol Press, 1989.

———. *The Macedonian State.* Oxford: Clarendon Press, 1989.

———. "The Macedonian Defeat Near Samarcand." *Ancient World* 22.2 (1991): 41–47.

———. *Philip of Macedon.* Baltimore: Johns Hopkins University Press, 1994.

———. *The Genius of Alexander the Great.* Chapel Hill: University of North Carolina Press, 1997.

Hanaway, William, Jr. "Anahita and Alexander." *Journal of the American Oriental Society* 102 (1982): 285–95.

Hanson, Victor. *The Western Way of War.* New York: Knopf, 1989.

Harmatta, Janos. "Alexander the Great in Central Asia." *Acta Antiqua Academiae Scientiarum Hungaricae* 39 (1999): 129–36.

Heckel, Waldemar. "Fifty-Two Anonymae in the History of Alexander." *Historia* 36.1 (1987): 114–19.

———. *The Marshals of Alexander's Empire.* London: Routledge, 1992.

Heckel, Waldemar, and J. C. Yardley. *Alexander the Great: Historical Sources in Translation.* Oxford: Blackwell, 2004.

Helama, Samuli, et al. "The Supra-Long Scots Pine Tree-Ring Record for Finnish Lapland: Part 2, Interannual to Centennial Variability in Summer Temperatures for 7500 Years." *Holocene* 12.6 (2002): 681–87.

Helton, Arthur. "Rescuing the Refugees." *Foreign Affairs* 81.2 (2002): 71–82.

Holt, Frank. "The Euthydemid Coinage of Bactria: Further Hoard Evidence from Ai Khanoum." *Revue Numismatique* 23 (1981): 7–44.

———. "The Hyphasis 'Mutiny': A Source Study." *Ancient World* 5 (1982): 33–59.

———. "The So-Called Pedigree Coins of the Bactrian Greeks." In *Ancient Coins of the Graeco-Roman World,* ed. W. Heckel and R. Sullivan, pp. 69–91. Waterloo, Ontario: Wilfrid Laurier University Press, 1984.

———. "Alexander's Settlements in Central Asia." *Ancient Macedonia* 4 (1986): 315–23.

———. *Alexander the Great and Bactria: The Formation of a Greek Frontier in Central Asia.* Leiden: Brill, 1988.

———. "Alexander the Great's Little Star." *History Today* 38 (September 1988): 31–39.

———. "Imperium Macedonicum and the East: The Problem of Logistics." *Ancient Macedonia* 5 (1993): 585–92.

———. "Response." In *Hellenistic History and Culture,* ed. Peter Green, pp. 54–64. Berkeley: University of California Press, 1993.

———. "Spitamenes against Alexander." *Historikogeographika* 4 (1994): 51–58.

———. "Alexander the Great and the Spoils of War." *Ancient Macedonia* 6 (1999): 499–506.

———. "Alexander the Great Today: In the Interests of Historical Accuracy?" *Ancient History Bulletin* 13.3 (1999): 111–17.

———. "Mimesis in Metal: The Fate of Greek Culture on Bactrian Coins." In *The Eye Expanded: Life and the Arts in Greco-Roman Antiquity,* ed. Frances Titchener and Richard Moorton Jr., pp. 93–104. Berkeley: University of California Press, 1999.

———. *Thundering Zeus: The Making of Hellenistic Bactria.* Berkeley: University of California Press, 1999.

———. "The Death of Coenus: Another Study in Method." *Ancient History Bulletin* 14.1–2 (2000): 49–55.

————. *Alexander the Great and the Mystery of the Elephant Medallions.* Berkeley: University of California Press, 2003.

Hopkirk, Peter. *The Great Game: The Struggle for Empire in Central Asia.* New York: Kodansha International, 1992.

Hughes, Lindsey. *Russia in the Age of Peter the Great.* New Haven: Yale University Press, 1998.

Imperial Hubris: Why the West Is Losing the War on Terror. Washington, D.C.: Brassey's, 2004.

Jalali, Ali Ahmad, and Lester Grau. *Afghan Guerilla Warfare: In the Words of the Mujahideen Fighters.* St. Paul, Minn.: MBI, 2001.

Junger, Sebastian. *Fire.* New York: W. W. Norton, 2001.

Kalita, Stanislaw. "Oblezenie, którego nie bylo? Uwagi na marginesie historii wojny Antiocha III z Eurtydemosem królem Baktrii." In *Studia Classica et Byzantina Alexandro Krawczuk Oblata,* ed. Maciej Salamon and Zdzislaw Kapera, pp. 47–55. Krakow: Uniwersytet Jagiellónski, 1996.

Kebric, Robert. "Old Age, the Ancient Military, and Alexander's Army: Positive Examples for a Graying America." *Gerontologist* 28 (1985): 298–302.

Keegan, John. "The Ordeal of Afghanistan." *Atlantic Monthly* (November 1985): 94–105.

Kinns, Philip. "Two Eighteenth-Century Studies of Greek Coin Hoards: Bayer and Pellerin." In *Medals and Coins from Budé to Mommsen,* ed. Michael Crawford, C. Ligota, and J. Trapp, pp. 101–14. London: Warburg Institute, 1990.

Klass, Roseanne, ed. *Afghanistan: The Great Game Revisited.* New York: Freedom House, 1987.

Knox, Robert. "Afghanistan's Archaeological Heritage: The Long Road Ahead." *Minerva* 14.4 (2003): 51–52.

Lahiri, A. N. *Corpus of Indo-Greek Coins.* Calcutta: Poddar Publications, 1965.

Lascaratos, John. "The Wounding of Alexander the Great in Cyropolis (329 B.C.): The First Reported Case of the Syndrome of Transient Cortical Blindness?" *History of Ophthalmology* 42.3 (1997): 283–87.

Latham, Ronald, trans. and ed. *The Travels of Marco Polo*. London: Penguin Books, 1958.

Lee, J. L. *The "Ancient Supremacy": Bukhara, Afghanistan, and the Battle for Balkh, 1731–1901*. Leiden: Brill, 1996.

Lerner, J. D. *The Impact of Seleucid Decline on the Eastern Iranian Plateau*. Stuttgart: Franz Steiner Verlag, 1999.

Litvinsky, Boris, and Igor Pichikyan. *Ellinisticheskiy khram Oksa v Baktrii (Iuzhnyi Tadzhikistan)*. 2 vols. Moscow: Vostochnaya Literatura, 2000.

Lunbaek, Knud. *T. S. Bayer (1694–1738): Pioneer Sinologist*. London: Curzon Press, 1986.

Lunin, B. V. "Uzbekskii arkheolog-liubitel' i sobiratel' drevnostei Akram-Palvan Askarov." *Obscestvennye Nauki v Uzbekistane* 6 (1960): 74.

Lunt, James. *Bokhara Burnes*. London: Faber and Faber, 1969.

Macrory, Patrick. *The Fierce Pawns*. Philadelphia: Lippincott, 1966.

————, ed. *Lady Sale: The First Afghan War*. Hamden, Conn.: Archon Books, 1969.

Mann, James. *Rise of the Vulcans: The History of Bush's War Cabinet*. New York: Viking, 2004.

Marsden, E. W. *The Campaign of Gaugamela*. Liverpool: Liverpool University Press, 1964.

Masson, Charles. "Second Memoir on the Ancient Coins Found at Beghram, in the Kohistan of Kabul." *Journal of the Asiatic Society* 49 (1836): 1–28.

Matinuddin, Kamal. *The Taliban Phenomenon: Afghanistan, 1994–1997*. Oxford: Oxford University Press, 1999.

May, Elmer, Gerald Stadler, and John Votaw. *Ancient and Medieval Warfare*. Wayne, N.J.: Avery, 1984.

McGirk, Tim. "A Dearth of Troops." *Time* 162.22 (December 1, 2003): 17.

"Mémoire historique sur la vie et les ouvrages de Mr. Bayer." *Bibliothèque Germanique* 50 (1741): 99–113.

Meyer, Karl. *The Dust of Empire: The Race for Mastery in the Asian Heartland*. New York: Century Foundation, 2003.

Meyer, Karl, and Shareen Brysac. *Tournament of Shadows: The Great Game and the Race for Empire in Central Asia.* Washington, D.C.: Counterpoint, 1999.

Milns, Robert. "The Army of Alexander the Great." In *Alexandre le Grand: Image et Réalité,* ed. Ernst Badian, pp. 87–130. Geneva: Fondation Hardt, 1976.

Mitchiner, Michael. *The Origins of Indian Coinage.* London: Hawkins, 1973.

———. *Indo-Greek and Indo-Scythian Coinage.* Vol. 1. London: Hawkins, 1975.

Momigliano, Arnaldo. *Essays in Ancient and Modern Historiography.* Middletown, Conn.: Wesleyan University Press, 1977.

Moore, Robin. *The Hunt for bin Laden: Task Force Dagger.* New York: Random House, 2003.

Narain, A. K. *The Indo-Greeks.* Oxford: Clarendon Press, 1957.

———. "The Greeks of Bactria and India." Pp. 338–421 in *The Cambridge Ancient History,* ed. A. Astin et al., vol. 8. Cambridge: Cambridge University Press, 1989.

Newell, Nancy, and Richard Newell. *The Struggle for Afghanistan.* Ithaca: Cornell University Press, 1981.

Newman, Cathy. "A Life Revealed." *National Geographic* 201.4 (2002): unnumbered.

Nikonorov, Valerii. *The Armies of Bactria, 700 B.C.–450 A.D.* 2 vols. Stockport: Montvert Publications, 1997.

Nojumi, Neamatollah. *The Rise of the Taliban.* New York: Palgrave, 2002.

Norris, James. *The First Afghan War, 1838–1842.* Cambridge: Cambridge University Press, 1967.

Nylander, Carl. "Darius III—the Coward King: Point and Counterpoint." In *Alexander the Great: Reality and Myth,* ed. Jesper Carlsen, Bodil Due, Otto Due, and Birte Poulsen, pp. 145–59. Rome: "L'Erma" di Bretschneider, 1993.

O'Hanlon, Michael. "A Flawed Masterpiece." *Foreign Affairs* 81.3 (2002): 47–63.

226 / *Select Bibliography*

Oldach, David, Robert Richard, E. N. Borza, and R. M. Benitez. "A Mysterious Death." *New England Journal of Medicine* 338 (1998): 1764–68.

Pearson, Lionel. *The Lost Histories of Alexander the Great*. London: American Philological Association, 1960.

Pellerin, Joseph. *Recueil de médailles de rois*. Paris: H. L. Guerin and L. F. Delatour, 1762.

———. *Additions aux neuf volumes de recueils de médailles de rois*. Paris: Desaint, 1778.

Philadelphia, Desa. "The Perils of Protest." *Time* 161.15 (April 14, 2003): 24.

Raimondo, Lois. "Long Road Home: A Story of War and Revelation in Afghanistan." *National Geographic* 201.6 (June 2002): 82–105.

Ramachandran, T. N., and Y. D. Sharma. *Archaeological Reconnaissance in Afghanistan: Preliminary Report of the Indian Archaeological Delegation*. New Delhi: Department of Archaeology, 1956.

Rapin, Claude. *Indian Art from Afghanistan: The Legend of Sakuntala and the Indian Treasure of Eucratides at Ai Khanoum*. New Delhi: Manohar, 1996.

Rashid, Ahmed. *Taliban: Islam, Oil, and Fundamentalism in Central Asia*. New Haven: Yale University Press, 2000.

———. *Jihad: The Rise of Militant Islam in Central Asia*. New Haven: Yale University Press, 2002.

Rea, J. R., R. C. Senior, and A. S. Hollis. "A Tax Receipt from Hellenistic Bactria." *Zeitschrift für Papyrologie und Epigraphik* 104 (1994): 261–80.

Renard, Marcel, and Jean Servais. "A propos du mariage d'Alexandre et de Roxane." *L'Antiquité Classique* 24 (1955): 29–50.

Rich, John, and Graham Shipley, eds. *War and Society in the Greek World*. London: Routledge, 1993.

Robert, Louis. "De Delphes à l'Oxus." *Comptes Rendus de l'Académie des Inscriptions et Belles-Lettres* (1968): 416–57.

Robinson, Charles A., Jr. *The History of Alexander the Great*. Vol. 1. Providence: Brown University, 1953; reprint, Chicago: Ares Press, 1996.

Robson, Brian. *The Road to Kabul: The Second Afghan War, 1878–1881.* London: Arms and Armour Press, 1986.

Roisman, Joseph. "Ptolemy and His Rivals in His Alexander History." *Classical Quarterly* 34 (1984): 373–85.

Romey, Kristin. "The Race to Save Afghan Culture." *Archaeology* 55 (May–June 2002): 18–25.

———. "Rebuilding the Bamiyan Buddhas." *Archaeology* 55 (2002): 23.

Roux, Emmanuel de, and Roland-Pierre Paringaux. *Razzia sur l'art.* Paris: Fayard, 1999.

Rtveladze, Edvard. "La circulation monétaire au nord de l'Oxus à l'époque gréco-bactrienne." *Revue Numismatique* 26 (1984): 61–76.

———. *Makedoniyalik Aleksandr i Baqtria va So'g'diyonada.* Tashkent: Academy of Fine Arts of the Republic of Uzbekistan, 2002.

Rubin, Barnett. "Human Rights in Afghanistan." In *Afghanistan: The Great Game Revisited,* ed. Rosanne Klass, pp. 340–44. New York: Freedom House, 1987.

———. *The Fragmentation of Afghanistan.* 2nd ed. New Haven: Yale University Press, 2002.

Rumsfeld, Donald. "Transforming the Military." *Foreign Affairs* 81.3 (2002): 20–32.

Sarianidi, Victor. *The Golden Hoard of Bactria.* St. Petersburg: Aurora Art Publishers, 1988.

Sbarounis, C. N. "Did Alexander the Great Die of Acute Pancreatitis?" *Journal of Clinical Gastroenterology* 24.4 (1997): 294–96.

Schmitt, H. H. *Untersuchungen zur Geschichte Antiochos des Grossen und seiner Zeit.* Wiesbaden: Historia Einzelschriften, 1964.

Schuyler, Eugene. *Turkistan: Notes of a Journey in Russian Turkistan, Khokand, Bukhara, and Kuldja.* New York: Scribner, Armstrong, and Company, 1876.

Sekunda, Nick. *The Army of Alexander the Great.* London: Osprey, 1984.

Shahbazi, A. S. "Iranians and Alexander." *American Journal of Ancient History* 2.1 (2003): 5–38.

Sherwin-White, Susan, and Amélie Kuhrt. *From Samarkhand to Sardis:*

A New Approach to the Seleucid Empire. Berkeley: University of California Press, 1993.

Smucker, Philip. *Al Qaeda's Great Escape: The Military and the Media on Terror's Trail.* Washington, D.C.: Brassey's, 2004.

Southard, Robert. *Droysen and the Prussian School of History.* Lexington: University of Kentucky Press, 1995.

Stadter, Philip. *Arrian of Nicomedia.* Chapel Hill: University of North Carolina Press, 1980.

Stein, Sir Marc Aurel. *On Alexander's Track to the Indus: Personal Narrative of Explorations on the North-West Frontier of India.* London, 1929. Reprint, Edison, N.J.: Castle Books, 2004.

Stewart, Andrew. *Faces of Power: Alexander's Image and Hellenistic Politics.* Berkeley: University of California Press, 1993.

Strauss, Barry, and Josiah Ober. *The Anatomy of Error: Ancient Military Disasters and Their Lessons for Modern Strategists.* New York: St. Martin's Press, 1990.

Tanner, Stephen. *Afghanistan: A Military History from Alexander the Great to the Fall of the Taliban.* New York: Da Capo Press, 2002.

Tarn, W. W. "Alexander the Great and the Unity of Mankind." *Proceedings of the British Academy* 19 (1933): 123–66.

——. *Alexander the Great.* 2 vols. Cambridge: Cambridge University Press, 1948.

——. *Hellenistic Civilisation.* 3rd ed. New York: Meridian Books, 1961.

——. *The Greeks in Bactria and India.* 3rd ed. Chicago: Ares Press, 1984.

Thompson, Margaret, Otto Mørkholm, and Colin Kraay, eds. *An Inventory of Greek Coin Hoards.* New York: American Numismatic Society, 1973.

Thompson, Mark, and Michael Duffy. "Is the Army Stretched Too Thin?" *Time* 162.9 (September 1, 2003): 36–43.

Todd, Richard. "W. W. Tarn and the Alexander Ideal." *Historian* 37 (1964): 48–55.

Toynbee, Arnold. *Between Oxus and Jumna.* Oxford: Oxford University Press, 1961.

————. *Some Problems in Greek History.* London: Oxford University Press, 1969.

Trail, Gail. "Tsyam Revisited: A Study of Kalasha Origins." In *Proceedings of the Second International Hindu Kush Cultural Conference,* ed. Elena Bashir and Israr-ud-Din, pp. 559–76. Oxford: Oxford University Press, 1996.

Tritle, Lawrence. "Alexander the Great and the Killing of Cleitus the Black." In *Crossroads of History: The Age of Alexander,* ed. Waldemar Heckel and Lawrence Tritle, pp. 127–46. Claremont, Calif.: Regina Books, 2003.

Trousdale, William, ed. *War in Afghanistan, 1879–1880: The Personal Diary of Major General Sir Charles Metcalfe MacGregor.* Detroit: Wayne State University Press, 1985.

Troxell, Hyla, and William Spengler. "A Hoard of Early Greek Coins from Afghanistan." *American Numismatic Society Museum Notes* 15 (1969): 1–19.

Ullman, Harlan. *Unfinished Business.* New York: Citadel Press, 2003.

Vaux, W. S. W. "On an Unique Coin of Plato, a King of Bactria." *Numismatic Chronicle* 15 (1875): 1–19.

Vogelsang, William. *The Afghans.* Oxford: Blackwell, 2002.

Wafadar, K. "Afghanistan in 1980: The Struggle Continues." *Asian Survey* 21 (1981): 172–80.

Waller, John. *Beyond the Khyber Pass.* New York: Random House, 1990.

Whitehead, R. B. "The Eastern Satrap Sophytes." *Numismatic Chronicle* (1943): 60–72.

Whitteridge, Gordon. *Charles Masson of Afghanistan.* Warminister: Aris and Phillips, 1986.

Wood, Michael. *In the Footsteps of Alexander the Great.* Berkeley: University of California Press, 1997.

Woodward, Bob. *Bush at War.* New York: Simon and Schuster, 2002.

Worthington, Ian. "Alexander and 'the Interests of Historical Accuracy': A Reply." *Ancient History Bulletin* 13.4 (1999): 136–40.

————. "How 'Great' Was Alexander?" *Ancient History Bulletin* 13.2 (1999): 39–55.

————. *Alexander the Great: Man and God.* New York: Pearson Longman, 2004.

————, ed. *Alexander the Great: A Reader.* London: Routledge, 2003.

Young, Rodney. "The South Wall of Balkh-Bactra." *American Journal
of Archaeology* 59 (1955): 267–76.

Yousaf, Mohammad, and Mark Adkin. *Afghanistan—the Bear Trap:
The Defeat of a Superpower.* Havertown, Pa.: Casemate, 2001.

INDEX

Abdullah-e Burj, 188n31

Achaemenids. *See* Persia

Aetion, 87, 91

Afghanistan, 16–17, 23, 30, 32, 38, 45–46, 53, 62, 85, 96–98, 101–102, 104, 106, 114–115, 120, 124–125, 128, 151–153, 167, 171; antiquities of, 136–145, 147–148, 150, 162–164; Britain and, 1–5, 9, 11, 18–19, 31, 59, 91, 131–133, 135; civil war in, 6, 44, 144–145; instability of, 9, 18, 20–21, 39, 73, 76, 108–111, 162; U.S. and, 1, 5–9, 15, 18–19, 24, 31, 58–59, 64, 67, 91, 112, 123; U.S.S.R. and, 1, 5–6, 9, 15, 18–19, 31, 59, 67, 91, 131; warlords and, 1, 2, 5–6, 10, 15, 19, 27, 29, 34, 39, 45, 48, 51, 57, 59, 64, 67, 69–70, 79, 84, 86, 90–93, 102, 105, 107, 112–113, 117, 126, 137, 144, 147, 152, 154, 162; women of, 88, 91, 143

Afghan War: First, 2, 34, 132–133; Second, 3–4, 136, 139, 150

Agathocleia, 136

Agathocles, 136

Ai Khanoum: ancient city located at, 16, 70, 154–155, 163; artifacts and remains discovered at, 142, 144–145, 156, 157–164

Alexander (III) the Great: adoption of Persian customs by, 30, 43, 86, 90, 93–96; appearance of, 43; army of, 20, 28, 53–54, 65–67, 85, 109–110, 159; background of, 10–13, 136; Bactria and, 23–27, 36–46, 67–84, 126–127, 132–135, 137, 141, 147; conspiracies against, 31, 95–96; foreign religions and, 25–26; frontier policies of, 46–48, 97–98, 101–102, 111, 113, 117, 120, 122, 128, 130, 163–164; heroicized, 17–18, 22, 63, 76, 151, 153,

HELLENISTIC CULTURE AND SOCIETY

General Editors: Anthony W. Bulloch, Erich S. Gruen, A. A. Long, and Andrew F. Stewart

Compositor:	Binghamton Valley Composition, LLC
Cartographer:	Bill Nelson
Text:	Granjon 11/15
Display:	Granjon
Printer and binder:	Friesens Corporation